Ethics and Organizational Leadership

Ethics and Organizational Leadership

Developing a Normative Model

Mick Fryer

UNIVERSITY PRESS

OXFORD
UNIVERSITY PRESS

Great Clarendon Street, Oxford ox2 6DP

Oxford University Press is a department of the University of Oxford.
It furthers the University's objective of excellence in research, scholarship,
and education by publishing worldwide in

Oxford New York

Auckland Cape Town Dar es Salaam Hong Kong Karachi
Kuala Lumpur Madrid Melbourne Mexico City Nairobi
New Delhi Shanghai Taipei Toronto

With offices in

Argentina Austria Brazil Chile Czech Republic France Greece
Guatemala Hungary Italy Japan Poland Portugal Singapore
South Korea Switzerland Thailand Turkey Ukraine Vietnam

Oxford is a registered trade mark of Oxford University Press
in the UK and in certain other countries

Published in the United States
by Oxford University Press Inc., New York

British Library Cataloguing in Publication Data
Data available

Library of Congress Cataloging in Publication Data
Data available

Typeset by SPI Publisher Services, Pondicherry, India
Printed in Great Britain
on acid-free paper by
MPG Books Group, Bodmin and King's Lynn

ISBN 978-0-19-959018-6

1 3 5 7 9 10 8 6 4 2

Dedication

This book is dedicated to the late Peter Gordon Lawrence: an eccentric pioneer and a most unconventional leader.

Acknowledgements

A number of people have made significant contributions to this book. Sixteen CEOs, MDs, and company directors participated in my empirical research, generously giving up their time to discuss with me the ethical challenges associated with their leadership roles. The material presented in the book started out as a PhD, and I am grateful to the PhD's assessors, Martin Parker and Donald Hislop, for their helpful comments. The feedback of OUP's commissioning editors and anonymous reviewers has also been a great help in refining the presentation of these ideas to their present form. Melissa Tyler, at Loughborough University, who was kind enough to read draft chapters of the PhD and the book, offered very useful feedback as well as fruitful suggestions regarding theory content. Louise Fryer has provided invaluable assistance with transcribing interviews and copyreading, as well as offering some helpful observations on presentation. But, most of all, I am especially grateful to Laurie Cohen and Peter Ackers at Loughborough University for their constant guidance and encouragement throughout the writing of my PhD and this book.

Contents

Introduction

It sometimes seems that contemporary Western society is fixated on leadership. From all directions we hear the clamour for more leadership, for better leadership, for leaders to show the way to a brighter future. Our faith in the capacity of leaders to make a difference verges on the cultish. So pervasive is that faith that the person at the top is often presumed to be more important to the electability of a political party than the talents of its members, the quality of its administrative systems, or even the nature of its ideology; it is party leaders, not theorists and planners, who win elections. Meanwhile, tales of charismatic champions, heroically steering their corporations to commercial riches, justify CEO remuneration that exceeds junior employees' pay by multiples of three figures. Such is our belief in the potency of leadership. But the cult of the leader extends beyond political and business management, intruding into the arenas of art, culture, and religion. Even in the modern sporting world, the leadership provided by team captains and coaches is often held to be decisive to competitive achievement on national and international stages. To be sure, this is not always good news for leaders. If they are held responsible for political, economic, and cultural achievement, so are leaders held to account when things go wrong. We are quick to malign those we once deified, and leaders who are thought to have failed are soon stripped of their honour.

Not surprisingly, a thriving industry exists to service this apparently insatiable craving for 'good' leadership. The shelves of popular and academic bookshops are crammed with explanatory accounts of triumphant leadership and with instructive prescriptions aimed at those who seek to invigorate their own career trajectory with the tag of 'leader'. A battery of academic journals also addresses the topic: the British Library currently lists over thirty serials whose titles include the word 'leadership'. And the ever-expanding profile of leadership coaching in the portfolios of corporate training providers, along with a proliferation of institutions dedicated to leadership development in a whole range of occupational arenas, offers further testimony to leadership's allure.

Despite all this, little academic attention has been paid to leadership's moral dimension. Joanne Ciulla, in her introduction to a rare text that does discuss leadership ethics, notes a willingness on the part of leadership commentators to 'genuflect at the altar of ethics and speak with hushed reverence about its importance' (1998: 1). However, Ciulla also notes that systematic treatment of leadership ethics is conspicuous only by its absence. The overwhelming preoccupation of leadership theorists has been to uncover the secrets of leadership effectiveness; few have paid much heed to the moral ramifications of their subject matter. This omission is regrettable, for leaders can be scary people. The political and business landscapes of the twentieth and early twenty-first centuries are littered with highly effective leaders who, in retrospect, are held to account for situations which many consider to be morally questionable if not downright deplorable. Clearly, being 'good' at leadership is no guarantee for being a 'good leader' in a moral sense. But as well as the possibility that leaders may lead in ethically undesirable directions, there is something troubling about the very notion of leadership; of individuals using exceptional influencing skills to move the masses. If leaders really do possess the potency that is commonly imputed to them, then such hegemonic power dynamics seem worryingly at odds with the democratic ideals that are held so dear throughout the Western world. This is perhaps why it is easy to detect, amongst some branches of organization and management studies, an air of suspicious disdain when the subject of leadership gets mentioned.

This book sets out to address this lacuna in the leadership literature by paying particular attention to leadership ethics,[1] with specific reference to leadership in organizations. This study has two aims. Firstly, the book will explore various ideas about what might constitute ethical leadership. These ideas are gathered from the leadership literature, from moral philosophy, and from my own empirical research. In exploring these ideas, I will be on the lookout for tensions. Those tensions might manifest themselves in conflicting responses to a particular, ethically oriented question. Alternatively, points of view that seem, on the surface, to make good moral sense might reveal troubling ramifications when examined more closely. Or, there may be ways in which a particular approach to evaluating ethicality becomes problematic when applied specifically to the realm of organizational leadership. It is by illuminating those tensions that I plan to work towards the book's second aim, which is to develop a normative model of ethical organizational leadership. I use the term *normative* to refer to 'a judgemental standpoint about what is

---

[1] Some philosophers make a distinction between 'morality' and 'ethics'. However, it is more usual in everyday speech to treat the two terms as interchangeable. I will follow the convention of common usage in this book, treating 'morality' as synonymous with 'ethics' and treating 'moral' as synonymous with 'ethical'.

(deemed to be) right and wrong' (Willmott, 1998: 78). So, that second, over-arching, normative aim is to develop a judgemental standpoint about what is right and wrong in relation to organizational leadership.

In order to achieve this normative aim, the book will adopt an approach that borrows selectively from the philosophical method pursued by G.W.F. Hegel in the *Phenomenology of Spirit* (1977 [1807]). Briefly, Hegel's approach was to consider various systems of thought, to draw out the implications of those systems and to see where they lead. This exploratory undertaking illuminated tensions within those systems of thought; tensions which offered a platform upon which an enhanced system could be constructed. For Hegel believed that there lies within each system of thought the potential for a more complete understanding. Furthermore, he believed that such progress can be achieved via consideration of tension; consideration which illuminates the insights that any given system of thought enables but which also highlights its problematic aspects. According to Hegel, then, we should not think of tension as retrogressive; rather, we should grasp the generative possibilities that it offers.

This, broadly, is what this book sets out to do. In presenting a range of different ways of thinking about the ethicality of organizational leadership and seeing where they lead, it will highlight tensions. In holding these tensions up for inspection, I propose to prepare the footings for a more adequate conception of leadership ethicality. The tangible outcome of this process will be the identification of a number of prominent themes. By 'themes', I mean a number of ways of defining ethicality in relation to leadership. These themes will be characterized by ambivalence: each will have something to offer to leadership's ethicality, but I will also highlight some significant challenges that each presents. The path to ethical leadership, I suggest, lies in sensitivity to both the morally generative potential within each of these themes and its morally problematic features.

Hegel believed that his method could be applied systematically and that he could thus build, layer by layer, an absolute understanding; a utopian culmi-nation of all of the systems of thought that he had reviewed. Furthermore, he seemed confident that this utopian end point had been reached in his own era and that it was revealed in his own philosophy. I make no such claim, either in relation to the possibility of a systematically derived, ultimate moral truth or in relation to this book. I am not proposing that a definitive version of ethical organizational leadership is waiting to be revealed, and I certainly do not offer the conclusions of this book as the last word on the subject. However, I do agree with Hegel that, by considering ethicality from a range of perspectives and by looking at both sides of these perspectives, we can improve upon them. This, then, is what I intend to do here: to build a normative model from a variety of different views on ethical leadership. But this normative model is not offered as the last word in ethical leadership. It is, rather, a step along the way; a step forward from those which precede it, but still no more than a platform from which further steps might be taken.

But if this book aims to use exploration of ideas about ethics and leadership to develop a normative model, then it is clear that the outcome will be significantly shaped by two factors: firstly, by the presuppositions and convictions of the person who undertakes that exploration; and secondly, by the landscape through which it travels. As far as the first of these factors is concerned, the exploration described in this book could not have been undertaken from a position of detached neutrality; the course that it follows is inevitably shaped by the sympathies of its author. Moreover, at regular intervals throughout the book, I will offer tentative observations on the significance of some of the material that I discuss. These observations will inevitably be personal. But if a clear exposition that is unencumbered by the baggage of my own presuppositions is unattainable, the least I can do is apprise readers of that baggage so that they can make their own allowances for the unavoidable peculiarities that it engenders.

When I began the research that is described in this book, I was working as a director of a fairly large, privately owned organization. However, the subject of leadership had occupied my mind for many years before this. A long time ago, during my years in full-time education, I had been asked to take on various positions of responsibility. Perhaps studying moral philosophy as an undergraduate had evoked reflection on the ethical ramifications of those roles, or maybe an innate interest in ethics had inspired my choice of degree. Whichever was the case, I found enough time between the usual diversions of undergraduate life to wonder about quite what levels of commitment I had a right to expect of those young people who were 'in my team'. Twenty-five years in various management roles followed; roles that carried customary expectations of showing 'leadership' to subordinates. These roles occasionally offered further cause for ethical reflection although, for most of that time, any major misgivings were subsumed by a managerialist self-assurance that left little space to question the hierarchical legitimation afforded by my status.

Oddly enough though, the further I moved up the hierarchical ladder, the less comfortable I became with the ethos of managerial prerogative with which I was increasingly confronted. I eventually returned to academia to study part-time for an MBA. This was a good move—not because of the promise of career riches that attracts many managers onto MBA courses, but because it reawakened a critical curiosity that had slowly atrophied since my departure from full-time education. The MBA raised as many questions as it answered. The familiarization that it afforded with the depersonalizing discourse and conventions of managerial capitalism helped me to move a bit more confidently through the world of intrigue into which my corporate responsibilities were, by then, leading me.[2] But, at the same time, the course evoked growing discomfort with many, although by no means all, of the foundations upon which that world was built. Shortly after graduating with an MBA, I resolved to undertake part-time PhD study with a view to exploring a little more systematically some of the ethical questions raised by managerial work and, particularly, by the Western preoccupation with business leadership. This aspiration eventually crystallized into the content of this book. It also, coincidentally, eventually led to my departure from the business world to focus on academic work.

As well as the authorial idiosyncrasies that unavoidably infuse a book's agenda, that agenda is also shaped by its content. In this respect, the sources upon which this book draws in order to elaborate its normative model are patently Western. The book reviews leadership theory that has been compiled mainly by British and North American researchers; it considers the implications of ethics theories that are drawn from the Anglo-American and European philosophical traditions; and it explores the views of leaders whose experience is mostly within UK-based organizations. So, how can I justify this manifestly Western flavour? Well, for a start, I have to place limits on the scope of this undertaking and it seems sensible to remain within the parameters of material with which I am familiar. But there are two further reasons why a characteristically Western study of leadership has merit. The first is that it is in the West, particularly in Anglo-American business and organizational thinking, that the cult of the leader seems particularly pervasive. It therefore seems appropriate to investigate this as a characteristically Western phenomenon. The second reason for concentrating on Western ideas is that many in the West seem particularly keen to export Western values to the rest of the world. Given the tenacity of Western political and economic imperialism, it seems sensible to expose to specific critique a phenomenon that comprises such a conspicuous aspect of the culture that is thus being exported. If we are to continue to foist a Western conception of leadership on the rest of the world, we should at least ensure that we get it right according to our own value commitments.

But the researcher's predispositions and the choice of researched material are not the only factors that influence a study of this type. Such an enquiry is also influenced by how one thinks about the subject under consideration. In this respect, popular notions of leadership, as well as most, but by no means all, academic leadership researchers, take the reality of leadership for granted. They assume that leadership actually exists as an object of exploration; that

---

[2] This 'intrigue' related mainly to an impending change of ownership structure of the company for which I worked. Acting in a support capacity to the company's owner, whose deteriorating health and advancing years had attracted the attentions of many suitors, I made the acquaintance of a posse of financial advisers, sellers of private equity, management buy-in candidates, corporate matchmakers, and assorted shysters.

some people are better at it than others; and that their effectiveness is the result of a bundle of personal traits and/or behaviours that these people exhibit in greater measure than their less successful counterparts. Researchers thus observe effective leaders in an effort to find out why they are so successful. Meanwhile, leadership development gurus draw upon the ostensibly stable findings of this research programme in order to share its secrets with their hopeful acolytes.

However, not all commentators are so convinced that leadership capability is a tangible object that is possessed by some and that can be studied, analysed, and taught by others. Some ask whether this thing called leadership actually exists at all or whether it is just a reassuring projection of special qualities on to those in positions of authority by dependent followers (Bennis and Nannus, 1985; Meindl, 1990); maybe an imaginative attribution, which flourishes as long as organizations are successful but which soon pales when they hit hard times (Bryman, 1987, 1992). Or perhaps it is partly the outcome of a post hoc, PR exercise on the part of skilled rhetoricians who are thus able to amplify the significance of their own contribution (Grint, 2000); something which is more about senior managers' esteem-enhancing identity creation than it is about what anyone actually does (Alvesson and Sveningsson, 2003; Carroll and Levy, 2008). Indeed, by imputing its objective certainty, the main body of leadership research has even been accused of creating, or at least perpetuating, the very beast that it seeks to capture (Smircich and Morgan, 1982; Gemmill and Oakley, 1992). In this case, not only might such research sustain an insidious chimera, it may also be culpable of propping up dualist depictions of leaders and followers; depictions which legitimize the hierarchical prerogative accorded by prevailing power relationships, and which conveniently keep in their place those less fortunate individuals who do not wear the leader's armband (Bennis, 1989; Knights and Willmott, 1992).

In other words, the leadership culture which seems so pervasive in the contemporary world may be nothing more than, at best, a colossal misunderstanding or, at worst, a maleficent con trick. Moreover, by wheeling out leaders as the culprits of political and economic misadventure, as well as crowning them as heroes when things go well, we may be shifting attention from systemic shortcomings that, in the long term, are just as important (it is easier to blame a CEO for corporate misadventure or a few greedy senior bankers for widespread economic collapse than it is to question the whole system atop which they sit!). Such concerns merit serious attention. The studies that they inspire offer invaluable pathways to a more nuanced understanding of the processes through which leadership is negotiated and enacted. They provide new ways of thinking about leadership; ways that enhance our understanding of what might be going on when leadership seems to be taking place. They also raise important questions about both the inevitability and the desirability of leadership per se. However, I do not believe that such issues need forestall ethical enquiry, for it seems to me that discussion about the reality or otherwise of leadership can be set aside from its impact. Regardless of whether leadership is a bundle of tangible qualities and behaviours or something that is socially negotiated, it figures prominently enough in the contemporary, organizational landscape for it to have a significant impact on the lives of many people. Real or constructed, leadership matters.

To be sure, studies that question its ontological surety might eventually serve to reduce leadership's impact, thus diminishing its ethical significance. However, this is a longer-term agenda, which I will leave others to pursue. Here, I will focus on what is, in many ways, a more pressing challenge. Some people find themselves in leadership roles. No matter how transitory, how imaginary, and how insubstantial the qualities that underpin their occupation of those roles may be, and regardless of the extent to which that occupation may be a negotiated achievement, the manner in which those people respond to their predicament is a matter of ethical significance. It may be a matter of ethical significance for them; it is probably a matter of ethical significance for those who bear the consequences of their leadership interventions; and it is also a matter of ethical significance for those who gaze in dismay over the social and environmental fallout from leadership that may, at one time and in some quarters, have been considered heroic. So, with those constituencies in mind, I will, in this book, leave aside the matter of leadership's ontological status and focus on the ethics of its enactment.

Overview of the Book

To recap, the agenda of this book is to bridge a notable gap in existing leadership literature by elaborating an understanding of what ethical organizational leadership looks like. It pursues this agenda by exploring a range of ideas about ethics and leadership. This exploration will illuminate a number of prominent themes, each of which seems to have something positive to say about ethicality but each of which also offers grounds for disquiet. By drawing attention to these solid foundations while illuminating the less-than-attractive edifices that sometimes spring from them, I hope to point the way towards an enhanced normative understanding. But this outcome should be regarded as no more than a step along the road. Although the book hopes to leave our understanding of ethical leadership in a better place than that in which it found it, that better place should be seen as a starting point for further reflection.

What, then, are the resources upon which the book will draw; where does it look to find those ideas about organizational leadership ethics that it seeks to explore? The book is organized into three parts, each of which focuses on a separate area that might be expected to have something to offer to this enquiry. Part I will look at what the leadership literature has to say about ethics. Although that literature tends to avoid sustained discussion of morality, it does contain enough ideas to offer at least a starting point for this study. I will concentrate on those theoretical contributions that have something explicit to say about ethics and on those that seem particularly evocative in a moral sense, either because they carry an intuitively moral tone or because they raise conspicuous moral questions. This discussion will be structured around the two ethical challenges associated with leadership that were mentioned earlier in this introduction: the ethicality of leadership agendas, and leadership's impositional overtones. After considering some responses that the literature offers to these challenges, I will say a little about the relationship between these ideas and broader trends within organization and management thinking.

Having looked at the relationship between ethics and leadership from the perspective of the leadership literature, the book will then explore that relationship from the opposite direction. Thus, Part II will view leadership through the lens of moral philosophy. The three chapters that comprise this section are organized under three contrasting *meta-ethical* headings; that is, under the rubric of three different ways of thinking about the nature of ethical validation. Chapter 2 will discuss some prominent principle-based theories. These theories tend to adopt an *objectivist* meta-ethical stance, assuming that there are real standards of ethical probity that apply to us all. Chapter 3 will consider existentialism, a theory which leans towards a *subjectivist* meta-ethic. In other words, existentialism challenges the idea that real, universal standards of moral legitimacy exist, proposing, instead, that ethicality is a matter of individual conviction. The last chapter in this section, chapter 4, will look specifically at *intersubjectivist* theory. Intersubjectivism, when applied to moral philosophy, locates ethical legitimation in agreement between people. In each of these three chapters I will outline some particularly influential contributions that fall under its respective meta-ethical heading, drawing out some implications of these contributions for organizational leadership. At the end of each chapter I will summarize a few key points that have arisen within that chapter. Then, at the end of chapter 4, I will look back over all three chapters in Part II, making some further comparative observations.

By this stage, a number of themes will begin to emerge that are broadly characteristic of different ways of thinking about leadership ethics. Also, a few tensions will start to become apparent in relation to these themes. Part III offers the opportunity to explore these themes and their respective tensions in more detail. These three chapters will depart from the theoretical focus that characterizes Part I and Part II, offering an account of empirical research.

Specifically, this section will discuss interviews with sixteen people who occupy formal, organizational leadership roles; interviews that sought to explore how these people think about the ethical implications of their jobs. Chapter 5 will describe three characteristic, 'ideal-type' ways of thinking about the role of an organizational leader with respect to ethics; three ways which resonate, in some respects, with the three meta-ethical stances explored in Part II. Chapter 6 will continue this tripartite classification, exploring a particular tension associated with each of these three ideal-type perspectives. Then, in chapter 7, I will consider some empirical responses to the two specific ethical challenges associated with leadership that are discussed in chapter 1.

The concluding chapter of the book pulls together a number of themes that have been highlighted in the preceding chapters, drawing attention to the equivocal character of each of these themes. It goes on to propose an approach to leadership that is best placed to capitalize on the morally generative potential of each of these themes whilst ameliorating its contentious aspects. The overall thrust of this concluding chapter and, indeed, of the book is that the managerialist expectation that pervades most leadership theory and practice presents a number of difficulties when applied to the field of ethics. I will say a little more about managerialism in chapter 1, but the basic idea upon which it is premised is that everyone will be better off if decisions in organizations are made by senior managers who have the necessary rational, technical expertise for such a task. This, I argue, is problematic when it comes to ethics. Conversely, I will propose an alternative conception of ethical leadership; a conception which builds upon the intersubjectivist meta-ethic outlined in chapter 4 and which presents leadership as a mediatory undertaking. The book will conclude with a few observations on the practical feasibility of such an approach in contemporary organizational contexts.

Part I
Leadership Literature and Ethics

1

A Review of the Leadership Literature

To begin this exploration of different ways of thinking about organizational leadership and ethics, it seems sensible to look at what the leadership literature has to say on the topic. As I have already suggested, it does not say much specifically about ethics. The overriding preoccupation of leadership theorists for the last eighty years or so has been to uncover the secrets of leadership effectiveness; there have been few attempts to address the issue of ethics head-on. However, one branch of the literature that has evoked a certain amount of ethically oriented discussion is *transformational leadership* theory. James Mac-Gregor Burns (1978) first developed the idea of what he referred to as 'transforming leadership' within the arena of political theory. Burns' work has subsequently been adapted and applied to organizational contexts, most notably by Bernard Bass (1985, 1990; Bass and Avolio, 1994), under its more common name. I will draw quite a lot on this material in the following discussion for, while aspects of transformational leadership theory are morally compelling, some of the ethical claims made in its name are also quite contentious.

Many other writers, while not explicitly discussing ethics, have offered accounts of leadership effectiveness that have an intuitively ethical tone. Prominent amongst these is the notion of *servant-leadership* (Greenleaf, 1977; Spears and Lawrence, 2002), which suggests that the role of a leader is to minister to the needs and aspirations of followers. Meanwhile, instrumental prescriptions that resonate with *Human Relations* approaches to management (for example, Lewin, 1939; Hemphill, 1955; Feidler, 1967; Skinner, 1969; Likert, 1979; Hersey and Blanchard, 1982; Blake and Morton, 1985) and those that explore characteristically 'feminine' leadership traits (such as Johnson, 1976, Hegelsen, 1990; Rosener, 1990; Cantor and Bernay, 1992; Grant, 1992) radiate a certain moral allure. As well as emphasizing the efficacy of participative leadership behaviour, these accounts seem to suggest that in order to be successful, leaders need to treat their people well. More recently, the democratic implications of *team leadership* and *distributed leadership* (for example, Gronn,

2002; Day et al., 2004; Woods, 2004; Woods et al., 2004) are ethically significant. Furthermore, a growing field of leadership studies that is driven by a social-constructionist commitment (such as Smircich and Morgan, 1982; Knights and Willmott, 1992; Collinson, 2005; Pye, 2005) has some interesting things to say to ethically oriented enquiry. Therefore, despite a lack of systematic treatment of morality (Ciulla, 1998), there is enough material tucked away within the folds of the curtains of the leadership literature to offer at least a starting point for ethical exploration. Accordingly, I will draw on these fields, and on some others, in the following pages.

In the introduction to this book I briefly alluded to two ways in which leadership might offer grounds for ethical disquiet. The first relates to the moral probity of the outcomes towards which leaders lead. The notion of leadership is imbued with images of prominent individuals who are able to apply exceptional influencing skills in order to rally support for a particular agenda. If those individuals, those people who are 'good' at leading, are either morally degenerate or morally injudicious, they may lead towards outcomes that, from an ethical perspective, are undesirable. Leadership flair becomes a dangerous tool when placed in the wrong hands. The second area of ethical concern relates to a vague discomfort that many people feel with the very notion of leadership. There seems to be something worryingly asymmetrical about leader–follower relationships; about the idea that leaders are expected to exert their agency over and above that of their so-called 'followers'. Effective leadership thus courts the challenge that the imposition of a leader's agenda erodes other people's capacity to fulfil their own aspirations, to pursue their own interests, to work towards realization of their own potential, or perhaps even to pursue their own moral agendas.

I propose to structure this chapter around these two principle areas of concern. I will explore the extent to which various leadership commentaries exacerbate these concerns and the extent to which various theorists respond to them, either explicitly or tacitly. I will suggest that each of these moral challenges is, in a sense, two-sided. In turning to meet challenges that are offered from one direction, we run the risk of opening ourselves to challenges that are launched from the other direction. Thus, to address questions about the ethicality of leadership agendas by pointing to the comforting prospect of leaders' altruism is to court the challenge of a narrowly focused altruism; one which prioritizes the organization and its interests over all other considerations. Similarly, the challenge of leadership's inherently suppressive character might be attenuated in several ways. Attention could be drawn to the apparently consensual nature of leader–follower relations, to the democratic tenor of successful leadership, or to the propensity for effective leadership to promote the interests of followers. However reassuring though such vindications might be, each also raises further questions concerning the constraints under which consensus might be accorded, limits that might be placed upon democratic participation, the distasteful prospect of emotional manipulation, and the challenge that majoritarian visions may present to individual agency.

These, then, are the issues I will explore in this chapter. My focus on the ethicality of leaders' agendas and on leadership's asymmetries should not be taken as an assertion that they are the only possible sources of moral discomfort with leadership, only that each is sufficiently compelling to merit attention during ethically oriented enquiry. Therefore, these two areas of concern are not proposed as a complete classification of grounds for moral disquiet. Rather, they are offered as a reasonable starting point for this enquiry on the basis that we have to start from somewhere but that the detail of that starting point may be subject to revision as the enquiry progresses. After exploring these issues in some detail, I will conclude this chapter by making a few general observations that arise from the discussion. I will also reflect on how various responses to these issues relate to contrasting perspectives within the broader field of organization and management studies.

The Moral Probity of Leadership Agendas

For Philip Selznick (1957), a defining characteristic of leadership is the capacity to infuse an organization with values; to lift it above the opportunistic quest for short-run efficiency; and to evoke a purpose that has a moral dimension. The frequent use of 'leadership' as an honorific, sometimes in comparison to rather dry, morally vacuous depictions of 'management' (such as Zaleznik, 1977), adds further credence to leadership's morally uplifting potential. Many such leaders spring to mind. History is packed with stories of exceptional individuals who were able to galvanize their followers, thus playing a pivotal role in the achievement of ethically laudable ends. But there are also plenty of cautionary tales of equally exceptional leaders who used their influence to bring about ends that are now considered morally deplorable: for every Martin Luther King, there is an Adolf Hitler; for every Anita Roddick, a Jeffrey Skilling; for each Florence Nightingale, there is a Charles Manson. So how are we to tell the heroes from the villains? Upon what basis can we judge that the remarkably potent gift of leadership is not misapplied?

Leaders' Altruism as a Moral Guarantor

One approach to distinguishing ethical from unethical leaders, offered most emphatically by transformational and charismatic leadership theorists, is to focus on the hazards presented by leaders' egotism: to portray altruistically motivated leadership as morally commendable and egotistically motivated leadership as morally degenerate. Bass and Steidlmeier thus distinguish 'authentic' transformational leaders from 'inauthentic' or 'pseudo' transformational leaders in order to tell those who wear the 'white hats of heroes' from those who sport the 'black hats of villains' (1999: 187). According to this depiction, authentic transformational leaders place the interests of followers above their own ambition for power and status. Pseudo transformational leaders, on the other hand, are those 'Inauthentic CEOs [who] downsize their organization, increase their own compensation, and weep crocodile tears for the employees who have lost their jobs' (1999: 187). Furthermore, authentic transformational leaders channel their need for power 'in socially constructive ways into the service of others' (1999: 189), whereas pseudo transformational leaders 'use power primarily for self-aggrandizement and are actually contemptuous privately of those they are supposed to be serving as leaders' (1999: 189).

Just as Bass and Steidlmeier use their pseudo-authentic distinction to tell villains from heroes, charismatic leadership theory has offered its own binary classifications to differentiate between the egotistic bad guys and the altruistic good guys. Jane Howell (1988) thus distinguishes between 'personalized' and 'socialized' charisma. The former is concerned primarily with the exertion of power and dominance over others: personalized charismatics only encourage the development of followers insofar as this may contribute to the personal goals of the leader. Socialized charismatics, on the other hand, are motivated by a collective ethic, by higher-order values, and by a desire to promote the personal development and intellectual stimulation of followers as an end in itself. Pursuing this same taxonomy, Conger and Kanungo (1998) draw attention to personalized charismatics' Machiavellian and narcissistic tendencies, also alluding to Musser's analogous distinction (1987) between 'negative' and 'positive' charismatic types, of which the former favour their own interests rather than internalizing the values and ideological goals that they are ostensibly promoting.

A slightly different take on altruism can be found in the work of Beverley Alimo-Metcalfe and John Alban-Metcalfe (2001, 2004, 2005), who have used research in British public-sector organizations to build upon the work of North American transformational leadership theorists such as Bass. Although Alimo-Metcalfe and Alban-Metcalfe note significant contrasts between their own findings and those of US models, 'where vision and charisma [of the leader] dominate' (2005: 57), they agree with their US colleagues about the significance of altruism. However, whereas the transformational and charismatic leadership theorists already mentioned offer their egotism–altruism distinction as a way of distinguishing morally degenerate, but nevertheless effective, transformational and charismatic leaders from their morally commendable counterparts, Alimo-Metcalfe and Alban-Metcalfe suggest that altruism may be intrinsic to transformational effectiveness. Noting that transformational leaders are inclined to value individuals and to show genuine concern for others' well-being and development, Alimo-Metcalfe and Alban-Metcalfe suggest that 'this factor is unequivocally the most important aspect of transformational leadership in the UK sample, explaining more variance than all the remaining factors together' (2005: 57). They also find a strong positive correlation between effectiveness and the leader's inclination to consider 'the good of the organization as more important than satisfying his/her own personal ambition' (2005: 60). Therefore, while the altruism–egotism dualisms offered by earlier researchers provide a handy litmus test for retrospectively telling morally sound, successful leaders from morally unsound, successful leaders, Alimo-Metcalfe and Alban-Metcalfe's reassuring message is that leaders need to have collective interests at heart if they are to be transformationally successful at all.

A link between altruism and leadership effectiveness is also apparent in Robert Greenleaf's discussion (1977) of *servant-leadership*. A key feature of servant-leadership theory is the idea that servant-leaders are fundamentally driven not by a desire to lead but by a desire to serve others. According to Greenleaf, despite the primacy of their desire to serve, such people agree to take on the mantle of leadership because they realize that this will permit them to serve others more productively than if they were to remain in a subservient role. Greenleaf contrasts such individuals with those who aspire to leadership because of its attendant trappings of power, privilege, and wealth. Greenleaf's depiction of servant-leaders resonates with Charles Handy's advocacy of 'unconditional positive regard' (1998: 135), which Handy equates with the unconditional love that many feel towards close members of their family. If such notions seem a little idealistic in respect to organizational leadership, subsequent researchers have added some practical relevance to Greenleaf's work by identifying correlations between servant-leadership and organizational achievement within certain contexts (Ruschman, 2002; Showkeir, 2002).

Altruism's Downside: Leaders' Limited Purview

To link moral probity with altruistic intent in this way is intuitively appealing. The idea that leaders who care about people are likely to be driven by ethically sound agendas seems to make sense. However, altruism's claim to be a guarantor of leadership ethicality is not as straightforward as it seems. A particular difficulty is that, by concentrating on the evils of egotistical leadership, we run the risk of overlooking an even greater moral hazard: that of narrowly focused altruism. As Joseph Rost puts it, even if, as transformational leadership theorists claim, leaders and followers can raise one another to higher levels of

motivation and morality, 'There is nothing in [this] notion of transformational leadership that speaks to organizations and societies being raised to
higher levels of motivation and morality' (1991: 164). Terry Price (2003)
pursues this point, suggesting that the vigour with which Bass and Steidlmeier
(1999) proffer their authentic–inauthentic distinction as a response to the
hazards of egotism only serves to magnify the danger of transformational
leadership agendas conflicting with wider, moral considerations. For Price,
Bass and Steidlmeier's effort to discredit egotism exacerbates the 'peculiar
cognitive challenge that leadership brings with it' (Price, 2003: 69): that is, a
pernicious, misplaced altruism.

Arguably, the dangers of narrowly focused altruism are illustrated most
emphatically by the case of Adolf Hitler, that popular stereotype of the villain-
ous, charismatic leader. Hitler is often portrayed as a power-hungry, self-
publicizing egotist who was primarily motivated by a desire for personal
enhancement. But an alternative view is that he was driven by a profound
mission to rejuvenate the economic and military status of Germany, and to
restore its people to what he considered their rightful position of European
pre-eminence (Hobsbawm, 1995; Grint, 2000). According to the latter interpretation, Hitler's vision of redemption for the German nation, unacceptable
though it is to most observers, was not the agenda of a narcissistic egotist. It
was the vision of a man who was so deeply committed to the well-being of *his*
people that he was prepared to place this agenda above all other moral considerations in initiating acts of barbarous atrocity.

Altruism, therefore, may not carry the unequivocal, morally generative
force that some theorists suggest. On the contrary, there seems to be a real
danger that the 'strong attachment to their organization and its people' (Bass
and Steidlmeier, 1999: 187), which Bass and Steidlmeier offer as indicator of
ethically uplifting 'authenticity', may cloud leaders' moral perspicacity, resulting in a collective abnegation of any broader, moral responsibilities. In
responding to this second line of criticism, this challenge of narrowly focused
altruism, leadership theory offers the basis for contrasting approaches: one
approach is to call upon leaders to be the arbiters of those broader moral
considerations; the other is to share this task more widely. The first of these
approaches is articulated most energetically by Bass and Steidlmeier in a
separate thread of their testimonial for authentic transformational leadership.
Here, they compare the role of the authentic transformational leader to that of
the moral sage, which, they suggest, figures prominently in Socratic and
Confucian philosophical traditions as well as within Judaic/Christian belief.
Their depiction of a moral sage is of an exceptional individual, a '(saint/holy
person) [who] exercises a transforming influence upon all those whom s/he
contacts' (1999: 196). They paint a compelling picture of organizational leaders who are blessed with exceptional moral insight; sagacious individuals

who have a clear personal understanding of moral truth and who are able to share the fruits of their moral acumen with their followers: thus 'the true transformational leader is to be, in Confucian terms, a "superior person"' (1999: 196).

Notably, Bass and Steidlmeier allow little space for followers to participate in the moral legitimation of leadership agendas. However, an alternative approach, which places a less onerous burden on leaders' moral judgement, is to trust in the desirability of outcomes that are reached through participative processes; processes which leaders may be able to facilitate and mediate. Many leadership theorists emphasize the merits of including followers, and perhaps even other organizational stakeholders, in decision-making. Generally, these encomia to participatory leadership amount to instrumental prescriptions rather than normative justifications: researchers are not necessarily advocating the ethical merits of participation; they are merely noting that those leaders who seem to involve followers in decision-making are more likely to achieve their desired outcomes. I will say more about these participatory leadership models shortly, but for now I will just note that despite their decidedly instrumental tone, such prescriptions at least make space for more comprehensive appraisals of the moral ramifications of organizational action. They thus place less reliance on the likelihood of 'compassionate corporate Bodhisattvas' (Western, 2008: 180) occupying leadership roles in organizations.

Leadership's Impositional Overtones

So much for the ethicality of leadership agendas. I will now consider a second ethically contentious aspect of leadership that I touched on in the introduction to this book. A great deal of the literature, as well as common conceptions of leadership, takes for granted the idea of prominent individuals, possessed of prodigious influencing skills, who use their extraordinary potency to move followers to do as they desire. Leadership tends to be thought of as an inherently asymmetrical undertaking—one in which leaders' capacity to assert their will over that of their followers is a measure of how good they are at leading. A glance at Joseph Rost's long list (1991) of definitions from the twentieth century gives some idea of the extent to which notions of imposition imbue leadership writing. For instance, eighty or so years ago, leadership was defined as 'the ability to impress the will of the leader on those led and induce obedience, respect, loyalty, and cooperation' (Moore, 1927, cited in Rost, 1991: 47). Half a century later it was located in a capacity 'to inspire others to undertake some form of purposeful action that is determined by the leader' (Sarkasian, 1981, Rost, 1991: 72). Peter Gronn succinctly summarizes the flavour of most of these definitions as lying in the notion that 'leadership is basically doing what the leader wants done' (Gronn, 2002: 424).

However, if leadership's impositional ramifications are morally problematic, the literature also offers ample grounds for reassurance. For a start, we might take comfort from the consensual character of leader–follower relationships. By drawing attention to the extent that followers consent, at least tacitly, to any disproportionate influence wielded by leaders, it may be possible to construct a sort of *social-contractual* legitimation of that influence. Secondly, we might emphasize the extent to which effective leadership is accompanied by a commitment to *democratic* inclusion. Since a lot of research suggests that effective leaders are characterized by their willingness to involve followers in decision-making, maybe leadership is not so impositional after all. And thirdly, the literature offers the basis for a *benevolent-paternalist* justification of leadership influence by noting that it tends to be wielded in the interests of followers. I will expand on each of these potential sources of reassurance, drawing attention to literature sources that, supportively or otherwise, illuminate them. It will become apparent that despite the potential reassurance that these themes offer, each also presents its own grounds for ethical concern.

Social-Contractual Legitimation of Leadership Influence

Despite a tendency for the literature to portray leadership as a top-down influence relationship and to cast the behaviour and characteristics of leaders as the prime object of study, some commentators have called for more attention to be paid to the processes through which leadership is accomplished. These writers also suggest that in order to understand those processes, we should take more notice of what is going on amongst followers. Chester Barnard observed, over fifty years ago, that discussions of leadership focus too much on what formally selected individual leaders are up to, and not enough on the emotional and relational complexities that constitute the choices made by followers to follow those leaders. According to Barnard, this conventional preoccupation fails to acknowledge that 'The test of the adequacy of leadership is the extent of cooperation, or lack of it, in relation to our ideals and this is largely a matter of the disposition of followers' (1997 [1948]): 108). For Barnard, formal authority cannot be sustained in the absence of informal acquiescence to the ideals manifested in that authority. To disregard the significance of the latter is to overlook the inevitability that 'in all formal organizations selection [of leaders] is made simultaneously by two authorities: the formal and the informal . . . the informal authority we may call acceptance (or rejection). *Of the two, the informal is fundamental and controlling.* It lies in or consists of the willingness and ability of followers to follow' (1997 [1948]: 108).

Several researchers who bring a social-constructivist perspective to leadership studies have also taken issue with the mainstream's tendency to focus on leaders rather than exploring the informal processes through which authority is accorded by followers. Smircich and Morgan (1982), considering leadership as an exercise in the management of meaning, observe that its success demands recognition by followers of leaders' right to shape meaning on the part of the collective: 'The leader exists as a formal leader only when he or she achieves a situation in which an obligation, expectation, or right to frame experience is presumed, or offered and accepted by others' (Smircich and Morgan, 1982: 258). On a similar note, David Collinson (2005) proposes that, rather than considering leadership through the lens of binary relationships such as control/resistance, more attention should be paid to the dialectical processes by which leadership legitimation is negotiated. Meanwhile, Annie Pye (2005) suggests that leader–follower relationships should not be cast as one-sided exercises in influence but as shared processes of sensemaking.

By focusing on the informal, dialectical processes through which followers' consent is negotiated, these commentaries draw attention to the prospect of that consent. Instead of casting leadership as one-sided application of influence by individuals who are privileged by formal status or by mysterious configurations of personal alchemy, they highlight the extent to which followers may be complicit in the construction of leader–follower relationships. They thus offer a basis for legitimation of leaders' influence: if followers have participated in the creation of leadership authority by signalling, through complex, informal processes, their consent to that authority, then perhaps we should not be too worried about the asymmetrical influence that characterizes it.

However, although the latent consensuality of leader–follower relationships may attenuate concerns about asymmetrical influence, some of these writers also raise important questions about the terms under which consensus is achieved. For example, Smircich and Morgan (1982) point out that the apparently informal processes through which organizational leadership is negotiated generally take place within formalized, institutional settings. Shared understanding is therefore shaped by predetermined authority relationships and patterns of interaction, comprising embedded roles, work practices, rules, and conventions. Similarly, David Knights and Hugh Willmott (1992) observe that although shared understanding between leaders and followers may be a negotiated achievement, such negotiation proceeds from bargaining positions that are fundamentally unbalanced. Apparently, intersubjective reality-construction thus becomes 'a product of "force" in the sense that followers are often disadvantaged—by a comparative lack of material and symbolic resources—in formulating let alone mounting a challenge' (1992: 766).

Consequently, acquiescence may be a more apt descriptor of followers' eventual responses than consent.

But concerns about the constrained nature of negotiated consensus do not stop there. Smircich and Morgan suggest that this institutionally restricted negotiation of meaning may result in 'overconcretized and dehumanizing' (1982: 260) relations in which followers surrender their meaning-making capacity; relations in which leaders expect to lead and followers expect to be led, generating a condition of 'trained inaction' (1982: 271) in the latter. David Collinson (2005) goes as far as to suggest that any lingering resistance to dominant leadership narratives is likely to get channelled into formats that propagate socially undesirable, stereotypical behaviour. Despite the multiplicity of forms that such resistance might take, Collinson notes a particular tendency for it to privilege, amongst men and women, a stereotypically laddish, shop-floor culture, which may exert its own pressures to conform, subordinating women and femininity and perhaps undermining other aspects of diversity such as race and ethnicity.

The apparently consensual tone of leadership processes therefore needs to be treated with caution. It may indeed be the case that the leadership will not succeed unless followers make tacit, informal choices to follow. However, we should not lose sight of the extent to which such choices may be shaped by unequal access to socially valued resources. Nor should we overlook the tendency for the accumulated momentum of systemic preconditioning to shape the self-understanding of individuals so that some acquire an inflated sense of self-worth, of their fitness to lead, while others are left with a sense of emasculation from which they seek refuge in demeaning, clichéd forms of covert resistance.

Democratic Comportment as a Legitimation of Leadership Influence

Another way to take shelter from leadership's morally disquieting, impositional overtones is to highlight the democratic demeanour that tends to accompany effective leadership. For a long time, commentators have noted that the most successful leaders are those who are prepared to involve followers in decision-making. Early, *behavioural* research (Lewin, 1939) drew attention to the limitations of autocratic leadership behaviour, indicating that leaders who encourage participation tend to foster higher levels of performance and less hostility amongst followers. Burns and Stalker's exploration (1959) of the relationship between leadership behaviour and context also noted that, at least some of the time, 'organic' approaches, which empower and delegate responsibility to lower level workers, are more successful than directive 'mechanistic' leadership. Descriptions of 'feminine' leadership style (Hegelsen, 1990; Rosener, 1990), in emphasizing the importance to leadership success of participation, power sharing, information sharing, listening skills, and open communication, also testify to the efficacy of consultation.

Research into *group-centred* leadership (Bradford, 1976) and *team leadership* (Day et al., 2004), which focuses on leadership *in* teams rather than leadership *of* teams, is also redolent of empowerment and shared decision-making. It expands the focus of leadership research 'to include ways that leadership is drawn from—instead of only added to—teams' (Day et al., 2004: 858). While team leadership theory does not preclude leadership that is external to the team, it draws attention to the need for 'external leaders' to adopt a highly participative style. After exploring relationships between external leaders and autonomous work teams, Manz and Sims thus advocate a set of supportive behaviours that help external leaders 'to influence the team and team members to be able to do it themselves, rather than . . . to exercise direct control or do it for the team' (1987: 114). A range of facilitative behaviours that have come to be associated more with mentoring management (Lewis, 2000) than with traditional, directive approaches to leadership are thus prescribed.

Some descriptions of *distributed leadership* also offer space for a less hegemonic style. This descriptor has been applied to many types of arrangement, from the sharing of authority amongst a small number of 'joint leaders' to a more widespread dispersal of decision-making authority throughout organizations. Peter Gronn (2002) dwells on the latter, describing distributed leadership theory as offering an alternative to dominant conceptions of 'focused' leadership, which, both descriptively and prescriptively, locate leadership firmly in the hands of individuals who occupy elevated hierarchical status. Gronn suggests that focused leadership approaches offer an inadequate response to the realities of contemporary organizational contexts, exploring instead the extent to which leadership might be distributed throughout hierarchical levels. Simon Western (2008) expands Gronn's analysis of the leadership needs of contemporary organizations, extending his prescription for democratic inclusion beyond organizational members to embrace less proximate stakeholders. According to Western, the imperatives and preoccupations that characterize contemporary organizational contexts have created the need for a new kind of 'eco-leadership'—a style of leadership that canvasses and responds to the expectations of multiple stakeholders within complex and diverse 'business eco-systems'.

In summary, there is a substantial body of research telling leaders that in order to succeed they must give their people a chance to participate in decision-making. A top-down, hierarchical approach will not suffice to drive organizational achievement. In that case, perhaps we should not bother too much about impositional leadership, for it is not likely to last for long. Leaders with a predilection for imposition will not achieve the results needed to get to the top and stay there. But before warming our hands too thankfully against the comforting glow of democratically tinged, instrumental prescriptions, it is as well to consider some ways in which democratic purity might be inhibited. Most notably, Woods et al. (2004), in their discussion of distributed leadership, highlight two particular ways in which distribution of authority might be restricted. Firstly, they note a tendency for leadership to be distributed according to expertise, where expertise is valorized in relation to its instrumental efficacy in meeting imperatives that are already given. A meritocratic prerogative of expertise is thus offered as an alternative to the hierarchical prerogative that is more usually associated with leadership. A qualified distribution of decision-making authority emerges; a distribution in which democratic inclusion is reserved for those employees who possess skills that are most congenial to the achievement of predetermined organizational objectives. The second criterion concerns the setting of those organizational objectives. In this respect, Woods et al. note that decision-making may only be dispersed insofar as it respects boundaries that are preset by formally constituted leaders. Overarching goals and values are seen as non-negotiable. Those to whom leadership is distributed are only able to participate in decision-making insofar as they respect the sanctity of those overarching goals and values.

Philip Woods develops this theme, noting a tendency for distributed leadership to be subject to dominant rationalities within organizations, which, he suggests, undermines its democratic credibility. He contrasts such conditionally distributed leadership with a notion of 'democratic leadership' that might evoke in individuals 'The capacity to author to some degree [their] own agency' (2004: 11). Woods suggests that such democratic leadership would need to be embedded within governance structures that respond to a 'thick conception' (2004: 11) of human beings as creative actors who are able to generate their own meanings and values. It should permit reflective, self-conscious choice on the part of individuals in the face of totalizing, organizational agendas. This requires decisional, discursive, and therapeutic arrangements, which, according to Woods, are often lacking in instantiations of distributed leadership. Most importantly, Woods proposes that in order for leadership to be truly democratic, the imperatives of market-driven, economic rationality must not be sacrosanct. Rather, their ethical merits should be up there alongside all other considerations to be debated amongst implicated parties.

Caring for the Interests of Followers

A third way of meeting the charge that leadership is fundamentally impositional is to point to the benefits that accrue to the followers of successful leaders. I highlighted, earlier in this chapter, the ethical reassurance that some theorists take from leaders' altruistic regard for followers. However, as well as being offered as an indicator of ethicality in evaluating leadership agendas, the well-being of followers might also assuage discomfort with leadership's impositional ramifications. Many theorists have pointed out that in order to be successful, leaders need to keep an eye on the well-being of their people. And if followers' material and spiritual well-being is served by leadership, why should we worry about the possibility that their agency might be eroded in the process? As I pointed out earlier, transformational leadership theory is particularly taken with the idea that ethical leaders are those who put the needs of their followers first. The way in which transformational leadership theory characterizes the needs of followers, and how these needs can be met, is particularly relevant to the issue of imposition. On the one hand, it might ameliorate concerns about imposition; on the other hand, it might attenuate them. I will discuss this matter shortly. Before doing so, though, I will take some time to consider more generally the extent to which ministration to the interests of followers is advocated in the literature. I will also draw attention to a worryingly Machiavellian tone that this lends to some leadership prescriptions.

Many theorists have noted a link between successful leadership and consideration for the needs of followers. Just as the Human Relations movement (such as Mayo, 1997 [1949]) drew attention to the limitations of Scientific Management (Taylor, 1997 [1912]) in achieving managerial effectiveness, leadership research has illuminated the shortfalls of leadership effectiveness recipes that focus uniquely on task achievement. This has been described as a displacement of an earlier, hard-edged discourse of the 'leader as controller' by a softer understanding of 'leaders as therapists' (Western, 2008). An early example of this change in focus, resulting from research carried out by the University of Ohio (Hemphill, 1955; Skinner, 1969), is the observation that effective leaders do not just deal with structural aspects of their role. They also tend to 'show consideration' for employees' needs. Later research at Michigan University (Lickert, 1970) found that 'employee-centred' leadership behaviours are as important as 'job-centred' behaviours in ensuring leadership success. Similarly, Robert Blake and Jane Morton (1985) describe successful leadership behaviour in terms of 'concern for people' as well as 'concern for results'. This Human Relations theme also features in gender-related studies (such as Johnson, 1976; Hegelsen, 1990; Rosener, 1990), which draw attention to the instrumental efficacy of 'feminine' behaviours that, as well as encouraging participation on the part of followers, manifest concern for followers' welfare.

More common than straightforward advocacy of ministration to the needs and aspirations of followers, though, are *situational* prescriptions. Situational theories point to the suitability of contrasting leadership behaviours to different circumstances. For example, Hersey and Blanchard (1982) propose that leadership style should be adapted in response to the 'favourability' of leadership situations, while Fred Feidler (1967) suggests that different stages of 'task-readiness' amongst followers call for varying mixes of relationship-building and task-orientation. Calls for an androgynous leadership style, which combines characteristically 'masculine' and 'feminine' traits (Grant, 1992), also valorize an apposite blend of assertiveness and empathy. The lesson of these theories is that in order to overcome the rich variety of challenges that the organizational world might throw up, leaders need to be able to step in and out of a range of personas: sometimes they must wear the mask of benevolent paternalism; at other times, the needs of their people must take second place to more compelling, overarching imperatives.

On the one hand, these relationship-focused prescriptions seem to offer sound, pragmatic reasons for leaders to take the well-being of their people into account. As such, they lend to effective leadership an intuitive moral appeal. However, they also have a potentially sinister side. If too much is made of the instrumental benefits of affecting concern for followers' well-being, and particularly if leaders are encouraged to turn on and turn off their responsiveness to followers' needs and aspirations as circumstances dictate, there is a danger that leaders will be encouraged to adopt relationship-oriented behaviours in order to get the job done rather than out of genuine solicitude for their people. Human relationships between leaders and followers, instead of being rooted in emotional responses and a sincere ethic of care, may become hitched to the bandwagon of organizational success as defined by leaders. Apart from the intrinsically discomfiting nature of such instrumental co-optation of emotions, this may even expose followers' vulnerability beyond the level already engendered by hierarchical power differentials. Followers may be tempted to place trust in leaders as a consequence of the latter's apparent solicitude, only to find their interests sacrificed to the leader's agenda when contingently apposite. For this reason, an unequivocally transactional, task-focused style may even seem morally preferable to the apparent, but conditional, kindness of relationship-sensitive leadership approaches. Although the former may not radiate the reassuring hue of benevolence that surrounds the latter, they at least offer the virtues of transparency and consistency.

The literature's endorsement of Human Relations-oriented leadership behaviour should therefore be treated with caution. Far from providing the reassurance against imposition that it promises, it could be read instead as a blueprint for ever more sophisticated modes of repression. As corroboration for the instrumental merits of compassion gathers momentum, it might come to be increasingly co-opted by leaders who wear it as a reassuring veil, not in order to promote an employment relationship that resonates with their personal values, but simply as a contingent means of evoking yet greater commitment to their personally defined agendas.

Building Commitment to a Common Purpose

An alternative source of reassurance against leadership's impositional overtones is offered by transformational leadership's contention that leaders can evoke followers' self-actualization by getting them to participate in a shared undertaking. Indeed, for James MacGregor Burns (1978, 2003), herein lies transforming/transformational leadership's moral vindication. According to Burns, transforming leadership is characterized by a leader's ability to encourage followers to subordinate their individual needs and wants to a collective agenda. Burns appeals to the essentially uplifting benefits of participation in a common conscience, suggesting that it is only through such participation that people satisfy their 'higher-order' needs and thus find true self-actualization. Therefore, in evoking fealty to a collective agenda, transforming/transformational leaders enable followers to rise above their illusory wants, thus facilitating agency on a more elevated level. Burns therefore calls upon leaders not only to move followers vertically up a Maslow-style needs hierarchy but also to move them horizontally towards an appreciation of the essentially social nature of their 'real' needs.

Bernard Bass (Bass, 1985, 1990, 1998; Bass and Avolio, 1994) follows Burns in stressing the need for leaders to transcend individualized, transactional exchanges by building a shared sense of purpose. Like Burns, Bass proposes that the ethical quality of transformational leadership lies in its capacity to divert attention from the individual to the collective. According to Bass, 'Leaders are truly transformational when they increase awareness of what is right, good, important, and beautiful; when they help to elevate followers' needs for achievement and self-actualization; when they foster in followers higher moral maturity; and when they move followers to go beyond their self interests for the good of their group, organization, or society' (1998: 171).

On the one hand, this emphasis on the self-actualizing propensity of participation in a shared purpose might alleviate misgivings about leadership's impositional connotations. If, rather than suppressing followers, leaders are actually able to raise them to a more elevated plane of being, then perhaps we should not be so concerned about the asymmetrical distribution of influence that leads to this happy outcome. By highlighting the capacity of transformational leaders to help followers to realize their true essence, Bass and his colleagues are showing us how leadership might liberate the human spirit, rather than shackling it. Why should we worry about the asymmetrical exercise of influence when that influence makes us better people? On the other hand, some critics find this veneration of shared agendas troubling. Michael Keeley (1998) takes particular issue with transformational leadership theory in this respect, pointing out that the efficacy of self-actualization as an ethical justification rests on the questionable assumption of homogeneity of followers' interests, values, and aspirations. Keeley questions this premise, concluding that transformational leadership presents an insidious version of majority rule, in which peer pressure is placed upon all followers to support the common vision generated by the leader regardless of its congruence with individual agendas. Under the thrall of transformational leadership, minority groups and individuals will thus be subjected to subtle coercion to conform, and 'unless leaders are able to transform everyone and create absolute unanimity of interests (a very special case), transformational leadership merely produces a majority will that represents the interests of the strongest faction' (Keeley, 1998: 124).

In responding to the challenge presented by the collective to the individual, different researchers adopt contrasting approaches. One approach is to suppose that the real interests of organizational members are in harmony and that apparent conflicts of interest are the result of misunderstanding or poor coordination. Thus, apparent tensions amongst followers, or between individuals and the collective, should be resolved in favour of the latter by morally sagacious and socially influential leaders. Unsurprisingly, this stance is articulated most explicitly by Bass in his direct response to Keeley's challenge (1998). Bass (1998) suggests that transformational leaders must attend to both 'transactional' and 'transformational' dimensions. In this way, transactional checks and balances will ensure adequate representation of individual interests while leadership's transformational elements build commitment to a common purpose. Bass downplays the likelihood of tension between those transactional and transformational dimensions, implying that the real interests of followers lie on the transformational side. The task of transformational leaders is therefore to make followers aware of those real interests and, using their leadership capabilities, to build commitment to the shared purposes through which they can be realized.

A contrasting response is to acknowledge a plurality of interests, aspirations, values, and perspectives amongst organizational members; a response which highlights the need for leaders to respond to such heterogeneity. Whereas Bass' ideas seem to be congruent with the first approach, the rather different transformational leadership model developed by Alimo-Metcalfe and Alban-Metcalfe (2001, 2004, 2005), to which I referred earlier in this chapter, is more supportive of organizational pluralism. Thus, Alimo-Metcalfe and Alban-Metcalfe highlight the congruence between effective leadership and respect for diversity, suggesting that 'the constructs of leadership emerging from our data . . . placed great importance on being sensitive to the agenda of a wide range of internal and external stakeholders, rather than seeking to meet the agenda of only one particular group' (2005: 63). Sensitivity to pluralism is also endorsed by the distinction that Alimo-Metcalfe and Alban-Metcalfe draw between their 'networking and achieving' factor and

Bass' 'inspirational charismatic' dimension. The former, they say, includes a 'crucially important additional aspect, which is "sensitivity to the agenda of different key players/interest groups, such that they feel they are being served by the vision"' (2005: 58).

Some General Observations

In this chapter I have explored what the leadership literature has to say about two particular ethical challenges associated with leadership. This has permitted the identification of a few prominent themes; themes which I will develop and augment as the book progresses. Before offering some general observations about the preceding discussion and saying a little about how the literature fits in with writing on management and organization more generally, I will recap these themes. I began the chapter by describing the reassurance that some theorists take from the morally uplifting force of leaders' altruism. These writers suggest that altruistic leaders are likely to lead in morally desirable directions, whereas the agendas of egotistic leaders are likely to be morally problematic. Therefore, by identifying the nature of a leader's intent, in accordance with a checklist supplied by the theorist, we can assure ourselves of the ethical probity of their agenda. Other researchers note an intrinsic, altruistic dimension to leadership. They suggest that leaders, if they are to be effective at all, need to be altruistically driven.

However, this preoccupation with leaders' altruism, compelling though it is, sets up another potential concern: that leaders' altruistic devotion to the members of the organizations they lead may occlude broader moral considerations. Given the far-reaching effects of the decisions made by leaders in organizations, such a narrowing of purview could have worrying repercussions. Contrasting responses might be offered to this challenge. One response is to trust morally perspicacious leaders to balance the interests of the organization against those wider considerations; to cast the leader as a moral sage; to put faith in the leader as arbiter of right and wrong on a broader scale. Alternatively, we might emphasize the instrumental or normative merits of shared decision-making. If effective leaders are inclined to consult, or if they did consult, then less reliance is, or would be, placed upon leaders' moral acumen.

I then moved away from the ethicality of leadership agendas to consider the issue of asymmetrical influence, along with its connotations of suppressed agency amongst followers. I began by drawing attention to the strong, impositional undertone that imbues a lot of the literature. Nevertheless, I pointed out that the literature also offers ample grounds for exonerating leadership from the charge of morally debilitating imposition. Firstly, I suggested that shifting the spotlight away from leaders and looking more broadly at the processes through which leader–follower relationships are negotiated illuminates the extent to which those relationships might be consensual. However, while the tacit, informal consent of followers may go some way to mitigating any suppression of their agency, such mitigation assumes that they have a realistic choice. If consent to the impositional yoke of leadership is accorded upon a negotiating platform that is systemically unbalanced, then its legitimating force is seriously undermined.

The widespread association of leadership effectiveness with democratically respectful leadership behaviour also seems to gainsay the charge of suppressed agency. If effective leaders tend to consult, then maybe leadership is not so impositional after all. However, the morally legitimating force of democratic processes may be eroded by the limitations and preconditions that are placed upon those processes. In particular, if organizations' democratic constituencies are too narrowly defined, or if the list of topics that are up for debate is overly censored, then organizational democracy may not be as democratic as it seems.

I ended by considering the suggestion that in order to succeed, leaders need to take care of their people. If successful leadership involves looking after followers, then perhaps we should not bother too much about suppressed agency: it will all be in everyone's best interests in the long run. But I also drew attention to the sinister, Machiavellian shadow that hangs over follower-responsive leadership prescriptions, particularly those that advocate contingent adaptation. The moral shine of benevolent paternalism is seriously tarnished if it is no more than a calculated, instrumentally driven affectation, particularly if it is switched on and off according to leader-defined imperatives.

But leaders' capacity to evoke support for a common cause also promises to relieve concerns about imposition. If participating in a common cause evokes people's self-actualization, then this may vindicate any undue influence used to encourage such participation. However, despite the intuitive appeal of participation in a collective undertaking, we should not lose sight of the challenge that the collective may present to the individual. Morally compelling though transformational leadership's advocacy of shared purpose is, that purpose should not be pursued so assiduously that it tramples over the heterogeneous aspirations, interests, and identities of followers.

In this discussion I may have given the impression that whatever a leader does is open to ethical critique. My review of the leadership literature might therefore be interpreted as a destructive undertaking; a pedantic, nitpicking exercise to show that organizational leaders are morally culpable whichever way they turn. However, this is not my intention. I am assuming that leadership has the capacity to be morally commendable as well as morally degenerate. I suggest, though, that morally commendable leadership is more likely if attention is paid to the themes explored here. It is important to note that each of these themes has its moral upside as well as its potential moral downside;

I have tried here to illuminate both the upsides and the downsides. To begin with, altruism undoubtedly confers ethical credit on leadership; but leaders' moral concern should surely extend beyond altruistic regard for organizational members. And, for sure, consensual agreement to leaders' extraordinary influence may go some way to legitimating that influence; but only if such agreement is freely given. Furthermore, few would argue with the moral attractions of democratically responsive leadership; but a democratic inclusiveness that rules out large numbers of affected parties is considerably less compelling. Moreover, that leaders care for the interests of their people undoubtedly confers moral credit on their leadership; but only if their care is genuine. And lastly, it is hard to disagree that participation in shared undertakings has the potential to be life enhancing; but only if the collective is not allowed to erode all dimensions of individuality.

Locating the Leadership Literature

To conclude this discussion of the leadership literature, I will relate some of the theories that I have discussed in this chapter to the broader field of organization and management studies. I will also say a little about some issues that follow from this brief orientation exercise. A lot of the literature that I have reviewed here can be characterized as being performative in its preoccupation and managerialist in its underpinning assumptions. I have already remarked upon the literature's preoccupation with effectiveness. It thus tends to be *performative* as defined by Fournier and Grey, who describe performative organization and management studies as having the 'intent to develop and celebrate knowledge which contributes to the production of maximum output for minimum input; it involves inscribing knowledge within means–end calculation' (Fournier and Grey, 2000:17). Another way of putting this is that the literature generally aims to help leaders to get the most out of their people and thus to enhance the performance of the organizations in which they lead. Perhaps this performative quality is unsurprising considering the prime target audience of a lot of this literature: that is, practising managers who look to leadership scholars to help them improve their ability to do what is expected of them in their managerial roles, which, most often, is to get the most out of their subordinates. It may also say something about the sources from which business schools, within which a great deal of this research has been carried out, derive much of their financial support (Alvesson and Willmott, 1996; Parker, 2002).

Closely linked to this performative characteristic of the literature are its *managerialist* (Burnham, 1972 [1945]; Enteman, 1993) presuppositions. The key premise of managerialism has been concisely summarized by Tony Watson as:

A belief that modern societies, and the institutions within them, should be run by qualified managers who can organise society rationally on the basis of expert knowledge—thus replacing the divisiveness and inefficiency of debate and democracy. (Watson, 2002: 53)

The faith in leaders' moral sagacity that characterizes some of the accounts described in this chapter sits comfortably within this managerialist perspective. These accounts take for granted that people who occupy formal leadership roles are innately better suited than are those at less exalted levels to make decisions that affect the rest of us. Such is the confidence that these accounts place in the proficiency of senior managers that this presumption of expertise extends even to the apprehension of moral probity. The extension of managerialism to the realm of organizational ethics is thus accorded normative legitimacy. The emphasis that charismatic and transformational theorists place on altruism as an indicator of moral probity is just one instance of managerialist faith in those who sit atop organizations. The onus that these theorists place on leaders' altruistic intent implies that, so long as the distractions of self-interest can be overcome, leaders' moral perspicacity will ensure ethically legitimate outcomes. If the apprehension of moral probity is a challenging undertaking for the rest of us, we can entrust this awesome responsibility to our leaders, safe in the knowledge that their superior aptitude sanctions such a role.

That managerialism permeates a great deal of leadership theory should come as no surprise given the overwhelmingly performative orientation of the latter. The quest to identify the secrets of effective leadership is generally undertaken in the interests of more effective management. It presupposes that managers will be better placed to manage if they can learn to lead effectively. The right of leaders, or managers, to lead is rarely questioned: In most leadership commentaries, that those who occupy formal positions of authority will dispense their responsibilities in the common interest is either taken as a given or is not subjected to rigorous interrogation. However, this managerialist presupposition presents some difficulties when considered from a moral perspective. The chief difficulties associated with managerialist accounts concern the expectation of unilateralism that they place upon leaders. These accounts tend to place the gavel of moral legitimization firmly in the hands of leaders. This asks an awful lot of those leaders, for ethics is rarely a simple matter. Reflection on the ethical ramifications of leadership decisions is a complex undertaking, requiring breadth of vision and moral perspicacity. It seems excessively hopeful to ask leaders to undertake such processes of moral reflection single-handedly. Possession of the social influencing skills that are widely associated with effective leadership, along with whatever additional technical and practical skills may be demanded of specific leadership roles, offers no guarantee that leaders will also be endowed with the moral sagacity required to legitimize unilateral, moral decision-making. Given the complexity of moral decision-making, its quality will surely be enhanced by contributions from diverse perspectives. Managerialism is broadly inimical to such breadth, leaving leaders to shoulder the burden of moral arbitration alone.

However, despite this preponderance of managerialism, some of the commentaries that I have discussed here are *critical* of it. I use the term 'critical' with a great deal of caution given the multiple meanings attributed to it in relation to organization and management studies (Alvesson and Willmott, 1996; Watson, 2001; Parker, 2002). I am using it here in the sense articulated by Alvesson and Willmott when they appeal for:

> a qualitatively different form of management: one that is more democratically accountable to those whose lives are affected in so many ways by management decisions…[where]…activities are determined through processes of decision making that take more direct account of the will and priorities of a majority of employees, consumers and citizens—rather than being dependent on the inclinations of an elite of self-styled experts whose principle allegiance is either to themselves or to their masters (Alvesson and Willmott, 1996: 40).

Some of the commentaries that I have reviewed in this chapter are explicitly critical in this sense. Falling into the category of overt critique are Smircich and Morgan's (1982) and Knights and Willmott's (1992) warnings that power structures within organizations may act to privilege leaders' versions of reality over discrepant constructions. Likewise, Price's (2003) and Keeley's (1998) critiques of the ethicality of transformational leadership constitute a direct challenge to Bass' performative and managerialist presuppositions. A critical tone is also apparent in Woods' admonition (2004) that situational, human relations-oriented, and dispersed leadership prescriptions may be harnessed to the wheel of corporate productivity with little genuine regard for followers' agendas or for democratic inclusion.

But if the unilateralism of managerialist accounts places upon leaders an unreasonable burden of moral sagacity, critically tinged commentaries present their own difficulties. Whereas managerialist expectations of leaders entail a unilateralism and a limitation of scope that is potentially damaging for ethical legitimacy, the difficulties confronted by critical accounts relate more to the practicalities of organizational life. If leaders adopt the responses to the moral challenges of leadership that are proposed by critically inclined theorists, there is a danger that they will not be perceived to be 'leading'. Leaders are generally expected, after all, to 'take the lead'. Managerialist expectations of imposition seem to be deeply embedded in popular understanding of leadership. As Martin Parker (2002) observes, despite 'managerialism's discontents', its pervasive influence is hard to avoid. So deeply engrained is it that it 'limits our capacity to imagine alternative forms of organizing' (2002: 11). As a consequence of this predicament, leaders who respond to the inevitable limitations of their own purview by sharing the burden of ethical reflection are likely to be perceived as shirking the responsibilities that accompany their elevated status and privileged remuneration: they are paid to 'lead'; therefore they must 'lead'.

A further difficulty with critically inclined accounts of leadership concerns the time-bounded nature of organizational life. People who occupy leadership roles are expected to make decisions with a minimum of delay so that others can get on with implementing those decisions. Democratic participation, on the other hand, can be a lengthy process. As a lot of the literature indicates, we tend to look for qualities such as decisiveness, self-assurance, determination, and resoluteness in our leaders. Enhancing the moral legitimacy of their decision-making via facilitation of consultative processes may be of little comfort to leaders who lose their jobs for pussyfooting. In view of these tensions, those models of leadership that place an onus on unilateral pronouncement by the leader may be more supportive of career enhancement than those which stress the ethically legitimating force of consultation.

Despite the pervasive thrall of managerialism and its penetration into common expectations of leadership, though, the focus placed by a lot of the literature on the instrumental benefits of democratic participation and heterogeneity indicates that leadership holds at least some space for critically resonant themes. Notwithstanding the warnings against manipulative co-optation, qualified diversity-responsiveness, and cynical, strategically driven consultation reviewed above, the (albeit instrumental) importance that has been attached to these themes during the last eighty years is testimony to their persistence. In the concluding chapter of this book I will discuss in more detail the possibilities that this tenacious, critical current may present for leadership approaches that challenge the managerial mainstream.

This discussion of leadership literature has permitted the identification of some prominent themes in the way that the relationship between organizational leadership and ethics might be conceived. These themes offer grounds for tension. Each seems to have something positive to say about ethical leadership, but each also presents its own moral drawbacks. Throughout the following chapters I will explore some of these themes in more detail, elaborating on the tensions already identified as well as highlighting some further issues. I will follow two additional avenues in order to progress this exploration. Later in the book, in Part III, I will look at what some practising leaders have to say on the subject of ethics. Before that overview of empirical findings, though, the three chapters that comprise Part II will consider leadership through the lens of ethics theory. I will, in each of these chapters, outline a different way of thinking about ethics and explore the implications that each approach holds for organizational leadership.

Part II
Moral Philosophy and Leadership

Part I of this book looked at what the leadership literature has to say about ethics. The purpose of that enquiry was to pick out some prominent themes and to identify areas of tension associated with those themes. Part II will continue this process, approaching the topic from a different direction. Having considered what leadership theory has to say about ethics, chapters 2, 3, and 4 will explore what Western ethics theory might have to say to leadership.

To ask what Western ethics theory has to say to leadership is to pose a very big question. Whereas the leadership literature considered in chapter 1 has accumulated over the last eighty years or so, the history of ethics theory spans more than two millennia. To do justice to such a heritage in the space of three chapters would be impossible, so my review has to be selective. However, I will try to embrace a representative cross-section of ideas by structuring this review around three *meta-ethical perspectives*, or three different ways of conceptualizing the status of ethical legitimation. This will give at least a flavour of the implications that various ways of thinking about ethics might hold for organizational leadership. Under the rubric of these three meta-ethical headings, I will focus on those theories within each group that have received most attention in the Western philosophical tradition.

The first meta-ethical group, which chapter 2 discusses, comprises theories that evaluate ethics in relation to principles that are held to be universally valid. To a large extent, these theories are characterized by an objectivist, moral ontology. The second group, which forms the subject matter of chapter 3, reveals a relativist or subjectivist commitment, considering ethics to be a matter of individual conviction. Within this group, I will focus specifically on existentialist theory. The third group, upon which chapter 4 is based, considers ethical legitimation as an intersubjective achievement. Chapter 4 pays particular attention to the theories of communicative action and discourse ethics developed by Jürgen Habermas, considering what this work might have to say about leadership in organizations.

As I pointed out in the Introduction to this book, in focusing on the Western tradition I am precluding consideration of moral philosophies from outside that tradition. I have already outlined my reasons for doing this, and it certainly should not be taken as an inference that non-Western traditions are any less compelling than Western philosophy, nor that they might not offer a useful basis for considering the challenges presented by leadership in contemporary Western organizations. Indeed, given the cosmopolitan make-up of contemporary Western society and the cultural interchange that is an inescapable corollary of a globalized organizational environment, such consideration would make a valuable adjunct to the ideas explored in this book.

Of course, even Western ethics theories of bygone eras were not offered as solutions to the moral conundrums associated with contemporary organizational leadership. They evolved in response to the idiosyncratic, philosophical preoccupations of their proponents, which in most cases were very different from those with which this book is concerned. Immanuel Kant, for instance, did not have in mind the CEOs of twenty-first-century business corporations when he penned his various formulations of the categorical imperative! Therefore, to take these theoretical offerings out of their context and apply them to that of contemporary, organizational leadership runs the risk of anachronism. However, although these philosophies were not developed in response to the challenges of organizational leadership, they are likely to have played their part in shaping the way we think about ethics today. It therefore seems reasonable for exploration of contemporary leadership ethics to embrace them. So, while I regret any misrepresentation that may arise from this anachronistic application, I believe such an appropriation to be justified.

My treatment of each of these three meta-ethical perspectives is a little different. Chapter 2, which discusses principle-based ethics, covers quite a lot of ground. This reflects the breadth of the range of principle-based theories that figure so prominently within the Anglo-American[1] tradition of moral philosophy, a representative selection of which I have tried to include. In order to give some consideration to each of these theories, that consideration has to be brief. I will reflect on some implications of these various ideas for leadership as I go along. I will then draw out some general points at the end of chapter 2. Chapters 3 and 4 on existentialist and intersubjectivist ethics, on the other hand, will discuss these respective theories in more detail. This is mainly because of the narrower focus of the material that these two chapters cover. Furthermore, I have also saved most of my reflections on the implications of existentialism and intersubjectivism for the end of their respective chapters. These contrasting structural approaches seem appropriate given the broad range of material covered in the principle-based chapter and the more concentrated focus of each of the other two chapters.

---

[1] In alluding to the Anglo-American tradition, I am not referring only to the works of British and American theorists but also to those European philosophers, such as Immanuel Kant, upon whom that tradition draws.

2

Principle-based Ethics and Leadership

Principle-based ethics theory holds that morally right action is action that is consistent with the application of certain principles. Therefore, in order to explore the moral challenges associated with leadership, we must consider them in relation to those principles. Principle-based ethics is characterized by a *universalist* commitment: the principles that define ethical conduct are generally believed to apply to all people. It also tends to be premised upon an *objectivist* moral ontology: a belief that certain moral principles have value whether we realize it or not. Principle-based ethics is thus contrasted to theories that view morality as culturally relative or as a matter of individual choice, and the task of moral philosophy is understood as being to identify those universal, objective principles that define ethical legitimacy.

Many approaches have been taken to this task. It is quite common to classify these theories in relation to the extent to which they display a consequentialist or a non-consequentialist character. *Consequentialist* theory judges the moral worth of an act in relation to the consequences that it brings about. It focuses on the desirability of states of affairs, proposing that actions are morally right or wrong insofar as they promote or detract from those desirable states of affairs. According to consequentialism, the manner in which these outcomes are achieved is of lesser importance in judging moral worth: consequences take primacy in moral evaluation, so the moral worth of a certain end justifies the means adopted to bring it about. Non-consequentialist theory, on the other hand, sees moral worth as intrinsic to an action. It proposes that certain types of action carry an intrinsic rightness or wrongness irrespective of the consequences that they bring about. Whereas consequentialist theory focuses on the ends of ethical action, non-consequentialist theory pays particular attention to the means adopted to bring about those ends.

In this chapter I propose to describe some of the consequentialist and non-consequentialist theories that have received most attention in the Western philosophical tradition. I will look at some ways in which these theories relate to organizational contexts and, in particular, I will draw out their implications for organizational leadership. The chapter will end with some general observations about principle-based theory and on some insights that it affords to leadership ethics.

Consequentialist Ethics and Leadership

When philosophers speak of consequentialist theory, they generally refer to *utilitarianism*. Utilitarianism proposes that a morally right action is one that brings about the greatest amount of good for the greatest number of people. In other words, morality is all about maximizing human well-being. Utilitarian analysis of leadership decisions therefore seems to be a straightforward matter: the morally right action for a leader to take is that which maximizes human well-being; that which brings about the greatest amount of good for the greatest number of people. This apparent simplicity is misleading, however, for using utilitarianism as a template for ethical leadership is beset with conceptual and practical difficulties.

The first problem is that the precise nature of 'good' – that well-being that leaders must seek to maximize – needs to be defined. Jeremy Bentham's seminal formulation of utilitarian ethics defined good in terms of pleasure. Bentham premised his theory on the principle of *psychological hedonism*, proposing that the only thing that humans pursue in its own right is pleasure and that the one thing that they avoid above all else is pain. As Bentham put it: 'Nature has placed mankind under the governance of two sovereign masters, *pain* and *pleasure*' (2000 [1789]: 87). Pleasure, according to Bentham, is therefore the only categorical good: all other supposed goods, such as wealth, status, and friendship, are only desirable insofar as they promote pleasure; they have no intrinsic value. Conversely, supposed evils such as poverty, rejection, or loneliness are only considered bad insofar as they bring about pain; they are not intrinsically bad. Since pleasure and the avoidance of pain are the only things that people desire in their own right, Bentham argued, maximization of pleasure must comprise the basis of ethical evaluation. A Benthamite utilitarian would therefore judge the ethics of leadership in relation to the amount of pleasure that it brings about. Benthamite analysis would expect a leader, when confronted with a moral choice, to take the option which brings the greatest amount of pleasure to the greatest number of people, while causing the least pain to the fewest people.

However, later utilitarians have taken issue with the psychological hedonism that underpins Bentham's theory, distancing themselves from its depiction of humans as 'a mad assembly of pleasure hogs constantly out for a buzz' (Goodin, 1993: 242). Even some commentators who agree with the principle of psychological hedonism question whether this entails *ethical hedonism*: it does not necessarily follow, just because pleasure *is* all that some people value categorically, that pleasure *ought to be* accorded intrinsic merit. Some critics even go so far as to propose that certain types of pleasure are intrinsically bad, such as the pleasure that some might take from witnessing a public execution (Dancy, 1993). In moving away from Bentham's hedonistic foundation, utilitarians have followed various paths. The first direction is taken by what Derek Parfit (1984) calls *desire-fulfilment theorists*. These place the satisfaction of people's desires, irrespective of what those desires are, at the centre of morality. A second direction, referred to by Robert Goodin (1993) as *welfare utilitarianism*, places people's long-term interests, as opposed to their immediate desires, at the centre of utilitarian calculation. A further variant, which Parfit (1984) refers to as *objective list theory*, holds that certain things are intrinsically good or bad for us no matter how much we might desire those things. Putative objective lists typically include such items as knowledge, aesthetic experience, self-actualization, and intellectual achievement.

Each of these variants of utilitarianism holds slightly different implications for leadership. Desire-fulfilment utilitarians would expect leaders to maximize the extent to which people can satisfy their desires, whatever those desires might be. This would seem to call for an attitude of laissez-faire facilitation, where leaders make it possible for people to do what they want to do and to achieve what they want to achieve. Welfare utilitarians, on the other hand, would judge leadership according to its propensity to maximize long-term welfare, regardless of whether people desire this in the short term. Similarly, objective-list theorists would expect leaders to maximize those states that are considered objectively good for people, regardless of their attitude towards those things. These last two variants are thus consistent with an attitude of benevolent paternalism on the part of leaders, where paternalism is understood as imposing some form of restraint on followers' freedom in order to secure their well-being (Kleinig, 1983). Unlike desire-fulfilment utilitarianism, welfare and objective-list utilitarianism both leave space for leaders to restrain people from satisfying their immediate desires on the basis that this is 'good' for them 'objectively' or 'in the long term'. Leadership's impositional connotations are not such an issue for these variants, as long as that imposition is ultimately in the best interests of its subjects. This approach resonates with transformational leadership theorists' advocacy of building commitment to a shared agenda, rather than negotiating around immediate, individualized interests. Since these theorists believe that people's real, long-term interests are realized through such collective participation, it would seem to be acceptable for leaders to use whatever means may be at their disposal to bring this about.

So, contrasting views about the precise nature of human well-being point to contrasting leadership approaches. But a further question that a utilitarian would have to address concerns the *universe of moral relevance*; that is, the composition of the group whose good must be taken into account by leaders' decision-making. For example, should it include only those people with whom the leader has regular, direct contact? Should it include all members of the organization for which the leader has responsibility? Should it comprise all those who depend upon the leader? Should it extend to all people who, in some small way, may be affected by the actions of that leader? This recalls an important question that was raised in chapter 1: the extent to which it is legitimate to limit the scope of leaders' moral concern to members of the organization that they lead. To restrict the universe of moral relevance to members of the organization would seem to require more than a utilitarian rationale. Other, non-utilitarian criteria, such as notions of duty or contractual obligation, would need to be enlisted to justify primacy of that limited group. If utilitarianism is to stand alone as a principle for ethical leadership, without support from non-consequentialist rationales, then its universe of moral relevance must have no limits; it must embrace every person who may be affected in some small way by the decisions and actions of that leader, either now or in the future.

But this still leaves unanswered a further question: whether we should limit ethical consideration to humans, or whether all sentient creatures, and perhaps even non-sentient beings, should be included in the universe of moral relevance. This question has a particular bearing for leaders of organizations that are involved with activities such as food production, clothing, cosmetics, and pharmaceuticals. Moreover, since nearly all organizations impact to some extent on the natural environment, the indirect impact on animals and other wildlife is of potential ethical significance for all leaders.

Utilitarian leadership is not free from complexity even after such questions as these have been answered, for once we have decided on the nature of good and the universe of moral relevance, the question of distribution of that 'good' within that 'universe of moral relevance' remains to be addressed. Should leaders aim for the greatest total good, which may justify substantial inequalities in distribution? Or should they aim to raise the minimum level of good experienced by every member of the universe of moral relevance? Such questions are important with regard to the distribution of reward within organizations; they are also relevant to the pricing and marketing of products and services. Moreover, would a considerable reduction of the good experienced by a few members of a universe of moral relevance be justified by small increases in the good experienced by a larger number? For example, is the major pain associated with making a few people redundant justified by the pleasure that many might derive from small material benefits associated with the consequent uplift in an organization's commercial performance?

Conceptual difficulties such as these do not necessarily preclude the claims of utilitarianism to provide a template for ethical leadership. They do highlight, however, the need for clarification of what is understood by 'the greatest good for the greatest number'. Conceptual difficulties do not exhaust the problems presented by utilitarianism though, for the leader who wants to maximize the good, however 'good' may be defined, must also confront some substantial practical challenges. Chief amongst these is the need to forecast the consequences of our decisions and actions. This is a particularly onerous undertaking given the nature of the leadership role. Those who occupy formal leadership positions in organizations are called upon to make many decisions. Those decisions are likely to impact on many people, so will be particularly influential on the store of common good. Therefore, in terms of both the quantity and potency of decision-making, utilitarianism imposes a heavy burden on leaders. Not only must they anticipate the likely effects of their actions on diverse groups of people, and maybe on other sentient and non-sentient beings as well, they must also carry out complex equations of the amount of good that might flow from alternative courses of action. To this complexity is added uncertainty: leaders can be sure neither of the outcomes of their actions nor of the degree to which those actions may bring about their intended consequences.

One response to these practical challenges centres on the distinction between *act utilitarianism* and *rule utilitarianism*. Act utilitarians propose that each specific act should be evaluated according to the amount of good that it promotes. According to act utilitarianism, a leader would have to weigh up every single action in accordance with its likely consequences in order to identify the right course; a seemingly impossible project. Rule utilitarians, on the other hand, acknowledge the impracticality of placing moral agents under such an arduous decision-making regime and base morality, instead, around a set of rules that, in general, can be expected to maximize the good. According to rule utilitarianism then, a leader would need to follow a set of moral principles that generally are found to promote the greatest good for the greatest number.

A rule-utilitarian rationale of this nature underpins some articulations of *market liberalism*: that the uninhibited workings of economic markets, although unkind to some in the short term, will ultimately promote the greatest good for the greatest number. Leaders of business organizations who are prepared to let market forces be their guide will therefore permit Adam Smith's 'invisible hand' (1998 [1776]: 292) to perform its beneficent role in the belief that this will, in the long term, be for the greater good of all.[1] There are,

---

[1] It is perhaps worth noting that at the other end of the ideological spectrum, a rule-utilitarian rationale might also be offered to justify the repressive cruelty of Stalinism.

of course, many who take issue with such a rule-utilitarian justification for economic liberalism. Some critics (such as Stiglitz, 2001; Turner, 2002; Kay, 2003) suggest that the utilitarian rule of unregulated economic markets does not maximize economic affluence in the long term (a contention to which the economic collapse of 2008 offers a great deal of support). Another group of critics (such as Galbraith, 1999 [1958]; Marcuse, 2002 [1964]; Hamilton, 2003) suggests that economic affluence does not offer a complete indicator of human well-being, so it should not be taken as an ultimate criterion of the greatest good. Such disagreements might be taken as an illustration of the difficulties associated with even a rule-utilitarian approach to moral legitimation when applied to practical contexts that are dynamic and complex.

I will make one last observation about utilitarianism before moving on to discuss some non-consequentialist theories. This is that, despite its conceptual and practical difficulties, utilitarianism has its uses. If we approach utilitarian calculation with an expectation of mathematical precision, then we are likely to be disappointed. But this need not undermine its worth. Neither should we conclude that utilitarianism is only suited to very simple decision-making scenarios, in which complexities of prediction and comparison are minimal. On the contrary, the merit of utilitarianism is that it encourages us to reflect on the consequences of our actions. In particular, it encourages us to think about the less obvious effects of those actions, their effects on those who are furthest away from us, or their effects on those who are least able to champion their own cause. To illustrate this point, as I write this book, oil is pumping into the Gulf of Mexico from a drilling pipe that was severed by the Deepwater Horizon accident, causing untold environmental and economic devastation. In deciding how to respond to this crisis, the leaders of BP do not need utilitarian reflection to draw their attention to the consequences of this leak; those consequences are being energetically represented by the politicians and media of the United States. However, the interests of those who are affected by frequent, socially and environmentally catastrophic oil spillages in and around the Niger delta (Vidal, 2010) are not represented with the same urgency. In the latter case, utilitarian reflection might offer a useful corrective to oil industry leaders as they consider their activities in that area.

Perhaps utilitarianism is best seen, then, as a handy reflective tool; a tool which helps us to think about how the things that we do affect those who are not so well placed to tell us themselves. Although utilitarianism may not come up with unequivocal responses to our moral conundrums, it still helps us to think those conundrums through before coming up with our own responses.

Non-Consequentialist Ethics and Leadership

Whereas consequentialist theory focuses on the outcomes of our actions, non-consequentialist theories give precedence to those actions themselves. According to the latter, actions are judged to be morally right or wrong according to their conformity to fundamental principles that carry universal, categorical worth irrespective of the states of affairs that they may or may not bring about. Therefore, whereas utilitarianism would judge the ethicality of leadership in relation to its propensity to maximize well-being, non-consequentialist perspectives would call upon leaders to respond to universal standards of moral rightness that have primacy over, and which may counter-mand, desirable consequences. These non-consequentialist theories tend to revolve around notions of duty and rights. I will discuss here two broad classifications of non-consequentialist theory along with two more specific fields. Each places a slightly different emphasis on rights and duties. The first, *rights theory*, embraces a range of theories that are primarily concerned with intrinsic rights, although they also speak of duties to observe those rights. The second, *Kantian ethics*, is a more specific field that is primarily concerned with categorical duties to behave in certain ways. The third embraces a range of *social contract theories*, which propose that rights and duties flow from tacit, contractual arrangements. The fourth stance, a *theory of justice* offered by John Rawls, steers a course between Kantian and contract theory, embracing aspects of both.

Rights Theory

The notion of universal human rights is firmly entrenched in the Western moral and political tradition. It provided a rationale for the American Independence movement, which championed the right to life, liberty, and the pursuit of happiness, while the French Revolution codified inalienable rights to liberty, property, security, and resistance to oppression (Almond, 1993). The perceived abuse of human rights has also offered a basis for the criticism of political regimes throughout the twentieth century and at the beginning of the twenty-first century. Unlike the negative protective framing of the seventeenth and eighteenth centuries, contemporary rights theory also offers a positive aspect by focusing on the provision of social benefits by the state, such as education and health care (Almond, 1993).

References to rights are also commonplace within the business context. On the one hand, large corporations have been criticized for complicity in state abuse of human rights (for example, Chomsky, 1999; Klein, 2001). Conversely, respect for human rights figures prominently in the self-legitimating claims that characterize the espoused social policies of many large corporations. More specifically, business ethics literature theorizes about the rights of particular groups, such as consumers, shareholders, suppliers, and local communities. Rights discourse is especially prominent in the way that employment relationships are often conceptualized: that is, as arrangements in which employees' rights and organizations' corresponding duty of care form one side of an equation that is balanced, on the other side, by a valorization of loyalty on the part of employees.

Given its resonance with contemporary thinking about political, business, and organizational morality, rights theory seems particularly apposite to the subject of leadership ethics. However, it is also problematic. Quite apart from the diverse ways in which rights might be framed, there is the challenge of balancing the presumed rights of different people where these justify conflicting courses of action. Nowhere are such conflicts more apparent than in corporate governance theory—a topic that connects closely to that of leadership ethics. On the one hand, shareholder theorists prioritize business executives' responsibility to maximize shareholder wealth. As well as the utilitarian rationale already referred to, shareholder theorists such as Friedman (1970) build on property rights theory (for example, Nozick, 1974; Locke, 1988 [1690]) in emphasizing business managers' *agentic* responsibility to respect the property rights of owners. They argue that business managers are appointed by owners—be they private owners or shareholders—to act as their 'agents' in running their business. This agency-forming relationship entails certain imperatives, the chief of which is that it is the right of owners to have their property (the company) used as they wish. And, since owners generally want to make the largest possible return on their investment in a company, it is the duty of executives to commit themselves to that task.

On the other hand, *normative stakeholder theory* (for example, Donaldson and Preston, 1995) draws attention to the rights of a broad range of stakeholders, including shareholders but also including other groups that interact with the business. Just because these other stakeholders do not all have an ownership relationship with a business, it does not mean that their rights should be overlooked. Clearly, there will be times when shareholders' rights to have their property used in the most remunerative way will conflict with the interests of other stakeholder groups. In such circumstances, which way should a business leader turn? Whose rights should take precedence? The persistence of the shareholder theory versus normative stakeholder theory debate, and the failure of either side to deliver a knockout blow, is an indication of the contentious and insoluble nature of rights conflicts. So, although rights theory offers a useful framework for drawing attention to leaders' responsibilities to particular groups, it does not necessarily provide a fail-safe mechanism for defining those responsibilities. Delicate choices still need to be made in balancing and prioritizing presumed duties to respect the diverse, sometimes irreconcilable, rights of different people.

Kantian Ethics

An alternative perspective on non-consequentialist ethics is provided by Immanuel Kant. Whereas rights theory tends to focus on people's rights, deriving moral obligations from other people's duty to respect those rights, Kant's preoccupation was with duty. Kant's moral philosophy needs to be understood within the context of his enquiry into the possibility of rational knowledge (Kant, 2003 [1787]). Kant proposed that we cannot have rational knowledge of the real world. This is because our experience of that real world is necessarily filtered by what he called the 'transcendental framework' of our senses and our conceptual understanding. We can, however, reflect on the nature of that transcendental framework and thereby acquire indubitable, universal knowledge about it. And by acquiring knowledge of our transcendental framework, we can acquire knowledge of how the world that is viewed through that transcendental framework will always appear. To draw a highly simplified analogy: if we always wear spectacles, and if we can acquire the knowledge that those spectacles are tinted green, we can be sure that everything we look at will also be coloured green. Everything may not really be coloured green; indeed, since we always wear green-tinted spectacles we will never know what colour things really are. But we can be sure that things will always look green to us.

Applying this process to moral enquiry, Kant derived transcendental truths about moral understanding (1948 [1797]; 1997 [1788]). In other words, by reflecting on the nature of our moral understanding, he identified fundamental presuppositions that will always hold true for moral judgement. Most importantly, for Kant, the notion of morality is inseparable from the notion of autonomy: it makes no sense to talk of someone being morally responsible for their actions unless we also assume that that person freely chooses those actions; in other words, that their choice is not preconditioned in any way. Therefore, in speaking of morality, we must assume human autonomy; autonomy from the influence of anything except what Kant called the 'practical rationality' of the moral agent. Kant thus deduced that moral action is action that is freely chosen with reference to nothing except our rational apprehension of our duty. It is not influenced by other factors such as desire, sentiment, or personal interest. According to Kant, it is this autonomy of the rational will that is ultimately deserving of ethical esteem, for it manifests the essence of humanity: that is, our capacity to make autonomous, rational choices. It is the sole principle of moral action and moral judgement. Therefore, the only acts that qualify for moral approbation are acts that are performed out of a rationally derived sense of duty.

The status of autonomy as a fundamental precondition of ethical action also provides a basis for determining the content of duty. Kant called the principle by which we determine our duty the *categorical imperative*. The categorical imperative is, for Kant, a basic principle without which the very concept of moral understanding would be meaningless. It is universally binding on all rational creatures because rational thought about morality presupposes it. Kant proposed a number of formulations of the categorical imperative, of which two have been particularly influential. The first of these is often referred to as the 'principle of universalizability'. It proposes that, since moral action must be based on the application of reason alone, and since reason is an homogeneous faculty that is shared with all other rational agents (unlike desires, which vary from person to person), then the principle upon which we act must be universalizable in order for it to be ethical. As Kant puts it: '*Act only on that maxim through which you can at the same time will that it should become universal law*' (1948 [1797]: 84). Many intuitively immoral acts would be conveniently proscribed by this principle since, were they to be universalized, they would be self-defeating. For example, telling a lie only achieves its desired objective if it is told against a general expectation that people will tell the truth: if everyone lied then there would be no point in lying because the liar would not be believed. To tell a lie whilst wishing for the universalization of lying would therefore be irrational and thus, according to Kant's dictum, it would be immoral.

To apply Kant's principle of universalizability to the leadership context would be to invite leaders to identify the principles upon which they are acting when they make ethically charged decisions and to ask themselves whether they would be happy for all people to act upon that principle in the same circumstances. It would call upon them to project themselves into the positions of those who are on the receiving end of their pronouncements and ask themselves how they, from that perspective of empathic engagement, would feel about the fairness of those pronouncements.

The second influential formulation of the categorical imperative is sometimes referred to as the 'principle of ends'. Given that autonomous beings are not just the agents but are also the repositories of all value, Kant proposed that they should always be treated as ends in their own right. This principle was expressed by Kant as: '*Act in such a way that you always treat humanity, whether in your own person or in the person of any other, never simply as a means, but always at the same time as an end*' (1948 [1797]: 91). Now, the application of the principle of ends to the world of organizational leadership seems, at first glance, to be rather impractical. For surely, at least part of what we expect of any leader is that they coordinate the resources at their disposal and that they apply these resources to the achievement of organizational objectives; in other words, that they use those resources as a *means* to the achievement of the *ends* of organizational objectives. Whatever those objectives may be, whether they relate to commercial accumulation, public service, or charitable ends, leaders are expected to use the resources available to them, including people, to achieve them. Thus, any stakeholders, whether they are employees, customers, suppliers, or whomever, are used as a means to the achievement of the organization's ends. And this seems to be prohibited by Kant's principle of ends.

However, a less rigorous, although more literal, translation of Kant's principle of ends avoids this apparent impracticality. Kant's precise wording of the second formulation does not necessarily preclude treating people as means to an end; it only precludes treating them *simply* as a means. It does not disallow treating people as a means as long as they are also treated *at the same time* as an end. According to this interpretation, it would be permissible to use people as a means to the achievement of an organization's ends as long as they are regarded, at the same time, as ends in themselves. Thus, it would be acceptable for a commercial organization to regard customers as a source of revenue as long as, at the same time, it treats them as ends in themselves. For example, it might regard the delivery of customer satisfaction not just as a means to making profit but also as a goal that carries intrinsic worth. Similarly, employees should not be viewed by leaders as purely instrumental to organizational success; rather, they should also be accorded intrinsic value. So, instead of cherishing employees as long as they offer the most cost-effective source of labour and then casting them aside as cheaper labour markets beckon, leaders should ascribe unconditional worth to their workforce. A similarly respectful approach should be extended to suppliers, shareholders, and to other groups upon whom organizational success depends.

To apply Kant's principle of ends to contemporary organizational contexts need not, then, morally invalidate the governance principles common to those contexts. To apply it as I have suggested, however, is to endorse a particular governance model. The principle of ends would invalidate an understanding of the organization that regards profitability and shareholder wealth as the overriding imperatives, and which calls for other stakeholder groups to be treated as no more than instrumental to the achievement of those ends. It therefore offers a further validation of the normative stakeholding (Donaldson and Preston, 1995) governance model already mentioned, which calls for the interests of all organizational stakeholders to be taken into account in corporate decision-making. On the other hand, it would morally invalidate the shareholder (Hayek, 1969 [1960]; Freidman, 1970; Sternberg, 1999, 2000) model of governance, which subordinates the interests of other stakeholders to those of shareholders, and which thus treats the former purely as means to the end of promoting the wealth of the latter.

Kant's rather convoluted reasoning thus delivers two principles which seem to offer a workable basis for thinking about the morality of organizational leadership. The principle of universalizability invites moral agents to consider whether they would wish the principle upon which they act to be universally adopted. It calls upon leaders to place themselves in the position of those who are affected by their decisions and to consider the rightness of those decisions from the point of view of those others. The second principle, Kant's principle of ends, might be otherwise described as a 'principle of respect for persons'. In a leadership decision-making scenario, it would call upon leaders to consider all stakeholders as having value in themselves.

Despite the apparent usefulness of Kant's categorical imperative, though, his theory does seem overrigorous in one respect. This is Kant's insistence that only acts performed out of a rational sense of duty carry moral worth. According to this stipulation, a leader who is driven by anything other than a rational sense of duty, but whose actions are nevertheless coincidental with duty, should not attract ethical merit. On the one hand, this criterion is intuitively appealing insofar as it precludes from moral approbation corporate social responsibility policies that pretend environmental or social concern but which are motivated purely by a desire to engender good public relations. So, for example, leaders who dedicate the resources of their organizations to charitable causes but who do so purely to gather the corporate kudos that such charitable action might attract would not, according to a Kantian evaluation, attract moral praise. This seems, intuitively, to be correct. However, Kant's stipulation that only acts performed out of a sense of duty should attract moral approbation also seems rather severe. It precludes emotionally motivated acts from moral approbation. Therefore, leaders who are driven by sentiments of altruism, charity, or benevolence to pursue intuitively appealing, moral agendas would not, according to Kant, attract moral praise. Kind people do not seem to have much moral worth in the Kantian system; attributions of worth are reserved for the rationally dutiful.

The distinction that some of Kant's commentators draw between *perfect duties* and *imperfect duties* addresses this point and also responds to a further limitation of duty-based ethics: that duty-based ethics tells us what we must and must not do; but it has little to say outside this morally legislative minimum. Although Kant does not offer an explicit and unambiguous definition of perfect and imperfect duty (Rosen, 1996), the distinction generally drawn from a broad reading of his work by his commentators (such as O'Neill, 1993) is that a perfect duty is a duty to which, under any circumstances, one is bound. Imperfect duties, on the other hand, respond to the inevitability of relations of mutual dependency between people. Based on this assumption of mutual dependency, it would be irrational for us to will that sentiments such as altruism, charity, and benevolence did not exist. However, these duties seem to be less complete than perfect duties since we cannot fulfil them absolutely: we cannot be completely altruistic, charitable, and benevolent to everyone in the world.

This distinction between perfect and imperfect duty seems to have something to offer to the organizational leadership context. On the one hand, we might use the principle of universalizability or the principle of ends to identify a leader's perfect duties. For example, we might thus identify obligations to certain groups who have a formal relationship with the organization: its shareholders, its employees, its suppliers, and so on. However, fulfilling these duties does not exhaust the possibilities of ethical leadership. Consideration for other groups who are affected by a leader's decisions, but with whom no formal relationship exists, might be included under the heading of imperfect duties. Although precedence is accorded to the leader's perfect duties, ethical leaders might also be expected to observe imperfect duties to communities that are affected by the actions of the organizations that they lead.

Contract Theory

Contract theory suggests that there are tacit contractual agreements between members of communities to abide by certain conventions and, in particular, to respect the rights and duties that those conventions entail. These tacit agreements generally place limits on the freedom of those members to act as they might otherwise choose. However, contract theorists propose that members freely agree to such curtailment of their liberty because it is in their long-term interest to do so. This idea figures prominently in the political and moral philosophy of Thomas Hobbes. Hobbes proposed that men and women are, by nature, free. However, they choose to accept limitations to their freedom because this brings about a state of affairs that is more advantageous for them than if everyone did whatever they wanted to do. Hobbes asks us to imagine a *state of nature* without controls on freedom, in which, he suggested, life would necessarily be 'solitary, poore [*sic*], nasty, brutish, and short' (1985 [1651]: 186). For Hobbes, the rationale for political rule lies in avoidance of the unpleasantness that this violent, combative state of nature entails. Applied to the ethical arena, contract theory suggests that we tacitly agree to limitations on the pursuit of our own immediate desires on the condition that others will do likewise. We thus avoid the unpleasant consequences that unbridled pursuit of short-term self-interest by everyone else would bring for us personally.

It is important to emphasize that the nature of the social contracts of which contract theorists speak is generally regarded as tacit. Few theorists would argue that an actual contractual agreement had ever taken place. Hobbes' application of the notion of contract appeals not to an historical event but to a conceptual notion that explains why it is in our enlightened self-interest to accept limitations to our liberty. The assumption that underpins contract theory is that in order to remain within a community and enjoy the benefits offered by membership of that community, we make a tacit agreement to abide by its conventions. Our continued presence in a community thus implies our fealty to its conventions and our acceptance of any restrictions on personal liberty that this may entail.

Contract theory offers a basis for thinking about leadership responsibilities, particularly insofar as it draws attention to tacit or implied agreements that may shape leader–follower relations within work organizations. To be sure, some of the contractual responsibilities that circumscribe workplace arrangements are legally enshrined, so have a compulsion that goes beyond moral imperatives. Formal contracts of employment provide a legally enforceable, minimum definition of the mutual rights and duties that define the employment relationship. However, in addition to legally defined, explicit commitments, relationships between organizational leaders and employees are also subject to tacit, mutual agreements that are not legally defined. Within contemporary human resource management theory, the term *psychological contract* has been adopted to describe the tacit conditions which define employers' and employees' expectations of one another (Guest and Conway, 2002; Conway and Briner, 2005). It generally refers to a set of imprecise expectations, based more on precedent than on formal statement of intent. It defines notions of fairness with respect to the balance between employee input and non-material rewards, including development opportunities, promotion, feedback, task allocation, and the nature of the working environment. It also embraces expectations of job security on the part of employees as well as expectations of employee loyalty on the part of employers. The psychological contract thus offers an example of how contract theory might be operationalized within contemporary organizational contexts. It also resonates with the idea discussed in chapter 1 that the perpetuation of leader–follower relations is partly dependent on tacit, consensual agreement on the part of followers to any asymmetries that those relationships entail.

To apply the Hobbesian notion of a social contract to the psychological contract is to understand it as a tacit agreement, rooted in enlightened self-interest, to the legitimacy of the principles of right and duty that circumscribe the relationship between an organization and its employees. Likewise, leader–follower relationships within organizations, viewed through the prism of contract theory, could be regarded as enlightened, tacit agreements by leaders and followers to the conditions that define those relationships. The relationship between employees, or 'followers', and organizational leaders is thus viewed as consensual predicament; one to which those followers tacitly agree because they realize that any apparent disadvantages that it entails are outweighed by its long-term benefits.

As some of the leadership theorists reviewed in chapter 1 suggest, though, such an interpretation acquires moral complexity from the possibility that those tacit contractual arrangements may originate from bargaining positions that are characterized by power differentials. Those power differentials may operate at an overt level (Haugaard, 2002), where followers agree to tacit contractual terms because they realize that they have little choice in the matter. The legitimacy of contract theory depends to a large extent on the assumption of choice: if remaining within a group is to be taken as a tacit accord on the part of group members to adhere to its conventions, then it is reasonable to assume that those group members have a choice; that they have somewhere else to go should they decide that that group is not for them. This is a problem for contract theory, in both its political and its organizational applications. The proposal that all citizens are free to leave a society if they do not find its conventions to their liking is nonsense. Equally, the contention that all members of a work organization can easily take their services elsewhere takes no account of either job-market realities or the switching costs involved in changing jobs. Although employees who are fortunate enough to possess sought-after skills (including proven leadership ability) may enjoy a degree of flexibility in their choice of workplace, as well a more solid platform from which to negotiate both tacit and explicit contractual commitments, the majority are not so well placed.

Of course, such power differentials may not only operate at overt levels. Bachrach and Baratz (2002 [1962]) draw attention to the covert manner in which some parties to a contractual agreement may limit the parameters within which that accord is reached. At a still more covert level, Steven Lukes (2002 [1974]) suggests that power differentials may be instrumental in shaping some parties' perceptions of their interests so that they willingly accord to contractual terms that are contrary to what they might, in a more enlightened state of mind, consider to be in their best interests. This, again, chimes with some of the objections made by those leadership theorists who question consensual legitimation of leadership influence. Considerations such as these need not preclude contract theory as basis for legitimating rights and duties within leader–follower relationships. However, if a tacit, informal contract is to offer such a basis, it is reasonable to expect agreement to its terms to be accorded under certain conditions. Those conditions include absence of coercion, the availability of alternatives, and access to information. Tacit, contractual agreements that are shaped by asymmetrical power relationships or misinformation, or where the only choice is to take it or leave it, provide a basis of moral legitimation that is, to say the least, questionable.

John Rawls' Theory of Justice

I will end this brief tour of principle-based ethical theory by mentioning a recent approach proposed by John Rawls (1971). Rawls' theory of justice incorporates elements of both contract theory and Kant's principle of universalizability as well as adding a vital third ingredient: the notion of fairness. It thus arrives at conclusions that avoid some of the difficulties associated with contract theory and which also refine Kant's approach. Like contract theorists, Rawls roots a system of rights in the idea of a hypothetical, pre-social condition, proposing that the duties incumbent upon moral agents are those that they would agree to were they placed in this imaginary situation. However, Rawls introduces the notion of a 'veil of ignorance'. He invites moral decision-makers to reflect on the contractual arrangements that they would agree to were they taken out of their present context, along with whatever status, talents, or potentials they enjoy in that context, and placed in an 'original position' in which they were ignorant of their own eventual status, talents, or potentials. Ethical behaviour, for Rawls, is that which 'free and rational persons [who are] concerned to further their own interests' (1971: 10) would accept if placed behind such a hypothetical veil of ignorance.

Applying Rawls' theory to leadership would invite leaders to assume this hypothetical original position; to undertake an imagined dismantling of the privileges that attend their rank; and to ask themselves how they might then appraise the fairness of their pronouncements. Of course, whether or not leaders can easily make the imaginative leap that is required in order to don Rawls' proposed veil of ignorance is open to question. Rawls' prescription supposes that people are able to stand back from the reality of their current circumstances sufficiently to make such hypothetical assessments. His theory has also been criticized (for example, MacIntyre, 1985 [1981]) on the basis that different decision-makers might tolerate different levels of risk in seeking to maximize their self-interest. Different people would therefore choose different standards of justice when placed behind the veil of ignorance: some would be willing to take a gamble on receiving a fortuitous allocation of talents, so would be inclined to adopt a less charitable disposition; whilst others would go for the safer option and opt for minimal differentiation in benefits.

Nevertheless, by introducing the veil of ignorance, Rawls goes some way to responding to the challenge of asymmetrical bargaining positions mentioned earlier in relation to contract theory. Leaders who follow Rawls' moral prescription would not just respond to tacit contractual commitments, which may be arrived at through positions of unequal power. They would be expected to reflect on the fairness of those commitments from a position of imagined impartiality. Rawls also responds to a criticism of Kant's principle of universalization. Kant's principle would invite leaders to ask themselves whether they would wish the maxim upon which they act to be universally adopted. However, it would be asking them to make that judgement from the perspective of their actual situation, along with its attendant privileges and potentialities. Again, Rawls takes things back a stage. He would require leaders to follow the course of action they would choose if placed in an original position where they were ignorant of their eventual status.

Some General Observations

I will end this discussion of principle-based theory with some general observations concerning its application to leadership contexts. The first observation is that principle-based ethics seems to offer a basis for unilateral, moral decision-making on the part of leaders. If morality is just a matter of applying the right rules, then leaders who are equipped with those rules, and who have the necessary moral perspicacity to apply them accurately, can single-handedly audit the ethicality of their actions and decisions. Principle-based theory therefore holds the promise of personally derived, moral authorization. However, while unilateral, ethical evaluation is thus legitimized in theory, its practice is no simple matter. Quite apart from choosing which to favour from a pantheon of principle-based theories—a question about which moral philosophers have yet to agree and about which I will say more shortly—the application of both utilitarian and non-consequentialist principles is fraught with practical difficulty. Utilitarian analysis demands clear definition of the common good. It also requires leaders to speculate about the likely consequences of their decisions for different groups and to weigh those consequences in terms of overall well-being. Although rule utilitarianism offers to relieve utilitarian decision-making of some of its complexity, it presents its own difficulties. Chief amongst these is that the identification of unproblematic, utility-maximizing rules is no simple matter. The application of non-consequentialist theories is no less equivocal. Apart from the conceptual difficulties that have already been mentioned, their employment in leadership contexts is likely to involve complex issues of interpretation as well as fine adjudications between perceived responsibilities to different people. However sensible and straightforward these principles may seem, their application to real-life scenarios demands intricate, qualitative evaluations that would tax any decision-maker.

While challenges such as these need not preclude the relevance of principle-based theory to leadership ethics, they place a heavy burden on any leaders who choose to impose a personally defined moral agenda on their organization. Quite apart from everything else that is required of leaders—including all those personal qualities that the effectiveness literature has identified—they would also need to be moral sages. It therefore seems sensible for leaders who choose to adopt a principle-based approach to ethical legitimation to share the onerous burden of morally auditing their actions and their decisions.

A second set of observations relates to the sheer breadth and variety of principle-based theory. In this chapter I have discussed some of the most frequently cited approaches, but there are many more. These theories 'speak in different voices, one praising what the other condemns. They clash and contradict each other, each claiming the authority the others deny' (Bauman, 1993: 20). The implications of this breadth and variety are twofold. On the one hand, leaders who look to principle-based theory for moral guidance may find themselves bewildered by the options that confront them, each of which seems sensible and intuitively appealing in its own right, but each of which may legitimize courses of action that others proscribe. Surrounded by such an array of alternative versions of right, it is difficult to know which way to turn.

In the hands of someone who is keen to do the right thing, then, the breadth and diversity of principle-based theory and the complexities of choice that this entails present a significant practical challenge. But perhaps the more pernicious implication of this breadth and diversity is that it may render moral judgement prone to expedient flexibility. Whereas leaders who are anxious to select an ethical course may find the profusion of principle-based ethics problematic, those who are more concerned with finding convenient moral rationales for their decisions than actually informing those decisions may be attracted to the possibilities that this wide choice entails. Leaders who do not look for moral guidance but who, instead, seek to legitimize decisions that they have already made on non-moral grounds may not have to look far to find a convenient justification. Given the range of theories and the range of interpretations to which each principle-based approach is subject, leaders should be able to find a suitable principle-based theory to justify whatever they want to do.

The worrying implications of this expedient flexibility are partly amelio-rated by a presupposition that principle-based theories hold in common: this is their presumption of consistency in application. A presupposition that underpins utilitarian and non-consequentialist rationales is that their respec-tive principles should apply for all people in all situations. The rationality common to principle-based theory entails this. Principle-based theories can-not be regarded as a quiver of rationales from which agents may select which-ever arrow matches the quarry they wish to bring down on that particular occasion. It is not ethically legitimate for leaders to pick-and-mix principle-based rationales in order to justify courses of action to which they may feel attracted on non-moral grounds. If a leader chooses to apply a particular theory in a particular way to justify a course of action in one scenario, it seems reasonable to expect them to apply the same criteria in other situations.

However, even the principle of consistency in application is not without its problems. Consistent application requires that if a principle is applied in a particular way in situation A then, if situation B arises in which all things are equal, the same principle should be applied in the same way. However, all things are never equal (Toulmin, 1990). Despite similarities between situation A and situation B, there will always be differences. The moral agent who chooses to apply a principle consistently in both situations does so because that agent has decided that the dimensions across which both situations approximate are morally relevant ones. Someone else may see things other-wise; another person may identify morally relevant dimensions across which the two situations differ and which therefore call for a different mode of application. The apprehension of sameness is subjectively defined. So, even consistency is not as reassuring as it may appear.

A third point relates to John Kaler's observation (1999) that ethics theory is of limited practical value for ethical decision-making in business contexts. Kaler's point is that we do not tend to think about practical moral problems in terms of principles such as 'maximization of the good' or by considering specific rights and duties and categorical principles. Instead, he suggests that we act on a sort of gut feel about what is the right thing to do in that particular instance. Kaler's point can be illustrated using the metaphor of a snooker player who is about to take a difficult shot. The snooker player does not calculate angles and velocities with the aid of tools and calculators, before applying the laws of applied physics to decide at what point, with what force, and with what degree of spin to strike the ball. The player takes a stroll around the table to familiarize herself or himself with the overall situation before striking the ball in a way that seems appropriate to those circumstances. Similarly, Kaler suggests that people confronted with business ethics decisions base those decisions not on the application of principles, but on an overall apprehension of what is the morally correct thing to do. Indeed, Kaler notes that we tend to test our moral theories with reference to our common-sense judgements of right and wrong, rather than the other way round. If a theoret-ical principle points in a direction with which we feel intuitively uncomfort-able, he suggests, we would be more inclined to ditch the theoretical principle than to act against our moral gut-feel.

If we go along with Kaler, then there would seem to be little need for principle-based theories in the evaluation of moral leadership: we should let intuitive moral judgement be our guide rather than going to the trouble of interpreting and applying theoretical principles. Combining Kaler's analysis with my earlier observations about the expedient flexibility of principle-based theory, we might conclude that the latter's prime purpose is a justificatory one: it is used purely to reassure ourselves and to persuade others of the ethical probity of the actions towards which our intuitive moral judgement has already pointed us.

Such criticisms of rationally based ethics theory have led some theorists towards the existentialist meta-ethical perspective that I will discuss shortly. Before doing so, though, I will say a few words in defence of principle-based ethics. The first point is that even if moral judgement normally relies on intuitive feel rather than on the application of principle, this need not undermine the worth of theoretical principles in addressing moral dilemmas. If we are able to identify principles that are important to us in those situations where the ethically sound course of action is clearly apparent, then it seems reasonable to appeal to those same principles for guidance in situations that are less clear-cut. Principle-based theory can thus be understood as an attempt to define moral imperatives that matter to us and to derive principles that will enable their application to real-life dilemmas.

My second point in defence of principle-based theory is that even if we believe that the quest for universally valid moral principles is conceptually misguided, we might nevertheless accede that various principle-based theories can serve a very useful purpose. That purpose lies in their capacity to draw attention to relevant aspects of ethically charged situations that we might otherwise overlook. A utilitarian perspective thus invites us to think of the long-term consequences of our actions, particularly as they affect people who might not spring readily to mind. Similarly, non-consequentialist theory serves the purpose of evoking sensitivity to the relationship that an organization has with less obvious stakeholders—particularly those who are not able to champion their rights as stridently as others. Even if we agree with Kaler that business people make moral decisions by applying a sort of moral gut-feel, we might still argue that the quality of those decisions can be enhanced if gut feel is exposed to a degree of critical reflection. And a leader's critical reflection may be enriched by looking at a moral dilemma through the lenses of a range of principle-based theories.

3

Existentialism and Leadership

Whereas the principle-based theories considered in chapter 2 seek to identify absolute bases of moral evaluation, the message that existentialism holds for ethics is that such a quest is futile. Existentialist philosophy can be characterized by both its *nihilistic* and its *emancipatory* themes. Its nihilistic message is that universal, objective foundations of moral truth cannot exist. The emancipatory implication of this declaration of moral nihilism is that, in the absence of absolute criteria of evaluation, the source of moral truth is to be found within each individual. According to existentialism, then, leaders who aspire to ethicality cannot appeal to external principles for guidance; they have to consult the font of moral authorship that is an inescapable aspect of their humanity.

This chapter will draw on the work of four key existentialist thinkers to elaborate the insights that existentialism has to offer to the topic of leadership ethics. It will start by describing how expressions of existentialism's nihilistic and emancipatory themes can be found in the writing of Søren Kierkegaard and Friedrich Nietzsche. It will then go on to summarize the contributions of Martin Heidegger and Jean-Paul Sartre, placing particular emphasis on these later writers' preoccupation with individual, moral autonomy and its centrality to what each considers an 'authentic' mode of human existence. I will reflect as I go along on how some of these ideas link with leadership before offering, at the end of the chapter, a more extensive discussion of existentialism's implications.

Critiques of Objectivist and Universalist Meta-Ethics

Søren Kierkegaard is widely regarded as a founding father of existentialist philosophy (Kaufmann, 1956; Langiulli, 1971; Gardiner, 1988; Barratt, 1990 [1958]), and it is in Kierkegaard's work that the roots of both the nihilistic and emancipatory themes of existentialism can be found. In *Fear and Trembling*

(1997*b* [1843]), Kierkegaard strikes a blow against dependency on conventional standards of morality when he contrasts a way of life that is lived in accordance with moral convention with a life that follows the dictates of faith. The former, for Kierkegaard, is fundamentally misguided insofar as it appeals to norms that claim an objective legitimacy that cannot exist. Moral convention, for Kierkegaard, can only comprise closed systems of reasoning that defy external legitimation. In other words, any part of a moral code can only be justified with reference to other parts of that same code; there can be no 'objective' source of justification that lies outside it. A life lived in accordance with faith, on the other hand, represents a positive choice to commit oneself to a given set of standards. And such a choice is made against an acknowledgement that there are no absolute, objective standards against which it can be justified: choice is its own legitimation.

I will say more, shortly, about Kierkegaard's endorsement of emotionally committed choice, which he articulates mainly in relation to religious faith but which has been adapted and applied in a secular fashion by Heidegger and Sartre in developing existentialism's emancipatory message. Before doing so, though, I will outline the nihilistic critique of morality that is delivered by Friedrich Nietzsche in *The Genealogy of Morals* (2003*b* [1887]), along with the idiosyncratic, emancipatory polemic that flows from it. In this work, Nietzsche refutes the objective, universal legitimacy of ethical standards on the basis that genealogical exploration of conventional morality reveals not only its origins but also the true nature of any system of morality. Nietzsche proposes that if we look back at how conventional morality has evolved, we will see it as no more than a set of standards that represent the interests of a particular group. Furthermore, Nietzsche suggests that all morality falls, and can only fall, into this same category. Any set of ethical standards is just a convenient fabrication that upholds the interests of certain types of people whilst repressing those of other, different types of people.

Nietzsche's analysis of morality draws heavily upon two presuppositions: a deterministic understanding of human capability and a particularly gloomy analysis of human motivation. His deterministic understanding of human capability proposes that people can be categorized according to 'type'. Nietzsche considers type to be determined by birth, so people have little or no control over their eventual psychological or physiological make-up. In elaborating the implications of type for ethics theory, he concerns himself with two particular types. On the one hand are the 'lower types', the 'herd', or the 'slaves', which include most people. On the other hand are the 'higher types', the 'over men', or 'super men': those exceptional individuals who are capable of a level of independence and creativity which elevates them above their fellow beings. Nietzsche points out that, due to the contrasting capabilities with which lower types and higher types are endowed, each type finds itself in very different circumstances. Consequently, the respective interests of each type are promoted by contrasting sets of moral principles. Higher types are blessed with greater intellectual and physical prowess, so their interests are likely to be served by egotistical and elitist standards that are consistent with the imposition of their interests over those of the masses. On the other hand, the masses, those 'lower types', are less well endowed with natural capabilities. Therefore, their interests are likely to be served by altruistic, egalitarian moral codes that alleviate the domination to which they would otherwise be subjected by 'higher types'.

A second presupposition of Nietzsche's nihilistic critique of morality is his belief that all people are fundamentally motivated by a desire to exert power over others. Our 'will to power' is thus, for Nietzsche, the driving force of human motivation. Any other motives that may seem to inspire our actions are ultimately reducible to the will to power because, when subjected to close analysis, they are found to be instrumental to it. According to Nietzsche, since this is the way that people are, it is futile to pretend otherwise. And it is equally futile to moralize about the consequences of this psychological inevitability. The strong impose their will on the weak because they can; the weak rail against this subjugation because it inhibits the expression of their own will to power. Nietzsche thus likens strong people to birds of prey, whereas weak people are as the young lambs upon which those powerful birds feed. According to Nietzsche, both the strong person and the bird of prey are acting in accordance with basic instinct. It makes no more sense to heap moral condemnation on those who impose their will on the weak from a position of strength than it does to condemn birds of prey for killing young lambs. Each is only doing what comes naturally. But just as the lamb will begrudge its oppression so, understandably, does the weak person: each does what they can to ease the burden of their hardship.

However, Nietzsche's genealogical exploration reveals that, despite the innate superiority of higher types, the morality of the lower types has prevailed. With sheer force of numbers on their side, and rallied by religious institutions—by the conniving 'priests of antiquity'—the morality of the lower types has succeeded in asserting itself over the elitist values that would otherwise privilege the interests of upper types. And, in the process, the self-interested struggle of the weak has acquired the force of morality. With the hegemony of slave morality, its imperatives have somehow come to acquire intrinsic value:

> This dismal state of affairs, this prudence of the lowest order, which even insects possess... has, thanks to the counterfeiting and self-deception of weakness, come to masquerade in the pomp of an ascetic, mute, and expectant virtue, just as

though the very weakness of the weak...were a voluntary result, something wished, chosen, a deed, an act of merit. (Nietzsche, 2003*b* [1887]: 26)

Values such as compassion, charity, and equality have thus come to dominate our moral intuitions: 'the morality of the vulgar man has triumphed' (Nietzsche, 2003*b* [1887]: 18). This triumph is not based on any objective superiority; it represents simply the successful imposition of the self-interest of the masses. The standards that are consistent with lower types' resistance to oppression have triumphed over those that uphold the interests of higher types. Nietzsche thus professes to have made an irrefutable case for the relativist nature of ethics, undermining any claims that the imperatives of 'slave moralities' might make to universal validity. Furthermore, because his analysis portrays the triumph of slave morality as 'an act of the *cleverest revenge*' (2003*b* [1887]: 17) which grew from the 'trunk of that tree of revenge and hate' (2003*b* [1887]: 17) and the 'festering venom and malignity' (2003*b* [1887]: 21) of the weak and oppressed, Nietzsche maintains that the basis of slave morality's hegemony lies in motives that it explicitly disparages. In this manner, he claims to have exposed not only the self-interested origins of slave morality but also its hypocrisy.

Thus far, I have emphasized the nihilistic message in Nietzsche's narrative. He sets out to undermine slave morality's pretensions and, in the process, he challenges the very notion of morality. However, Nietzsche's intention is not just to commit an act of moral vandalism, for this demolition is undertaken in the interests of an overarching, emancipatory agenda. Nietzsche's task is not just to dismantle traditional values; it is to effect a revaluation of values. He is driven by a passionate conviction that not only do the principles of conventional, ascetic, slave morality lack objective validity but that they also constrain human progress. Nietzsche's disquiet about slave morality relates particularly to the ways in which it holds back the elite. Its values have insinuated their way into our ideological presuppositions so that altruism is placed above self-love; equality is preferred to inequality; the quest for happiness, peace, and tranquillity inhibits our capacity to endure suffering, risk, and danger.

A major theme of the *Genealogy of Morals* is that this cultural hegemony of ascetic principles will inhibit 'higher types' from realizing their potential to further human excellence. Precisely what this human excellence consists of is not clear from Nietzsche's narrative. It seems to correspond to some vague notion of the self-actualization of the human species. Furthermore, Nietzsche's presentation of Goethe, Beethoven, and, indeed, himself as its embodiments (Leiter, 2002) suggests that he judges excellence largely in terms of intellectual accomplishment and cultural achievement. Despite his equivocation in defining the substance of excellence, though, Nietzsche offers an unambiguous description of the conditions necessary for its attainment. For excellence, in Nietzsche's view, cannot be achieved without suffering. It also requires prioritization of the interests of higher types over those of other people; it is inherently unequal. Furthermore, it cannot be achieved without a high tolerance of risk, and it demands the expression of instinctual drives. The crux of Nietzsche's concern, then, is that the values of slave morality, having become embedded in our culture, are constraining nascent higher types from cultivating and giving expression to those traits that are essential for the realization of their potential and thus for the advancement of humankind. The quest for excellence has thus been smothered under a blanket of flaccid mediocrity.

Now, in championing the pursuit of excellence, Nietzsche might be interpreted as evincing an objectivist meta-ethic. Despite his apparent repudiation of any objective basis of moral evaluation, his call for a revaluation of morality seems to appeal to notions of excellence and human progress; notions which reveal an objectivist commitment. This apparent ambivalence has been widely debated amongst Nietzsche commentators (such as Clark, 1994; Foot, 1994; Danto, 2002). To become too tied up with the question of whether or not Nietzsche contradicts his own apparent moral relativism is, however, to divert attention from a key aspect of his contribution to ethics theory. This is that Nietzsche casts a shadow of doubt over the universal desirability of qualities such as charity, benevolence, compassion, and equality; qualities whose veneration has pervaded the mainstream of Western ethics. Conversely, he offers a basis for the valorization of very different human qualities and, in particular, with his call for the 'super men' to assert themselves (or perhaps for the 'super man' or 'super woman' that resides within each of us to assert itself[1]) he provides an alternative template for ethical leadership.

Nietzsche's overarching preoccupation is with the pursuit of human excellence. Ethical leadership that is consistent with a Nietzschean revaluation of values would therefore be leadership that promotes the realization of human potential that he holds so dear. Furthermore, according to the reading of Nietzsche outlined here, the methods adopted to pursue excellence need not be constrained by the scruples of conventional morality. Nietzschean leaders would be change-evoking 'super men' or 'super women' who are able to apply their exceptional talents in order to unite people towards the flourishing of excellence. This Nietzschean Holy Grail could only be achieved if the more capable elite were encouraged to join the leader in fulfilling their potential,

---

[1] A less literal interpretation of Nietzsche's work is that, rather than proposing an elitist social ethic, he is merely calling upon every individual to strive for their own self-actualization and to release their own potential for excellence. It seems unlikely, though, that the polemical narrative of the *Genealogy of Morals* was only intended by Nietzsche to be read metaphorically.

unrestrained by considerations of equality, compassion, and altruism. Nietzsche thus provides the basis for a particularly elitist and meritocratic understanding of leadership; one in which, because of their innate superiority, leaders are justified in asserting their own agendas over weaker people; in which gifted visionaries inspire the more capable amongst their followers to follow their personal example, thus realizing their own potential for excellence and optimizing human progress.

It is perhaps worth noting that Nietzsche's philosophy has been co-opted to justify some of the most appalling leadership agendas of the twentieth century. Many of Nietzsche's commentators (such as Kaufman, 1956; Langiulli, 1971; Leiter, 2002) point out that to paint Nietzsche with the brush of Nazism is unfair, since he despised both German nationalism and anti-Semitism and would have been appalled by the selective misappropriation of his philosophy by the National Socialists of 1930s Germany. Nevertheless, given Nietzsche's biological determinism, his unashamed elitism, and his repudiation of many of the values trodden on by Nazi inhumanity, this misappropriation is unsurprising.

But there is also another, rather different message tucked inside Nietzsche's nihilistic analysis of moral convention; a message which may also have something to say to leadership ethics. By drawing attention to the extent to which our ethical commitments may be shaped by considerations of self-interest, Nietzsche offers good reasons to be cautious of moral conviction. In particular, he alerts us to the possibility that the ethical commitments of a leader may be at least partly shaped by the interests of the community of which that leader is part. If the 'will to power' of 'lower types' has been so influential in the overall direction of moral convention, then it is equally feasible that the will to power of specific, influential communities shapes the convictions that are articulated by the members of those communities. We need not commit wholeheartedly to Nietzsche's nihilistic meta-ethic in order to be suspicious of ethical pronouncements that are delivered with self-assured unanimity from within a particular interest group.

Personal Commitment as a Basis for Moral Legitimacy

The stark, nihilistic message contained within Kierkegaard's and Nietzsche's writing is that there are no universally valid principles in accordance with which ethical dilemmas can be resolved. Responsibility is therefore thrown back upon each individual to define his or her own ethical standards. In developing the emancipatory ramifications of this nihilistic commitment, Kierkegaard takes a rather different tack from Nietzsche. Whereas Nietzsche calls for a revaluation of values, a transformation in moral understanding that will emancipate superior beings from the altruistic and egalitarian shackles of conventional morality, Kierkegaard champions the self-actualizing qualities of individual choice. For Kierkegaard, the legitimacy of moral sentiment derives not from its conformity to some objective, universal reality but from the fervour with which it is experienced. Kierkegaard thus challenges the Cartesian notion of true belief as comprising correspondence between belief and reality. In *Concluding Unscientific Postscript*, Kierkegaard proposes a subjectivist notion of truth as an alternative to the objectivism of the Cartesian position, using this notion of subjective truth to legitimize Christian faith. As far as Kierkegaard is concerned, spiritual verity does not derive from the relationship between what is believed and what is; it concerns the relationship between the believer and their belief:

> The issue is not about the truth of Christianity but about the individual's relation to Christianity, consequently not about the indifferent individual's systematic eagerness to arrange truths of Christianity in paragraphs but rather about the concern of the infinitely interested individual with regard to his own relation to such a doctrine. (Kierkegaard, 1997c [1846]: 189)

Therefore, the criterion of religious truth does not lie in correspondence with a supposed external reality but in the sincerity with which a believer believes: 'The passion of the infinite, not its content, is the deciding factor' (Kierkegaard, 1997c [1846]: 206). It is this passion, this emotional engagement, which, for Kierkegaard, is absent from conformity to moral convention. By resolving moral dilemmas in accordance with conventionally accepted, ethical principles, a decision-maker adopts a passive relationship with his or her decision. This passivity is inherently limiting because the decision is thus deprived of emotional commitment. According to Kierkegaard, the application of conventional, principle-based morality comprises rational accounting in accordance with rules; rules which do not only lack the external legitimacy they claim but which also offer an inadequate basis for meaningful, personal engagement. Decisions that derive from direct, personal faith, on the other hand, are characterized by the vibrancy of emotional resolve.

For Kierkegaard, the importance of personal commitment is not confined to the validation of religious faith. In *Either/Or*, he stresses the self-actualizing force of choice per se, proposing that, by the very act of making choices, we become better people. Thus, the act of choosing is its own reward: it is by making emotionally engaged choices that the human spirit flourishes; deprived of such choices, it 'withers away in atrophy' (Kierkegaard, 1997a [1843]: 72). So, the value of choice is intrinsic to the act of choosing. It derives not from the consequences of what is chosen but from the degree of emotional fervour that is invested in making that choice: 'What is important in choosing is not so much to choose the right thing as the energy, the earnestness, and the pathos with which one chooses' (Kierkegaard, 1997*a* [1843]: 73–4).

Leaders who measure themselves according to Kierkegaardian standards would therefore need to be comfortable with the responsibility entailed in acts of choice. They would need to weigh their decisions not in accordance with rational accounting of conventionally accepted norms but in relation to the strength of their personal conviction. The right course of action, for Kierkegaardian leaders, would be that to which they could wholeheartedly apply themselves. In the Kierkegaardian model, external measures of ethical rightness must give way to a leader's heartfelt commitment as the sole criterion of legitimacy. In a celebration of non-conformity that resonates with charismatic leadership theory, Kierkegaard notes that this affirmation of personal commitment often requires sustained challenge to the status quo: the Kierkegaardian champion may have to stand alone against convention; he (or she) 'must comprehend that no one can understand him, and must have the constancy to put up with it that human language has for him naught but curses and the human heart has for his sufferings only the one feeling that he is guilty' (Kierkegaard, 1967 [1845], cited by Gardiner, 1988: 62).

Heidegger, Sartre, and the Nature of 'Being'

Whereas Kierkegaard's acclamation of personal commitment and choice is both polemical and imbued with religious fervour, Martin Heidegger and Jean-Paul Sartre deliver separate endorsements of individual responsibility that are more sober and secular in style and which are constructed upon more systematic rationales than Kierkegaard's. Heidegger's *Being and Time* forms part of an incomplete, ontological exploration of the nature of being. It addresses specifically the question of what it is to *be* human, or, in Heidegger's words, the nature of *Dasein*,[2] that (human) being, for which 'in its very Being, that Being is an issue for it' (1962 [1926]: 32). A significant outcome of Heidegger's enquiry is his conclusion that individual, agentic responsibility is intrinsic to any 'authentic' embodiment of the human condition. Sartre reaches a similar conclusion in *Being and Nothingness*, in his case via an exploration of the nature of consciousness. For Sartre, 'authenticity' demands acknowledgement of the ineluctable autonomy that defines human consciousness. For Sartre: 'What we call freedom is impossible to distinguish from the being of

---

[2] When discussing Heidegger's work I have followed the German convention, applied by the author and also by his translators and most of his commentators, of capitalizing the first letter of many of the key terms that he uses to elaborate his ideas.

"human reality". Man does not exist first in order to be free *subsequently*; there is no difference between the being of man and his *being-free'* (2003 [1943]: 49).

Heidegger derives his notion of authentic being from consideration of three aspects of the human condition or, to put it in Heidegger's terms, three characteristics of *Dasein*: firstly, its 'Being-in-the-World'; secondly, its temporality (its 'Being-in-time'); and thirdly, its intersubjective character (its 'Being-with-others'). By 'Being-in-the-World', Heidegger refers neither to *Dasein's* physical containment within its surroundings nor its physical proximity to other worldly entities. He refers, rather, to the interdependent processes of signification by which the 'World' that *Dasein* is 'in' is accorded meaning and in relation to which *Dasein* defines itself. In other words, we inevitably define ourselves with reference to our surroundings whilst, at the same time, experiencing those surroundings within the context of our own self-definition. The 'World' within which *Dasein* dwells, in a Heideggerian sense, is therefore a world of mutual signification and reference.

A key aspect of *Dasein's* Being-in-the-World is the inevitability of *care*: 'the Being of Dasein itself is to be made visible as *care'* (Heidegger, 1962 [1926]: 83–4). When Heidegger uses such terms as 'care', he does not do so in the sense of custodial care or guardianship, nor do these terms carry any implication of benevolent or compassionate intent (Polt, 1999). He simply means that each person's 'World' matters for that person, not in the obvious sense in which it sustains their biological and emotional needs, but in the sense that they cannot interact with it other than with some affective predisposition towards it. For Heidegger, as with Kierkegaard, we do not encounter our world from the position of a neutral, detached observer; we can only encounter that world within the context of our projects and preoccupations. That world, therefore, necessarily takes on meaning in relation to those projects and preoccupations.

For Heidegger, the way in which 'care' defines *Dasein's* relationship with its World must be grasped within the context of *temporality*. That is, care can only be conceived in terms of *Dasein's* past and future. The disposition that defines our caring relationship with our world is not a cognitive one but is manifested through 'moods'. And these moods, which define how we respond to our World, derive from what Heidegger refers to as our *attunement*, or our *thrownness*. Our past experiences 'attune' us, or 'throw' us, in certain ways, and the consequent *mood* in which we relate to our World defines the nature of that relationship: '*Dasein's* openness to the world is constituted existentially by the attunement of a state-of-mind' (Heidegger, 1962 [1926]: 176). And this attunement does not derive only from our first-hand personal experiences. It also comes from absorbing the ideas and values that permeate our generation. Thus, *Dasein* 'is its past, whether explicitly or not.... Its own past—and this always means the past of its "generation"—is not something which *follows along* after *Dasein*, but something which already goes ahead of it' (Heidegger, 1962 [1926]: 41).

However, the extent to which our past defines the nature of our Being-in-the-World should not obscure the significance of our future. For, just as our Being-in-the-World is temporally defined in relation to our past, it is also defined in relation to our understanding of our future potentials: in Heidegger's terms, not only are we 'thrown'; we are also 'throwers'. *Dasein* and its Being-in-the-World cannot be conceived in terms of a fixed present that is the outcome of attunement. It must also be conceived in relation to the totality of its 'disclosive potentiality-for-Being' (Heidegger, 1962 [1926]: 183). We define ourselves and our relationship with our World in terms of potentials that are important to us, so the way in which our past attunes us is structured by our understanding of our future potentiality. Equally, that understanding of our future potentiality is attuned by our past experiences and by absorption of the experiences and values of our generation. Present, past and future must therefore be conceived not as separate instances of a linear progression but in terms of inescapable interrelatedness: each temporal dimension is impacted by the other temporal dimensions while, at the same time, each impacts upon the others. This temporal relationship might be conceptualized in terms of three convex mirrors, facing one another from the corners of an equilateral triangle. One of the mirrors represents our understanding of our past; one represents our present understanding of what we are now; the third represents our vision of our future potentials. To look in any of the three mirrors is to see the reflection of the others. No mirror has causal primacy; to look in any of the three is to see an infinite regression of interrelatedness between itself and the other two.

A third existential characteristic of *Dasein*'s Being-in-the-World is that *Dasein* is necessarily 'in-the-World' with other *Dasein*. So, our world of signification is not encountered in a solitary manner; it is an *intersubjective* endeavour. And this sharing of the world is not just a contingent circumstance that could be otherwise; it is a fundamental aspect of our Being: Being-with is 'an existential statement as to [*Dasein's*] essence. Even if the particular factical *Dasein* does *not* turn to others, and supposes that it has no need for them or manages to get along without them, it *is* in the way of Being-with' (Heidegger, 1962 [1926]: 160). Furthermore, our intersubjective situation entails a mutual engagement of worlds of signification within which all parties have significance for one another: not only are others significant for me; I, as well as other 'others', are also significant for them. And, of course, just as I am 'in-the-World', not as a detached observer but with an attitude of 'care' that is temporarily located in relation to my past and my future, so are these others in-the-World; just as I care so do they care: 'They are not encountered as person-Things present-at-hand: we meet them "at work", that is primarily in their Being-in-the-World' (Heidegger, 1962 [1926]: 156).

Some key points that I take from this reading of Heidegger are that each person's 'Being' can be conceived in terms of three existential characteristics. The first characteristic is that we cannot relate to our respective worlds from an attitude of detached neutrality. The way in which each person perceives his on her own world is inevitably shaped by his or her respective projects and preoccupations: as Heidegger would put it, we cannot 'Be-in-the-World' other than with an attitude of 'care' for that World; and that attitude of care will shape our understanding of that World. The second ineluctable characteristic of being is that it must be understood in terms of its interrelatedness with its past-facing attunement and its future-facing apprehension of its potentialities. Although we are shaped by our experiences and the experiences of our generation, the way in which we receive and respond to those experiences is shaped, in turn, by our future projects. And these future projects, in turn, are shaped by our past, and so on. The third inescapable characteristic of each person's being to which Heidegger draws our attention is its intersubjective quality: we find ourselves living in the same world as other people. Even if we choose to lead a solitary existence, avoiding contact with these others, their presence nevertheless shapes our relationship with our world. And just as my relationship with my world is shaped by my projects and preoccupations, so is every other person's relationship with their world shaped by the nature of their respective 'care'. Moreover, each of these other people is just as subject to his own interrelated, temporal embeddedness as I am.

Whereas Heidegger's conclusions flow from his exploration of the nature of Being, Sartre's proceed from his elaboration of the nature of consciousness (2003 [1943]). According to Sartre, human subjectivity must be understood in relation to consciousness, for consciousness *is* human subjectivity. But like Kierkegaard and Heidegger, Sartre rejects the Cartesian notion of a detached subjective 'mind' that looks out dispassionately at an objective world. Sartre focuses on the emptiness of subjectivity: for Sartre, consciousness, in itself, is nothing; it only takes on substance in relation to the objects that it experiences. In Sartre's vernacular, the 'for-itself' (subjectivity/consciousness) only takes on form in relation to the 'in-itself' entities (objects) of which it is conscious. But just as consciousness only takes on substance through its relationship with the in-itself, those in-itself entities are nothing but featureless matter until given form by consciousness; by the for-itself.

Sartre's elaboration of the relationship between consciousness and the entities which comprise its objects—between the 'for-itself' and the 'in-itself'—thus resonates with the interrelatedness that Heidegger envisages between *Dasein* and the attuned, temporal, intersubjective world that it inhabits. This resonance is also apparent in the significance of *facticity*, which, for Sartre, is a key aspect of existence. Just as Heidegger speaks of the 'attunement' which shapes our care for our world—those past circumstances that shape our understanding of our present and our future potentialities—Sartre describes the facticity that impacts on our situation. We do not choose what we are and what our position in the world is; these are given to us by a facticity that is the outcome of our past. Nevertheless, although we are partly conditioned by facticity— just as, in Heidegger's scheme of things we are 'thrown', or 'attuned', by our past experiences and the experiences of our generation—we are nevertheless free to choose how to respond to this predicament.

A conclusion about the human condition that is drawn by Heidegger and, with a great deal more emphasis, by Sartre, concerns our ineluctable freedom of choice. For both Heidegger and Sartre, our dependency on the world that we inhabit is not absolute; there is always a place in our interrelationship with our world for agency. For Heidegger, we are not powerless in our 'attuned', 'temporal', and 'intersubjective' situation. Our preoccupations and our relationships with time and with others leave space for autonomous choice. These are not causal relationships in which *Dasein* is inexorably driven along a certain path; they are arrangements of interrelatedness in which *Dasein* has a say. Similarly, for Sartre, although consciousness is shaped by the entities of which we are conscious, those entities owe their form to whatever consciousness makes of them. And although our situation may be shaped, largely, by 'facticity', we are nevertheless free to choose how we respond to that facticity. Facticity provides reasons for us to act in a certain way but, as far as Sartre is concerned, we choose whether those *reasons for* action should become *causes of* action. We are thus, as Sartre puts it, 'condemned to be free' (1973 [1946]: 34): we cannot escape being makers of choices.

Inauthenticity and Authenticity

Heidegger and Sartre develop the notion of *inauthenticity*[3] to describe responses to the human condition that fail to acknowledge our autonomy and our capacity for personal engagement. Inauthenticity has two faces. For Heidegger, the first face consists of overlooking the predisposed nature of our 'care' for our World, denying our 'attunement', and repudiating our 'intersubjective' context. To be inauthentic in this first sense is to regard the subject as standing apart from the purposeful, temporal, and social processes through which it constructs its reality. Inauthentic people thus assume that they can

---

[3] Sartre uses the term 'mauvaise foi', which his translators render as 'bad faith' rather than 'inauthenticity'. However, for clarity I will use the word inauthenticity here when referring to the work of both Heidegger and Sartre.

construct the nature of their 'Being-in-the-World' without reference to the forces that have defined each moment of that process of construction. They imagine that the construction of their reality is an act of unilateral, rather than interrelated, signification. They pretend a moodless neutrality, disregarding the attunement, or thrownness, that inevitably shapes the way in which they interact with their situation. Furthermore, they assume that they can stand apart from their intersubjective context. They fail to acknowledge that even those who pursue a life of reclusive self-sufficiency cannot escape the inevitability of co-presence. For Sartre, too, the avoidance of inauthenticity requires reconciliation with those features that comprise the inescapable 'facticity' of one's context: features such as one's past, one's social class, one's nationality, one's experiences, one's gender, and one's physical attributes. To deny facticity is to deny the reality of one's past; a past which constitutes the resistance against which future choices are made.

However, despite the temptations of this first mode of inauthenticity, it is to its second face that both Heidegger and Sartre believe that we are more likely to succumb. For Heidegger, this is to deny our capacity for choice: to suppose that the World in which we live is constituted independently of our own signification of it; to deny that our attunement is shaped by our own understanding of our potentialities; and to overlook our agentic capacity in the face of intersubjectivity. Of particular concern to Heidegger are the temptations of 'falling', 'averageness', and 'disburdening'. To *fall*, in a Heideggerian sense, is to go unreflectively where we are 'thrown'; to permit the momentum of our 'attunement' to carry us wherever it may. Heidegger notes that we are inclined to use the routines and superficialities of everyday situations as props to avoid committing ourselves to choices about who we are and what we are doing. 'Falling' thus ignores the essential interrelatedness of our temporality; it acknowledges that we are 'thrown' whilst failing to acknowledge that we are also 'throwers'.

Averageness, for Heidegger, is the tendency of *Dasein* to lose its identity in intersubjectivity. Thus, in Dasein's everyday 'Being-with-others', its Being is taken away by those others: 'This Being-with-one-another dissolves one's own *Dasein* completely into the kind of Being of "the Others"' (Heidegger, 1962 [1926]: 164). The outcome of averageness is that an individual *Dasein* comes to think of herself or himself not as 'I' but as part of 'they'. That individual's actions thus come to be shaped by what is expected of that commonality. Heidegger describes this loss of individuality as a *disburdening* of individual responsibility: 'the particular *Dasein* in its everydayness is *disburdened* by the "they". Not only that; by thus disburdening it of its Being, the "they" accommodates *Dasein* if *Dasein* has a tendency to take things easy and make them easy' (1962 [1926]: 165). So, disburdening is a tempting cop-out of one's individual, agentic capacity. Moreover, once embarked upon it can only lead to further emasculation as 'the "they" retains and enhances its stubborn dominion' (1962 [1926]: 165).

For Sartre, this second face of inauthenticity comprises the assumption of passivity in the face of facticity. Sartre stresses that although we are impacted by features of our social, hereditary, physical, and intellectual circumstances, we are nevertheless free to choose how we interpret and respond to these features; we are thus free to 'transcend' facticity: 'The basic concept which is thus engendered, utilises the double property of the human being, who is at once a *facticity* and a *transcendence*' (Sartre, 2003 [1943]: 79). To deny one's transcendence is to objectify oneself; a futile attempt by the 'for-itself' to identify itself as some form of 'in-itself' entity; something which it can move towards but which it can never become.

Heidegger and Sartre introduce the notions of 'anxiety' and 'anguish' to describe different aspects of our response to the ineluctable autonomy of the human situation. According to Heidegger, *anxiety* is the emotion that attends realization of the inadequacies of the inauthentic mode of Being. For Sartre, *anguish* is a response to the vertigo-inducing realization of our own autonomy. Faced with the terrifying awareness that we are nothing except that which we choose to be, that we have no essence other than that which we construct for ourselves, we are racked by anguish.

The opposite of inauthenticity is *authenticity*. If the two faces of inauthenticity comprise either denial of the influences that shape our predicament or an assumption of helplessness before these influences, authenticity involves coming to terms with both the 'facticity' and 'attunement' of our past and the 'transcendent potentialities' of our future. Sartre is particularly explicit in his endorsement of authenticity and autonomy. These themes pervade his literary and philosophical works, and their moral implication is clearly articulated in the advice he gives to a student whose agonized, moral prevarication he recounts in *Existentialism and Humanism*: 'You are free, therefore choose—that is to say, invent' (1973 [1946]: 38). For Sartre, 'authenticity' can be understood as a form of enlightenment. It represents realization of our transcendent freedom and requires us to come to terms with the anguish that this presents. Authenticity, though, should not be thought of as a once-and-for-all achievement, for to suppose that one has now come to terms with one's freedom and that one is now an 'authentic person' would itself be a manifestation of inauthenticity. It would suppose that one has become something through an act of choice; a something that precludes the need for future acts of choice. This is a something that, as far as Sartre is concerned, we can never be. Authenticity therefore demands that we confront the ever-present possibility that we will slip back into inauthenticity and deny our freedom: we can always choose not to choose. It thus requires continual renewal and constant reaffirmation. Authenticity is not an achievement; it is a never-ending project.

Sartre's Look and Heidegger's Authentic Solicitude: Contrasting Analyses of Intersubjectivity

Despite their agreement on the autonomy of the individual and the nature of authentic being, a topic upon which the writings of Sartre and Heidegger point in rather different directions is that of interpersonal relationships. Sartre, at least in his earlier work, focuses on the conflictual quality of inter-subjectivity, dwelling on the challenge that one person's authenticity neces-sarily presents to the creative autonomy of other people. Heidegger, on the other hand, describes contrasting types of interpersonal relationship. Although certain forms of interaction may suppress the autonomy of indivi-duals, Heidegger also envisages relationships in which the authenticity of one person can actually be enabled and encouraged by another person. He thus leaves space for the possibility of mutually authentic coexistence. I will briefly review Sartre's perspective before outlining Heidegger's more optimistic stance.

Sartre (2003 [1943]) introduces the notion of the *Look* to draw attention to the potentially conflictual nature of intersubjectivity and to account for the destructive turn which many interpersonal relationships take. The reason for this conflictual quality is that intersubjectivity necessarily entails challenge to each party's creative autonomy. Sartre offers an account of one person encountering another in a park to illustrate this intersubjective tension. I may be sitting on a park bench, quietly contemplating my surroundings, alone in my situation. All of a sudden, I become aware of the presence of another person in the park. That person may present no physical threat and may make no attempt to engage with me. Nevertheless, my awareness of that person's presence immediately changes my situation: instead of being the only 'for-itself' entity amongst a field of 'in-itself entities', my 'for-itself-ness', or my subjectivity, and thus my authorship of my world is now shared with another. I am no longer a subject surrounded by a world of objects; another subject, another author, is now present. Of course, the other under-goes the same process, at which point a struggle for centrality and ownership of our (now) shared world ensues. I can only get back 'my' world if I can reduce the other person to an in-itself entity within that world and they likewise for me. So, I inevitably embark on the fruitless process of trying to reduce them in this way; fruitless insofar as they are, and cannot be other than, 'for-themself': despite both of our efforts to objectify the other, each of us cannot but be a subject. We thus derive the significance of the 'Look' of another person. That significance lies not in the impact of the eyes but in my awareness that my subjective autonomy is threatened by the gaze of another.

In contrast to Sartre's conflictual analysis of intersubjectivity, Heidegger offers the possibility of harmonious coexistence with fellow *Dasein*. As I pointed out earlier, one of the key characteristics of Being, for Heidegger, is 'Being with' other people. Heidegger proposes that this intersubjective quality of Being is not just something that happens to be that way but which could, conceivably, be otherwise. Rather, it is an existential necessity; an inescapable aspect of being human. So, one person cannot conceive of their world other than as incorporating other people. Thus far Heidegger is on similar ground to Sartre: for Sartre, too, intersubjectivity is inescapable: we are 'condemned' to be with others. But whereas, for Sartre, 'Hell is Other People' (1965 [1944]: 185), Heidegger envisages the possibility of benign coexistence.

The basis for that benign coexistence can be found in Heidegger's presentation of contrasting attitudes that one *Dasein*, or one subject, might adopt towards another. The attitude—the type of Heideggerian 'care'—that characterizes this intersubjective relationship with other *Dasein* is referred to by Heidegger as *solicitude*. And Heidegger differentiates two extreme kinds of solicitude: an 'inauthentic' mode and an 'authentic' mode: 'that which leaps in and dominates and that which leaps forth and liberates' (Heidegger, 1962 [1926]: 159). *Inauthentic solicitude* would occur if one *Dasein* were to

> take away 'care' from the Other and put itself in his position of concern: it can *leap in* for him. This kind of solicitude takes over from the Other that with which he is to concern himself. The Other is thus thrown out of his own position; he steps back so that afterwards, when the matter has been attended to, he can either take it over as something finished and at his disposal, or disburden himself of it completely. (Heidegger, 1962 [1926]: 158)

To be sure, inauthentic solicitude is not presented by Heidegger as a necessarily vindictive endeavour: for one person's solicitude towards another to be described as inauthentic need not imply malevolent intent. Indeed, Heidegger's depiction of inauthentic solicitude seems as apposite to altruistic paternalism as it is to self-interested domination. Any negative quality associated with inauthentic solicitude derives not from an assumption of manipulative or exploitative intent but from its suppression of the other person's agency.

In contrast to this inauthentic extreme is *authentic solicitude*: a relationship that facilitates agency rather than suppressing it. For Heidegger, authentic solicitude comprises

> a kind of solicitude that does not so much leap in for the other as *leap ahead* of him in his existential potentiality-for Being, not in order to take away his 'care' but rather to give it back to him authentically as such for the first time...it helps the other to become transparent to himself *in* his care and to become *free for* it. (Heidegger, 1962 [1926]: 158-9)

Heidegger thus presents authentic solicitude as an interpersonal relationship in which one party enables authenticity in the other; a relationship in which one helps the other to come to terms with their autonomy. Whereas inauthentic solicitude is suppressive of agency, authentic solicitude has a liberating quality: it puts the other in touch with their own authenticity.

For Heidegger, then, Being necessarily involves 'Being-with' others and it would be inauthentic of us to repudiate the influence that those others have on our self-understanding. Furthermore, Heidegger proposes that we are prone to respond to this interdependence in an overly dependent manner: to 'disburden' our agentic potentiality; to 'fall' in the direction taken by others rather than self-reflectively asserting our own autonomy; to lose ourselves in 'averageness'. Given the lure of this 'real dictatorship of the "they"' (Heidegger, 1962 [1926]: 164), we are more amenable to inauthentic solicitude on the part of other people than we are to authentic solicitude. However, this need not be the case. Although inauthentic solicitude is the easier and more attractive option, the capacity resides within each of us to grasp our own agency. Furthermore, the capacity also lies within each of us to adopt an attitude of authentic, rather than inauthentic, solicitude towards others; to put them in touch with their own authenticity rather than, out of either repressive malignance or paternalistic altruism, stepping in to undermine their agency.

Now, in describing the place that Heidegger holds out for an authentically facilitative form of intersubjective relationship, I am not imputing to him approbation of it. Despite his apparent commendation of authenticity, Heidegger's is not an explicitly ethical agenda: he is more concerned with the ontological nature of Being than with normative ethics. Indeed, unlike Sartre, who 'condemns and approves with the confidence of a pope' (Danto, 1975: 144), Heidegger adopts a notably non-prescriptive stance. Nevertheless, in drawing attention to the facilitative, emancipatory potential of intersubjective relationships, Heidegger points towards an alternative to the necessarily conflictual picture painted by Sartre. He therefore offers part of the foundation upon which his one-time protégée, Jürgen Habermas (Matuštík, 2001), builds the systematic valorization of intersubjective ethics that I will review in chapter 4.

Existentialism's Implications for Leadership

Existentialism's stark message for leaders is that there are no universally valid principles against which they can measure the moral probity of their actions and decisions. Morality is not a matter of conformity to principles; it is a matter of individual commitment. Therefore, leaders who wish to follow an ethical course of action must do without external guidance; they must come to terms with their own moral authorship. However, this does not entail amoralism: just because conventionally prescribed, ethical principles can offer no firm guidance for organizational leadership, it does not follow that organizations are morality-free zones. Nor does existentialism legitimize the unbridled pursuit of self-interest by those in charge. Existentialism does not invalidate ethics; it simply places the onus of moral authorship fairly and squarely on the shoulders of the agent. Applied to the domain of leadership, existentialism would call upon leaders to acknowledge that responsibility; to grasp the moral autonomy that it entails; and to continually reaffirm that autonomy by making ethical choices.

Existentialism's preoccupation with authenticity holds some particularly significant implications for organizational leadership. To follow Heidegger's and Sartre's injunctions, leaders need to come to terms with the relationship of mutual signification that pertains between them and their organizational contexts. They must acknowledge that the 'facticity' of their situation provides their being with significance but that they are nevertheless free to interpret and attribute meaning to the predicaments within which they find themselves. They may have compelling reasons for acting in certain ways, but it is up to them to decide how they are to respond to those reasons; to decide whether these *reasons for* action should become *causes of* action.

On the one hand, leaders must acknowledge their 'thrownness', their 'attunement', and their 'facticity'. They must concede that their outlook on the world and their responses to that outlook are partly shaped by their prior experiences and the experiences of the community of which they are part. For those who lead within business organizations, the conventions of market capitalism and the associated expectations of social and professional peers are likely to figure prominently in that facticity. Furthermore, leaders cannot overlook the extent to which their own material circumstances, along with those of their dependents, are reliant upon their conformity to those conventions. Those who lead in other types of organizational context may be less securely shackled to market capitalist imperatives, but their outlooks will nevertheless be influenced by the preoccupations of those people who shape their respective organizational agendas. Both Sartre and Heidegger alert us to the need to acknowledge those influences; to concede this 'facticity', this 'attunement' of our situation. To do otherwise would not only be 'inauthentic'; it would also be unrealistic. Furthermore, reflection on the facticity of their predicament may also serve an important supplementary purpose for leaders: it may illuminate the extent to which their own thought processes, priorities, and judgements are shaped by the circles within which they move. Indeed, Heidegger's and Sartre's observations support Nietzsche's nihilistic conclusions in alerting us to the extent to which moral conviction might be a response to the self-interested agenda of a particular community.

But if, on the one hand, leaders need to be sensitive to the extent to which their context is influenced by 'facticity', by 'thrownness', and by intersubjective contact with peers, they must also, if they are to avoid 'inauthenticity', grasp their agentic capacity to interpret, to respond to, and to transcend those influences. The material and social circumstances that characterize their roles and their professions may well shape leaders' agendas, but they are always free to choose how they respond to those circumstances. So, although the economic realities of capitalist enterprise may shape the preoccupations of business leaders, moral choices are still theirs to make. They and only they are accountable for those choices and they must take ownership of their consequences. Similarly, leaders in public and charitable sectors may be subjected to more varied imperatives that characterize their particular organizational contexts, but their responses to those imperatives are no more predetermined than are those of business leaders. Other, more powerful actors may disagree with the choices that leaders make; they may even veto those decisions. Leaders' ethical agendas may thus be frustrated. In extreme circumstances, fealty to their moral conviction may even undermine leaders' job tenure or their career prospects. Nevertheless, those choices are always the leader's to make.

Phrases such as 'I had no choice' or 'I had to do what was expected of me' therefore have no currency in existentialist ethics. For Heidegger, such phrases would be manifestations of 'disburdening' and of 'averageness'; of renouncing one's agentic capacity for autonomy; of blending with one's intersubjective context. For Sartre, they would represent an 'anguished' flight from one's irrevocable moral autonomy. Existentially moral leaders are those who take responsibility for their decisions. They make decisions in response to the depth of their moral conviction; not in response to the expectations of their role. They accord with Nietzsche's depiction of a Zarathustran super person whose sense of moral ownership acknowledges only the 'unknown sage', the 'mighty commander' that is self. (Nietzsche, 2003a [1885]: 62)

I have discussed so far how existentialism would applaud leaders who make morally committed choices; who accept the burden of their own moral autonomy. However, if commitment on the part of a leader is to be accorded merit then so, surely, must it be desirable on the part of followers. If, as Kierkegaard suggests, committed choice has inherent value, then that inherent value must pertain as much to choices made by followers as it does to choices made by leaders. And the emphasis that Heidegger and Sartre place on authenticity must also apply as much to followers as it does to leaders: if ethical leadership demands of leaders that they come to terms with their own autonomy, it must also call upon them to put followers in touch with their own autonomy. And if we are to denigrate leaders who 'disburden' their own agentic capacity, then surely we must also call upon them to respect the need for followers to avoid blending into the 'averageness' of *their* intersubjective contexts.

To appraise leadership according to existentialist criteria, then, is to take account of the extent to which leaders enable committed moral choice and facilitate authenticity in those whom they lead. Different existentialist perspectives entail contrasting responses to this requirement. Nietzsche's elitist and deterministic analysis would call upon those exceptionally gifted 'super men' and 'super women', whose privileged talents set them apart from the common herd, to assert themselves over 'lower types' in order to evoke the flourishing of humanity. Although Nietzschean leaders might be expected to facilitate self-actualization in the occasional gifted subordinate, Nietzsche would have no truck with the notion of 'super beings' facilitating authenticity in lesser mortals. However, this is not the conclusion towards which Kierkegaard's, Heidegger's, and Sartre's analyses would point. For these writers, if coming to terms with our own autonomy is to be valued, there seems to be no basis, unless we accept Nietzsche's elitist exclusionism, for us not to place similar worth in evocation of authenticity in all other people. This, then, seems to be a key existentialist criterion of ethical leadership: that the leader encourages followers to grasp their own moral autonomy, thus facilitating authenticity in those followers. Existentialist leadership, then, has decidedly facilitative connotations.

Now, here we confront a difficulty, because contested moral authorship presents a possible terrain of conflict. Indeed, for Sartre, intersubjective tension is unavoidable: the 'Look' of a leader will necessarily challenge the creative autonomy of followers and vice versa. Intersubjective engagement thus entails, for Sartre, unavoidable confrontation between competing authorships; confrontation from which the only escape is the triumph of one person's authenticity over all others. Despite his enthusiastic advocacy of authenticity, then, when applied to leadership, Sartre's theory drives us towards an unfortunately Nietzschean impasse. Given Sartre's conflictual analysis of intersubjectivity, a battle of Nietzschean 'wills to power' seems the most likely outcome; a battle in which successful leaders will be those who are able to assert their own moral authorship over and above that of their followers. Only thus can they preserve their authenticity: the authenticity of followers must necessarily be sacrificed to that of the leader.

Heidegger, on the other hand, seems to offer a route out of this impositional impasse. By drawing a distinction between authentic solicitude, which facilitates agency, and inauthentic solicitude, which erodes it, Heidegger leaves space for leaders to realize their own authenticity whilst also enabling authenticity in those whom they lead. Whereas inauthentic solicitude is necessarily emasculatory, authentic solicitude offers a template for empowerment. So, what might inauthentic and authentic solicitude look like in a leadership context? Perhaps inauthentic solicitude might consist of 'leaping in' and making moral choices on behalf of followers. Or perhaps it might involve offering comforting rationales that help followers come to terms with doing what, deep down, they consider to be wrong: 'don't feel bad about it; you had no choice'. Alternatively, it might comprise over-emphasizing the merits of fealty to a common agenda; of asking followers to 'disburden' their agentic individuality; and to sink into the 'averageness' of a shared undertaking. Authentic solicitude, on the other hand, would involve creating space for followers to respond to their own deeply felt convictions; to participate in the collective whilst retaining their capacity for choice. I will explore in more detail how this might be achieved in chapter 4, which, in exploring the implications of intersubjective ethics, elaborates a facilitative model of leadership that resonates in some ways with Heideggerian authentic solicitude.

4

Intersubjectivist Theory and Leadership

Intersubjectivist theory offers a basis for evaluating leadership ethics that differs from those considered in chapters 2 and 3. The principle-based theories reviewed in chapter 2 seek to identify universally valid foundations of moral legitimacy. Existentialism, as discussed in chapter 3, proposes that no such foundations can exist and that each individual must be the author of his or her own standards of moral rightness. While the former tends towards an objectivist meta-ethic, the latter offers a basis for moral relativism. Intersubjectivist ethics, on the other hand, is neither objectivist nor relativist: it holds that ethical legitimacy does not comprise correspondence with objective, universal standards, but neither is it a matter of individual commitment on the part of the agent. According to the intersubjectivist position that I will elaborate here, ethical legitimacy is created and sustained through processes of ongoing dialogue. An ethical leader, according to this intersubjectivist stance, would thus be a person who facilitates and responds to the outcomes of such dialogical processes. Furthermore, a leader's ongoing occupation of a leadership role can only be legitimated through such processes.

In order to elaborate this third meta-ethical stance, I will begin by reflecting on how Aristotelian virtue theory points us in the direction of intersubjectivist ethics. Following this Aristotelian preamble, the main body of the chapter will describe a particular approach to intersubjectivism offered by Jürgen Habermas, drawing attention to an increasingly explicit preoccupation with ethics that runs through Habermas' earlier discussion of social theory and his later exploration of communication and discourse. I will then spell out some implications of Habermas' discourse ethics theory for organizational leadership, before outlining a few challenges that subsequent writers have offered to aspects of Habermas' work. The insights afforded by these critiques will permit modifications to the Habermasian model of intersubjectively ethical organizational leadership already presented. The chapter will conclude with a few general thoughts about the discussion of ethics theory and leadership that has occupied this chapter and chapters 2 and 3.

Virtue Theory: Pointing the Way towards Intersubjectivism

In judging the ethical quality of an act, virtue theory focuses on the character of the agent who performs that act. It proposes that an ethical act is one that is performed by a person who embodies the standards of virtue that prevail within a particular community. Stated as simply as that, virtue theory seems to offer a relativist analysis of morality: if ethics is all about standards of virtue that are accepted within a particular community, then surely this pushes us towards the Nietzschean understanding discussed in chapter 3. However, some virtue ethicists avoid the slide into cultural relativism by emphasizing certain characteristics of communities whose value systems are thus accorded legitimacy. Those characteristics feature prominently in the descriptions of virtue offered by Aristotle (1999 [334–322 BC]), the philosopher whose moral and political teachings have inspired contemporary virtue theory. As far as Aristotle was concerned, ethical behaviour is behaviour that conforms to the virtuous standards of the community within which he spent a large part of his life: the Ancient Greek city-state of Athens. And the characteristic of Athens in the fourth century BC that, for Aristotle, lent moral legitimacy to its standards of virtue was the involvement of its citizens in key decisions that affected them. For the Athenian, political system comprised a type of direct democracy in which the citizens regularly met to discuss and decide on how the city-state should be run.[1]

Aristotle considered our capacity to participate in such direct, democratic processes to be a defining characteristic of humanity. He believed that this capacity for political participation distinguishes us from other creatures and thus offers a foundation for the attribution of moral probity. However, it is important to note that Aristotle did not ascribe the morally legitimizing force of direct democracy to its efficacy in identifying ethically right outcomes. To adopt such a stance would have been to presume an objectivist meta-ethic; to assume that there is an objectively 'right way' and that democratic debate is the most effective way of identifying that right way. This is not Aristotle's position. For Aristotle, the fact that an issue has been decided upon in democratic fora, involving people who display democratic 'virtues', confers moral legitimacy. Direct democracy is not a means of *identifying* moral probity; it is an institutional arrangement that *confers* moral probity.

---

[1] The democratic purity of ancient Athenian politics was undermined by a restricted definition of citizenship, which excluded all women and certain strata of men from the political process, and by its institutional dependency on slavery. However, the desirability of broadening this understanding of who falls into the category of 'citizen' need not divert attention from the overriding principle of Aristotle's political and moral philosophy: that all citizens should be included in decision-making that affects them.

More recently, Alasdair MacIntyre has adapted this Aristotelian notion, suggesting that ethical legitimation is not only accorded by internal disputation but also through exposure to external critique. Whereas Aristotle's focus is on democratic process within a particular community, MacIntyre (1985 [1981], 1988) also refers to the ethically legitimizing force of discourse between different communities of thought. MacIntyre proposes that the standards of virtue that prevail within any given community, or 'tradition', are partly validated by the extent to which that tradition is open to engagement with the competing ethical perspectives of other traditions.[2]

In the writing of philosophers such as Aristotle and MacIntyre, then, discourse is offered as a foundation of moral legitimation. Both writers propose that the legitimacy of the standards of virtue that prevail within a particular community of thought is largely dependent upon the extent to which members of that community of thought are prepared to expose their agendas to internal debate and to imaginative engagement with alternative, competing perspectives. Although not generally associated with virtue theory,[3] Jürgen Habermas follows the Aristotelian lead, offering a systematic philosophical justification for intersubjectivist ethics as well as spelling out some procedural conditions to which discourse would need to conform in order to confer moral legitimacy on its outcomes.

The focus in Habermas' writing has evolved from his early emphasis on social theory (1974 [1963]; 1987 [1968]; 1987 [1969]), through his exploration of the ethically legitimating potential of communication (1979 [1976]; 1984 [1981]; 1987 [1981]), his discussion of discourse ethics (1990 [1983]; 2001 [1994]), and his recent preoccupation with applied moral philosophy and political commentary (2006 [2001]; 2006 [2004]). I will concentrate here on his work on social theory, communication, and discourse ethics, for it is from this work that a sustained, systematic rationale for an intersubjectivist meta-ethic can be extracted. Notwithstanding those commentators (such as Giddens, 1985) who lament discontinuity between the work that precedes Habermas' so-called 'linguistic turn' (Pusey, 1987) and that which follows it, I propose that the discussion of critical, social theory found in Habermas' earlier writing offers a backdrop for the increasingly explicit treatment of

---

[2] Virtue theory, as interpreted by MacIntyre, has a great deal more than this to say about organizational ethics. Other notable insights are MacIntyre's Weberian-influenced critique of the amoralism that pervades management thought, to which I will refer in the concluding chapter of this book, and his discussion of notions such as 'excellence', 'practices', and 'institutions' in relation to organizations. Furthermore, Robert Solomon (1993) illuminates the benefits of considering business and virtue through the Aristotelian lens of *telos*, or purpose. However, Aristotle and MacIntyre's common focus on dialogue is the most pertinent to the present topic.

[3] Indeed, although he acknowledges his own debt to Aristotle, Habermas is quite critical of some branches of what he refers to as 'neo-Aristotelianism' (for example, 2001 [1994])—particularly those which co-opt Aristotelian theory to support conservative agendas.

normative ethics that characterizes his later work. I will therefore begin this discussion of Habermas's work by outlining his early discussion of the need for a type of rationality that will inform critical social theory. I will then explain how the model of communicative action and the principles of discourse ethics developed in his later work respond to that need.

A Normative Role for Social Theory

A major preoccupation of Habermas' earlier work (for example, 1974 [1963]; 1987 [1968]; 1987 [1969]) is the quest to establish a normative role for social theory and to define a form of rationality that would be suited to the fulfil-ment of that role. In other words, Habermas was keen to show that social theory can be used to critique social arrangements; that social theory is not just about describing, understanding, and manipulating prevailing states of affairs but that it can also concern itself with normative evaluation of those states of affairs. Social theory, according to Habermas, should be able to tell us what 'ought to be', not just what 'is'. Habermas' critical social theory thus shares an agenda that, at least on a tacit level, infuses most applied ethics theory: it seeks to explore the normative legitimacy of political and social structures, using the insights afforded by this exploration to loosen con-straints that inhibit progress along the path towards human enlightenment.

In Habermas' vernacular, social theory should thus enable entry into the domain of *critical-emancipatory* knowledge. It should deliver critical-emancipatory truth that is concerned with 'progress toward the autonomy of the individual, with the elimination of suffering and the furthering of concrete happiness' (1974 [1963]: 254); truth which 'advances the interest of reason in human adulthood, in the autonomy of action and in the libera-tion from dogmatism' (1974 [1963]: 256). In order to deliver such truth, a form of rationality is required that is up to the task. And since the forms of rational-ity that prevail in the realms of natural science and social science are not suited to this normative role, there is a pressing need to develop an alternative form that is. Therefore, in order to facilitate a normative role for social theory, a type of critical-emancipatory rationality must be developed; one that augments both the positivistic rationality that informs the natural sciences and the hermeneutic rationality that prevails within social science.

However, the development of such a form of rationality, one that will furnish normative truth, is problematic for two reasons. On the one hand, Habermas (1987 [1968]; 1987 [1969]) points out that several hundred years of spectacular progress in the natural sciences have generated an overwhelming confidence in the *positivistic* rationality that has enabled that progress. Rapid advances in disciplines such as physics and biology have greatly enhanced our capacity to understand and control our physical environment and our inter-action with it. Human beings, or at least some human beings, are thus able to lead considerably longer, more comfortable lives than their forebears. As a result, the rationality associated with these achievements is accorded hege-mony in scientific understanding. So, any notion of truth that does not conform to the criteria of rationality that brought these life-enhancing devel-opments to fruition is viewed with suspicion: we expect 'truth' to be derived from systematic, empirical observation, undertaken in controlled conditions and enabling the identification of founding principles and causal relation-ships that consistently enhance our ability to predict and control what goes on in our world. We tend to mistrust any truth claims that are not 'scientifi-cally proven' in this manner. And since critical-emancipatory knowledge cannot conform to such criteria of truth, doubt is cast upon the possibility of such knowledge. The scientific hegemony of positivistic rationality thus problematizes the very notion of a critical-emancipatory rationality.

On the other hand, the prospect of critical-emancipatory knowledge is also under attack from the *hermeneutic* (or interpretive) approach that figures so prominently in social science. Positivism's limited relevance to social science has been exposed, which has led to a widespread perception that a hermeneu-tic agenda, which seeks to understand and explain people's reasons for acting, should prevail in enquiry into human activity. And a hermeneutic agenda does not sit easily with the notion of normative critique. A key supposition of hermeneutic enquiry is that, in order to really understand a person's reasons for acting, we must be able to identify with those reasons: 'only to the extent to which the interpreter also grasps the *reasons* why the author's utterances seem rational to the author himself does he understand what the author meant' (Habermas, 1990 [1983]: 30). Since all people—all 'authors'—presum-ably have reasons to act that are legitimate to them, if we have truly under-stood their reasons for acting we must have got inside these conditions of legitimacy. Therefore, as Habermas points out: 'There is a sense in which any interpretation is a *rational* interpretation' (1990 [1983]: 31). Hermeneutic success seems, then, to preclude rational, normative critique, leaving us to conclude that a hermeneutic undertaking necessarily commits us to a relativ-ist conception of normativity.

Therefore, a key task facing Habermas is to counter, on the one hand, calls for critical-emancipatory propositions to conform to the positivistic criteria of rationality that prevail within the natural sciences; within what Habermas calls the domain of 'empirical-analytic' knowledge. On the other hand, he must counter the hermeneutically influenced expectations that prevail within what he refers to as the domain of 'historical-hermeneutic' knowledge; expectations which entail that all forms of rationality must necessarily be culturally and historically relative. Habermas thus sets out to demonstrate the possibility of a 'critical-emancipatory' rationality that can move beyond both in order to validate normative truth claims.

It is important to note that Habermas is not an enemy of either positivistic or hermeneutic rationality per se, for he believes each to be suited to its respective knowledge domain. Indeed, he applauds the achievements of empirical-analytic knowledge over the last few centuries as well as more recent applications of historical-hermeneutic method. Positivistic methodology is fine within the realm of empirical-analytic knowledge, for it enables the identification of truths that meets the human needs that are relevant to that realm: that is, control and prediction in the natural world. Furthermore, since historical-hermeneutic, social-scientific enquiry is driven by a need to generate understanding, a hermeneutic preoccupation is well suited to it. The problem comes though, as far as Habermas is concerned, when positivistic and hermeneutic rationalities leap outside the boundaries of natural and social science and try to shape the world of normative, critical-emancipatory enquiry; in other words, when they try to 'colonize' the realm of applied ethics. In this respect, Habermas echoes MacIntyre's critique (1985 [1981]) of the 'Failure of the Enlightenment Project'. MacIntyre describes how Enlightenment moral philosophers' search for universally valid, founding principles that describe an external, absolute reality is doomed to failure. Similarly, Habermas suggests that the call for critical-emancipatory propositions to conform to the same criteria of rationality as natural science will necessarily frustrate the quest for the former. On the other hand, just as MacIntyre rues the slide into moral relativism that has followed the Enlightenment Project's inevitable demise, Habermas observes how postmodernism's conclusion that all forms of rationality must necessarily be culturally and historically relative has prompted the abnegation of normative legitimacy within critical-emancipatory enquiry.

So, Habermas' project is not to refute the legitimacy of positivistic and hermeneutic rationality within their respective knowledge domains. His project is, rather, to validate an alternative form of rationality that is suited to the domain of critical-emancipatory knowledge. Furthermore, although he believes that the pathway to enlightenment lies in carving out a separate terrain for critical-emancipatory rationality, the formation of this critical-emancipatory terrain can benefit from selective appropriation from the domains of natural science and social science. For, just as the methodological presuppositions of those domains can deflect from the elaboration of critical-emancipatory knowledge, so they can contribute to it.

As far as the empirical-analytic world of natural science is concerned, Habermas (1987 [1981]) observes that the attribution of scientific truth entails a tacit assumption of rational consensus amongst a scientific community. In other words, for a scientific proposition to be considered 'true' within a scientific community, it is assumed that this proposition would be agreed to by all those members of that community who were in possession of all relevant information and who were driven only by a quest for understanding. Habermas borrows this idea of 'unforced, rational consensus' as offering a basis for attributions of 'truth'. He applies it in order to define those processual conditions that constitute the basis for critical-emancipatory legitimacy. Furthermore, since the attribution of scientific truth implies liberation from the dogmas and cultural prejudices which threaten to undermine rational consensus, it offers a methodological precedent for a critical-emancipatory social theory that sets out to clear a pathway towards enlightenment by dismantling any ideological barriers that impede it.

The contribution that historical-hermeneutic enquiry can make to the evolution of critical-emancipatory rationality also stems from its communicative connotations. Habermas (1987 [1981]) notes that hermeneutic understanding can only be achieved through interaction between an interpreter and the perspective that is interpreted. He proposes that, just as an interpreter constitutes meaning in what is being interpreted he or she is, in turn, constituted by that meaning: just as I seek to understand you, I must inevitably become changed somehow by that act of understanding. Hermeneutic achievement thus offers a template for the dialogical creation of shared, normative understanding by which, as we shall see, Habermas suggests that critical-emancipatory knowledge is legitimated.

In a short while I will offer some further observations on the communicative aspects of the processual model of normative legitimation that Habermas develops in his later work on communicative action and discourse ethics. Before doing so though, I will briefly outline a few further sources to which Habermas turns in order to elaborate his processual model. I do this in the hope that a little background information might make the rationale behind this model a little clearer. One particular debt that Habermas (1990 [1983]) acknowledges is that which he owes to Lawrence Kohlberg and Jean Piaget, for his model conforms to the assumptions of these theorists in two important respects. Firstly, the models of developmental moral psychology proposed by both Kohlberg and Piaget offer a processual, rather than a substantive, conception of ethical legitimation. These writers envisage stages of moral development through which human beings progress, proposing that, as a consequence of evolution to higher stages of development, people are able to make choices that are more ethically sound than those that they would have made at earlier stages. But the superiority of those later choices is not based upon their correspondence to some supposedly external standard of moral rightness. It is legitimated by the fact that those choices are made from the perspective of a higher stage of development. The attainment of that higher stage of development intrinsically validates the choices that it enables.

To be sure, Habermas is not overly attracted to the notion that humans progress through stages of moral development. Nevertheless, he holds on to the idea of processual legitimation that it entails. In his case, processual normative legitimacy derives not from a decision-maker's evolution to a higher stage of moral development; it derives from the quality of the dialogical processes by which a decision is reached.

A second feature that Habermas borrows from Kohlberg's and Piaget's systems is their suggestion that we can judge the inadequacy of an earlier stage of development from the position of enhanced critical insight that is afforded by having reached a later stage. As Habermas puts it: 'the learner can *explain*, in the light of his second interpretation, why his first interpretation is false' (1990 [1983]: 34). Thus 'A subject who moves from one stage to the next should be able to explain why his higher-stage judgements are more adequate than those at lower stages.' (1990 [1983]: 38). Habermas appropriates this 'internal logic of an irreversible learning process' (1990 [1983]: 34) by proposing not only that the perspectives which result from processes of dialogical engagement are necessarily superior to those that precede such engagement but, also, that those who have passed through such processes can appreciate the reasons for that superiority. Here, once again, Habermas is on common ground with Alasdair MacIntyre (1988), who proposes that the insights afforded by one 'tradition' of thought can help us to perceive the limitations of earlier, less evolved traditions.

Habermas also draws upon, as well as departing from, the notion of *immanence* that is found in the work of G.W.F. Hegel. Hegel (1977 [1807]) had looked at the evolution of human understanding as a process of immanent development. In other words, he believed that each stage of that evolution contained the potential for successive stages. Those successive stages were thus immanent in it. Furthermore, Hegel saw this as a progressive process: each stage of development offered the basis for successive, more adequate stages. In the same way, Habermas proposes that the moral truth for a certain community of discourse is immanent in that community; it comprises a potentiality that is already contained within that community of discourse. Where Habermas departs from Hegel, though, is in the latter's faith in an ultimate, utopian destination (Pusey, 1987). Hegel believed that the process of immanent development would eventually arrive at a predetermined, fixed point; a destination that we may not yet have reached but which nevertheless awaits us. In advocating the moral potential of communication, Habermas renounces this hint of moral objectivism that lingers within Hegelian theory; he eschews any notion of a fixed point that awaits those engaged in that communication. For Habermas, moral legitimacy does not flow from communication's capacity to 'arrive' at a particular destination; it derives purely from the quality of the journey that is undertaken.

So where does all this leave us? Thus far, I have outlined Habermas' quest to develop a form of rationality that is suited to the domain of critical-emancipatory enquiry; a domain that I take to be broadly analogous to the domain of applied ethics. I have described how Habermas differentiates the knowledge that this critical-emancipatory form of rationality would provide from that offered by positivistically driven natural science and hermeneuti-cally inclined social science. I have briefly explained the challenges that the hegemony of positivistic method and the prevalence of hermeneutic commit-ment present to the credibility of such a form of rationality. I have also described how Habermas' model of critical rationality productively draws on certain aspects of these other two knowledge domains. I have begun to outline this model of critical rationality by explaining how Habermas identifies, in developmental moral psychology, a test case for a model of ethical legitima-tion which is processual and which appeals to the enhanced insights enabled by retrospective comparison. I have also mentioned how he builds upon the notion of immanence; of moral legitimation as being derived from within a community of thought rather than from outside it. In the next stage of this elaboration of Habermasian theory I will offer a broad outline of how Haber-mas builds on his earlier observations about critical-emancipatory knowledge in order to develop the idea of communicative rationality as a source of ethical legitimation; how communicative rationality comes to offer the basis for critical-emancipatory legitimation that he envisages in that earlier work.

The Social Nature of Humanity

I pointed out earlier how Habermas' discursive, processual model of ethical legitimation resonates with Aristotelian virtue theory. A key feature of Haber-mas' work, which he shares with Aristotle, with contemporary Aristotelian-inspired theorists (such as MacIntyre, 1985 [1981]; Taylor, 1991; Walzer, 1995), and, incidentally, with his erstwhile mentor Heidegger (see chapter 3) along with many other theorists, is that it emphasizes the social nature of humanity. These writers challenge the atomistic individualism that characterizes a lot of post-Enlightenment philosophy. Along with the likes of MacIntyre, Habermas proposes that the social understanding that underpinned Classical theory has been lost to the modern era and that modern philosophy is poorer for it.

A great deal of modern ethics theory is premised upon the idea that human beings are discrete entities, moving independently through their worlds but necessarily making occasional contact whilst pursuing their individualized agendas; rather like self-absorbed drivers on a dodgem ride who sometimes bump into one another. Within this atomistic understanding, moral philoso-phy is cast as a means of defining appropriate rules to govern these inevitable social encounters—as with the rules of usage on the dodgem track. MacIntyre (1985 [1981]) attributes the 'Failure of the Enlightenment Project' to this deficient understanding. According to MacIntyre, the principle-based theorists of the Enlightenment were as scientists trying to piece together the incomplete fragments of a once complete system of thought. Their vain efforts at reconstruction could only end in failure because they were deprived of the vital ingredient that gave this system unity and meaning: the Aristotelian focus on humanity's social predicament. Habermas (1974 [1963]; 1990 [1983]) also describes the fundamental error of Enlightenment philosophers as lying in their individualist presuppositions; their conception of men and women as independent rather than as interdependent creatures. And, for both MacIntyre and Habermas, the 'emotivist' (MacIntyre, 1985 [1981]), relativist stances that have superseded the breakdown of principle-based ethics fare no better: by privileging the subjective over the intersubjective and by rooting moral impulse in individualized responses, emotivist philosophies such as existentialism are just as culpable of marginalizing humanity's social character as their Enlightenment predecessors.

But not only does the social analysis of humanity to which Habermas and virtue theorists appeal contrast with atomistic individualism; it also sets their work apart from a couple of other perspectives which have a social flavour but which reach very different conclusions to theirs. Firstly, a distinction needs to be drawn between the intersubjectivist position elaborated here and the understanding that underpins the *social contract* theories reviewed in chapter 2. Despite its name, social contract theory tends to be premised upon individualism. It seeks to establish a basis for the validity of social rules. However, this endeavour starts from the premise that humans are, by nature, solitary creatures who surrender their independence and some of its associated liberties in order to enjoy the fruits of social living. It thus commences from an atomistic rather than a social understanding of people; it seeks to rationalize social arrangements with reference to the economic and political needs of individuals. As Michael Walzer notes, it thereby gets things back to front, since it fails to acknowledge that: 'we are by nature social, before we are political or economic beings' (1995: 16).

A second school of socially oriented theory focuses on the creation and sustenance of *social capital*. Social capital generally refers to unifying bonds between people within families and communities; bonds which, it is suggested by theorists, can contribute to desirable outcomes such as enhanced levels of educational achievement (Coleman and Hoffer, 1987) or economic development (Fukuyama, 2002). An assumption that tends to characterize celebrations of social capital is that its value is seen to lie in its capacity to bring about desirable states of affairs: social capital is seen as a means to the achievement of ends that are, in themselves, beneficial for those individuals who participate in them. As Charles Taylor puts it: 'the relationship is [seen as] secondary to the self-realisation of the partners' (1991: 43); social cohesion is thus valorized because individuals benefit from it.

In contrast to these notions of social contract and social capital, which portray a means–end relationship between sociality and the achievement of individual purposes, Habermas' understanding descends from a lineage that flows from Aristotle through Hegel and Marx. Hegel (1977 [1807]) had proposed that individuals will only achieve self-realization if they are able to come to terms with their interrelationship with the broader system of which they are part. Importantly, in order for this realization to take place, the individual and that broader system must evolve to a state of mutual compatibility; there must be a form of mutual adaptation. The broader system that Hegel had in mind was 'universal spirit', of which Hegel believed every particular individual to be part and which he also believed is embodied in those particular, individual forms. He proposed that we must come to terms with our place in that universal spirit and that it, in turn, must evolve to an extent that it is reflective of the particular, individual components that comprise it. Habermas drops this idea down from the level of universal spirit to that of a community of interaction. The individuals who comprise that community of interaction are ineluctably defined by it[4] but, for them to feel at home in it, it also needs to be reflective of them. Thus, the individual and the community of interaction must evolve in such a way as to become mutually reflective of one another.

Of course, that mutual evolution may not happen. There may be too much onus placed upon individuals to reflect the community and too little emphasis on the need for the community to evolve at the same time to reflect the individuals that comprise it. This will result in a situation that is, to use a Marxian term, *alienating*. In other words, individuals will experience the community as something that is fundamentally 'other'; something which stands over them rather than being something within which they can find themselves. In order to avoid this alienating state of affairs, it is crucial that the common understanding of that community of interaction evolves in response to the individual understandings of its members. Meanwhile, those individual understandings will, themselves, evolve in response to that of the community.

In summary, Habermasian and neo-Aristotelian perspectives share a common focus on the social constitution of humanity; a focus which contrasts with the atomistic individualism that informs a great deal of Enlightenment and post-Enlightenment ethics theory. That social constitution should not be thought of as an instrumentally expedient arrangement that enables the

---

[4] This resonates with the inescapably intersubjective dimension of 'human being', or *Dasein*, to which Heidegger drew our attention (see chapter 3).

achievement of individually valued ends; rather, it should be conceived as the means by which we define ourselves as individuals. But, while our social predicament is critical to our self-definition as individuals, for a mutually compatible relationship between the social and the individual to occur, it also needs to be expressive of our individuality. The uniquely Habermasian edifice, which is constructed upon this analysis of the relationship between the individual and the social, is his proposal that the achievement of shared understanding is vital to the maintenance of our social predicament and his elaboration of a framework of 'communicative action' which enables this shared understanding. It is to this edifice that I will turn next.

Communicative Action, its Criticality to Social Existence, and its Primacy over Strategic Action

For Habermas, communication is fundamental to the maintenance of those social relations that are an ineluctable aspect of the human condition. Without communication, it would not be possible to establish the bases of understanding and cooperation upon which social relations depend. However, communication can take two contrasting forms (Habermas, 1979 [1976], 1984 [1981], 1987 [1981]), each of which enables the achievement of a different purpose. The first of these forms is referred to by Habermas as *communicative action*, which enables the achievement of shared understanding. The second is *strategic action*, which is aimed at manipulating our environments and putting them to effective use. So, whereas communicative action is about understanding one another, strategic action is the means by which people achieve their desired agendas.

Despite the differences between these two purposes and their corresponding types of action, though, there is a sense in which strategic action is dependent upon communicative action. This is because even strategic action needs to be socially coordinated. We are not able to achieve our strategic goals unless we first establish shared bases of understanding; in Habermas' words: 'If the hearer failed to understand what the speaker was saying, a strategically acting speaker would not be able to bring the hearer, by means of communicative acts, to behave in the desired way.' (1984 [1981]: 293). Habermas concludes that communicative action, carried out in an endeavour to achieve shared understanding, is therefore the primary function of communication. Strategic action, on the other hand, is a derivative usage that is contingent upon achievement of this primary role. The fundamental purpose of speech is thus to achieve shared understanding, or, as Habermas puts it: 'Reaching understanding is the inherent telos of human speech. . . . The concepts of speech and understanding reciprocally interpret one another.' (1984 [1981]: 287).

Communicative action, aimed at achieving shared understanding, is therefore integral to the human condition. Given the inescapability of this proposition, Habermas suggests that we can work towards a notion of communicative rationality that will offer a basis for normative legitimacy:

> If we assume that the human species maintains itself through the socially coordinated activities of its members and that this coordination is established through communication—and in certain spheres, through communication aimed at reaching agreement—then the reproduction of the species *also* requires satisfying the conditions of a rationality that is inherent in communicative action (Habermas, 1984 [1981]: 397).

An important ingredient of Habermas' presentation (1984 [1981], 1987 [1981]) of communicative action is what he calls an *ideal speech* situation. In other words, he proposes a model of dialogical engagement which permits communicative action to realize its fundamental purpose—its 'inherent telos'—of reaching understanding. Central to this notion of ideal speech is the raising and challenging of *validity claims*. What Habermas means by this is that, when a person speaks—in Habermas' terms, when they perform a 'speech act'—that person implicitly asks listeners to accept certain assumptions concerning, firstly, the factual content of what they are saying; secondly, their authority to say what they are saying; and thirdly, what they hope to achieve by saying it. If the listener does not share these assumptions, then shared understanding has not been achieved through the performance of that speech act. Therefore, listeners must be at liberty to question these validity claims, these assumptions about factual content, authority, and intent, in order to verify their acceptance of them. Any disagreements that are thus identified can then be negotiated in order to bring about the harmony across each of these three dimensions upon which shared understanding depends.

I will illustrate this idea about raising and challenging validity claims with a simple example. Suppose Irene is Curtly's line manager at work. Irene tells Curtly that the project he is currently engaged in is so important that he ought to focus all his efforts on it. Irene's 'speech act' (as Habermas would call it) appeals to a shared understanding of the *factual content* of 'important'. Irene and Curtly may have different ideas about what 'important' means in this particular context. Irene may be thinking of importance in terms of commercial performance, or in terms of the priorities of senior managers. Curtly, on the other hand, may appeal to different criteria of importance; perhaps the project's contribution to the company's social responsibility profile, or its significance in terms of the welfare of his colleagues. Understanding has not been reached unless Curtly establishes precisely what Irene means by 'important'.

Secondly, Irene and Curtly need to agree on Irene's *authority* to tell Curtly that the project is important. So, once they have agreed on criteria of importance, they must also agree on Irene's authority to rate the project against those particular criteria. Suppose they establish that senior management prioritization is the criterion of importance to which Irene is appealing. It may be that Irene is basing her 'speech act' on nothing more than a hunch; that she has not actually spoken to senior managers about their priorities but that she is making an inspired guess. But Curtly might have different expectations of authority. He might expect Irene to have been party to an explicit articulation by senior managers of their priorities before she made such a speech act.

And lastly, Curtly is likely to assume that Irene's *intention* in telling him that the project is important is that she wants him to complete it as soon as possible. Of course, Irene may have some more sinister reasons for persuading Curtly to focus his efforts on this particular project. Perhaps she wants to distract his attention from other projects, which she wants to hold back for personal reasons. The important thing is that shared understanding between Irene and Curtly demands commonality across each of these three dimensions. By advising Curtly as she does, Irene is implicitly raising validity claims across each dimension. Curtly must be at liberty to challenge these validity claims if he suspects any points of divergence. He must be free to ask why she thinks this particular task is important (to assure agreement of *factual* content); how she knows managers value it (to assure her *authority* to make that statement); and what she hopes to achieve by asking him to focus his efforts on it (to confirm her *intent* in making that statement). Only after any departures have been recognized and negotiated, only after Curtly has had the opportunity to check that he and Irene are both on the same wavelength across each dimension of Irene's speech act, can it be said that Irene and Curtly have reached shared understanding.

For Habermas, then, achieving understanding through communication is not about linguistic familiarization but, ultimately, it is about raising validity claims and being able to challenge the validity claims raised by others across each dimension of a speech act: 'The speech act of one person succeeds only if the other accepts the offer contained in it by taking (however implicitly) a "yes" or "no" position on a validity claim that is in principle criticizable.' (1984 [1981]: 287).

Thus, integrating insights from Habermas' earlier and later work, we are moving towards a form of rationality which is apposite to the domain of 'critical-emancipatory knowledge' and by which the validity of the normative and regulative statements that are made within that domain can be judged. This is the notion of communicative rationality; a rationality which validates moral truths. As Habermas puts it:

This concept of *communicative rationality* carries with it connotations based ultimately on the central experience of the unconstrained, unifying, consensus-bringing force of argumentative speech, in which different participants overcome their merely subjective views and, owing to the mutuality of rationally motivated conviction, assure themselves of both the unity of the objective world and the intersubjectivity of their lifeworld (1984 [1981]: 10).

To recap the nucleus of the Habermasian ideas that I have highlighted so far: truth, insofar as it relates to the realm of critical-emancipatory knowledge, is rooted in communicative rationality. This is the form of rationality that enables social theory to fulfil a normative role; to go beyond descriptive statements about what *is*; and to make critical statements about what *ought to be*. As I interpret this, communicative rationality is thus the basis of ethical legitimation. Ethical legitimation therefore lies in communicative processes that are aimed at reaching shared understanding; in Habermasian 'communicative action'. This presumption flows from the social predicament of humanity—a predicament to which social coordination through the achievement of shared understanding is essential for, without shared understanding, we would not be able to live our human lives in a satisfactory manner. And the achievement of shared understanding entails being able to raise and challenge validity claims in relation to the truth of, the authority of, and the reasons for making those speech acts through which understanding is negotiated. Insofar as decisions, actions, and situations are the outcome of such processes, then, they have ethical legitimacy. Insofar as they eschew such processes, they are deprived of ethical legitimacy.

Communicative Action and Discourse Ethics

Habermas thus claims to have presented a *transcendental-pragmatic* valorization of communicative rationality as the basis of normative critique. It is *pragmatic* insofar as it is related to the fulfilment of human needs: if the conditions of communication that Habermas envisages were not met, the human needs that communication seeks to satisfy would not be met. And it is *transcendental*, in a Kantian sense, insofar as it defines the fundamental presuppositions upon which any endeavour to meet those needs must be premised. It concerns 'the general symmetry conditions that every competent speaker who believes he is engaging in an argumentation must presuppose as actually fulfilled' (Habermas, 1990 [1983]: 88). This is that of an 'unrestricted communication community' (1990 [1983]: 88) in which the force of the better argument is allowed to prevail unaffected by external or internal coercion and which 'neutralizes all motives other than that of the cooperative search for truth' (1990 [1983]: 89).

But how realistic is this as a practical model of normative legitimation? How likely are we to engage in the quest for shared understanding that Habermas envisages? If ethical legitimacy is only accorded to decisions, actions and scenarios that proceed from Habermasian ideal speech, then ethical legitimacy may well be in short supply, particularly in contemporary organizational contexts. On this question, Habermas acknowledges that the ideal speech situation that he portrays is indeed an ideal, since we rarely engage in communication in a state of disinterested neutrality. Communication is usually situated within strategic contexts insofar as we communicate in order to achieve some agenda that we value, so we generally have some degree of emotional commitment to, or vested interest in, the outcome of that communication. Nevertheless, by establishing common ground across each of the three dimensions of the speech act, non-coerced, shared understanding can still be achieved. Specifically, even when acting strategically, as long as validity claims are made apparent by the speaker, as long as all parties to communication are at liberty to challenge the validity claims raised by other parties, and as long as such challenges are responded to with transparency and sincerity, shared understanding can still be achieved.

In *Moral Consciousness and Communicative Action*, Habermas explicitly discusses the implications that his earlier work on communicative action hold for ethical legitimation. In particular, he builds upon his earlier analysis of ideal speech in order to identify a number of practical principles that would have to be met for ethical legitimation to occur. Specifically, these principles of discourse ethics are that:

> Every subject with the competence to speak and act is allowed to take part in the discourse.
> Everyone is allowed to question any assertion whatever.
> Everyone is allowed to introduce any assertion whatever into the discourse.
> Everyone is allowed to express his attitudes, desires and needs.
> No speaker may be prevented, by internal or external coercion, from exercising his rights as laid down [by the above principles]. (Habermas, 1990 [1983]: 89).

Thus, we come to the holy grail of discourse ethics; the overriding principle which provides normative legitimation; 'the transcendental-pragmatic justification of a rule of argumentation with normative content' (1990 [1983]: 94): this is the principle that 'only those norms can claim to be valid that meet (or could meet) with the approval of all affected in their capacity as participants in a practical discourse' (1990 [1983]: 93).

Implications for Organizational Leadership

So what does all this mean for organizational leadership? Well, for a start, it means that leaders cannot measure the ethicality of their decisions and actions with reference to universal principles such as the greatest good for the greatest number, inalienable rights, rationally derived duties, or social-contractual fairness. But nor can they seek legitimacy in the fervour of their own moral assurance. What it means is that the ethicality of leadership interventions is dictated by the extent to which those interventions are consistent with Habermas' principles of discourse ethics. If 'only those norms can claim to be valid that meet (or could meet) with the approval of all affected in their capacity as participants in a practical discourse' (Habermas, 1990 [1983]: 93), then ethical legitimacy is accorded to organizational agendas insofar as they emanate from such 'practical discourse'. In other words, organizational agendas are legitimate insofar as they are the outcome of ideal speech situations that embrace all those who are affected by them. The role of leadership thus becomes one of facilitating and responding to such conditions of practical discourse.

The task of leaders in organizations, then, is not to rally support for unilaterally defined visions, no matter how much ethical goodwill they may have invested in those decisions. It is to facilitate the ethically legitimating, processual conditions of ideal speech and to ensure that their own conduct meets those conditions. More specifically, drawing on the principles of discourse ethics outlined above, ethical leaders will ensure that the voice of every person who is affected by a decision can be heard; that all can question any assertion, including those made by the leader; that all are able to introduce any assertion whatsoever into discourse; that all are permitted to express their attitudes, desires, and needs; and that no person is prevented, by either internal or external coercion, from participating in this manner. No participant in discourse should be prevented from challenging the validity claims raised by fellow participants. Furthermore, sincerity and mutual understanding across the dimensions of factual content, authority, and intent should be encouraged amongst organizational members, including those who occupy formal leadership roles.

Ethical leadership, then, according to this model, would be leadership which envisages a work organization as an 'unrestricted communication community' (Habermas, 1990 [1983]: 88); one in which the force of the better argument is allowed to prevail unaffected by external or internal coercion; one which 'neutralizes all motives other than that of the cooperative search for truth' (1990 [1983]: 89). And 'truth', in this sense, is understood as a processual achievement rather than as lying in correspondence to some external, supposedly objective standard. Importantly, if asymmetrically distorted communication is to be avoided, not only should these principles prevail during discourse between junior organizational members; they should also govern relationships between leaders and those whom they are supposed to lead. Furthermore, any barriers that might distort communication by restricting participation, by precluding challenges to validity claims, or by otherwise inhibiting ideal speech, should be identified and dismantled.

A significant aspect, perhaps *the* most significant aspect, of relationships between leaders and followers concerns the processes by which those relationships come to be and by which they are sustained. Looked at through the prism of intersubjectivist theory, the position of the leader should not be taken for granted. That position, along with everything else, must be up for intersubjective authorization. Intersubjectivist ethics offers more than a facilitative template by which leaders can justify the decisions that they generate on behalf of their organizations; it also offers a constitutional procedure by which their right to generate those decisions has to be justified. The leadership of a leader, in itself, demands intersubjective legitimation. This recalls the emphasis that several of the researchers reviewed in chapter 1 place on the processes by which leadership comes about. In highlighting the processual nature of leader–follower relations, these theorists offer a consensual basis of legitimation for such relationships. In other words, by drawing attention to followers' consent to leadership, they suggest that maybe we should not worry too much about any asymmetrical influence that leaders wield. However, some commentators also express reservations about the extent to which such consensus might be forced, thus undermining that basis for legitimation. Habermasian theory, for its part, offers a template of consensual purity that might avoid such reservations.

Some Challenges to Habermas' Intersubjectivist Theory

So far, this chapter has focused mainly on the work of Jürgen Habermas, highlighting a particular thread that runs through his work, culminating in his principles of discourse ethics. However, although Habermas has written a great deal about intersubjectivist ethical legitimation, he is by no means alone. I propose now to expand this discussion by drawing upon a few of the many other theorists who have contributed to intersubjectivist theory, as well as a few who, although not falling strictly into the intersubjectivist camp, offer insights that are relevant to the present discussion. This continuation will be structured around some direct challenges that have been offered to Habermas' work; challenges which, although broadly sympathetic to his understanding of intersubjective ethical legitimation, take issue with some of its detail. By considering these challenges, and by augmenting the Habermasian notion of leadership outlined above in ways that may defuse them, I hope to shed further light on intersubjectivism's implications for organizational leadership.

Privileging Certain Types of Rational Articulation

Habermas' model of intersubjectivist legitimation has been criticized on the basis that it is liable to perpetuate the very exclusiveness that it seeks to undo. Specifically, it has been proposed that Habermasian discourse ethics only allows those who are able and willing to adopt particular discursive conventions to take part in processes of ethical legitimation. Iris Young (1996), for example, suggests that Habermas's emphasis on rational argumentation entails exclusive entry to modes of articulation that are emotionally controlled and logically presented. In Young's opinion, a characteristically white, male, upper-class style of communicative engagement is thus privileged, which may marginalize gender, ethnic, and socioeconomic groups that do not conform so readily to this template. Indeed, certain people may even self-deselect from Habermasian communicative action as a consequence of an 'internalized sense of the right one has to speak or not to speak, and from the devaluation of some people's style of speech and the elevation of others' (Young, 1996: 122). If the oratorical hegemony of which Young warns is to be avoided, it is important not to interpret Habermas' depiction of ideal speech too strictly. Young points to the need to expand permissible modes of discourse to include those with which otherwise marginalized groups might feel more at ease.

But as well as making more diverse communication media available, there are also steps that leaders might take on an attitudinal level to help understanding. In particular, leaders whose entry to positions of hierarchical privilege may have been facilitated by their command of the modes of rational articulation to which Young draws our attention should adopt a flexible attitude to what others have to say and how they say it. As well as encouraging communicative media that may foreground perspectives that differ markedly from their own, leaders must be prepared to open up their own minds to opinions that may be couched in less conventionally valorized terms. That a perspective is not enunciated with the mellifluous self-assurance of socioeconomic privilege should not deprive it of an audience; that it should not confer special authority upon it. The same might also be said of the mesmerizing techno-babble of management-speak that so often seems to attract credibility within contemporary organizational discourse (Watson, 2001; Parker, 2002).

There may be a lesson here in Alasdair MacIntyre's veneration (1988) of 'imaginative engagement'. MacIntyre proposes that in order to empathize with perspectives that are articulated from within cultural traditions that differ from our own, we need to make a proactive effort to engage with speakers on their terms, rather than trying to translate what they say into the dialect of our own cultural proclivities. Luce Irigaray's elevation (2004 [1984]) of an attitude of 'wonder' also has something to say in this respect: Irigaray points to the merits of a sense of philosophical humility; one which embraces another person's point of view as something that we can positively learn from rather than something of which we are obliged to take account.

The Challenge of Asymmetrical Power Relationships

But the availability of variegated communicative media, along with leaders' genuine desire to hear what others have to say, may not be enough to encourage people to say what they think. However committed a leader may be to the principles of ideal speech, it is still asking a lot of junior employees to overcome what Nancy Fraser calls 'informal impediments to participatory parity that can persist even after everyone is formally and legally licensed to participate' (1992: 119). In particular, subordinates may struggle to disregard the status differentials that are deeply etched into the very notion of leadership. So, even the most solicitous leaders may have trouble persuading others that their own 'validity claims' are up there to be challenged alongside everybody else's.

It may help to make spaces available where those who are less confident to tread the main stage of discourse, or who perhaps seek a sheltered environment within which to explore their own points of view, can cultivate their ideas without the unnerving presence of hierarchical superiors. On this note, deliberative democracy theorists speak of the importance of 'subaltern counterpublics' (Fraser, 1992: 123) or 'protected enclaves' (Mansbridge, 1996: 57) or 'homeplaces' (bell hooks, cited by Honig, 1996: 268). Clearly, trade unions and other forms of employee organizations may have a role to play in this respect. Such safe havens may be as vital to communicative action within organizations as they are to deliberative democracy on a macro-political scale. Leaders who truly aspire to intersubjectivist legitimacy should therefore ensure the availability of intimate fora where less assertive, less forthright, and less conventionally articulate individuals might develop their points of view as well as their discursive confidence. In order to do so, leaders may have to overcome an inclination to view such sheltered enclaves with suspicion; to regard them as incubators for organizational insurrection.

The Paradox of Coercion

Lying behind most of this discussion of Habermasian communicative action as a model for intersubjectively ethical leadership is a knotty problem. Even if leaders in organizations observe fealty to the processual conditions of Habermasian ideal speech, it cannot be assumed that those people who look to them for leadership will necessarily do the same. It is by no means certain that organizations are populated by Habermas devotees who are just waiting for their leaders to see the light. People in work organizations may be unwilling to discard or declare their emotional commitments and hidden agendas; issues of power and vested interest may intrude into communicative fora. Furthermore, participants in communication may find it hard to adopt the requisite attitudes of 'imaginative engagement' (MacIntyre, 1988) and 'wonder' (Irigaray, 1996) towards their fellow interlocutors that intersubjective legitimacy seems to demand. It falls to those who wear the cloak of leadership to encourage fealty to these conditions of ideal speech. Whilst privileging discourse that is devoid of hierarchical impediment, then, this leadership model also prevails upon leaders to use whatever means are at their disposal to encourage others to conform to Habermasian processual imperatives. This seems paradoxical: on the one hand, an 'unrestricted communication community' that is devoid of hierarchical constraint is envisaged; on the other hand, hierarchical constraint is legitimized insofar as it enforces conditions of ideal speech within that community.

Jane Mansbridge's discussion (1996) of deliberative democracy tackles the issue of coercion head-on, and two of her observations seem particularly apposite to this paradox. The first point is that a certain amount of coercion may always be necessary, even under a deliberatively democratic constitution. As Mansbridge puts it: 'Even regulations that succeed primarily because citizens cooperate freely from public-spirited motivation usually need some coercion around the edges to keep the occasional defector from turning the majority of cooperators into suckers.' (1996: 48). Whereas, for Mansbridge, such interventions would comprise legitimate applications of state-sponsored coercion, within organizational contexts they would delineate the proper application of the administrative apparatus and social influence wielded by those who occupy leadership roles.

To be sure, defences would need to be put in place to protect against misapplication of these coercive apparatus, whether such misapplication is intentional or not. In this respect, the second of Mansbridge's observations is pertinent. This is that institutional arrangements are needed that will forestall such misapplications, either by calling to order the leader's fidelity to dialogical processes or even by instigating a vote-of-no-confidence in the leader's right to lead. Just as such institutional safeguards can prevent overly enthusiastic applications of coercive power, they might also regulate leaders' personal fealty to conditions of ideal speech. It therefore seems essential that leaders who aspire to intersubjective ethical legitimacy should endorse institutional arrangements that will ensure their own dialogical integrity as well as safeguarding against illegitimate coercion on their part. In short, they must be willing to lay traps to bring down any flights of their own monological intemperance that might attempt to break free from the boundaries of inter-subjectivist legitimation.

The Unlikelihood of Consensus

The practical feasibility of Habermasian leadership seems to rest upon the likelihood that ideal speech will end in agreement; it assumes that, once validity claims have been raised, challenged, and resolved, once shared under-standing between all parties has been reached on the levels of factuality, authority, and intent, all parties will agree on a common agenda. This, partic-ularly in work organizations that are characterized by plurality of aspirations, interests, and values, seems improbable. However, the improbability of con-sensus need not undermine the notion of intersubjectively ethical leadership. It only does so if the latter is regarded in absolute terms; if we assume that any dilution of intersubjective purity completely eliminates legitimacy. This need not be so. Absolute consensus may indeed be a rare achievement. Further-more, all of the other legitimating conditions spelled out by Habermas may seldom be realized in practice. Nevertheless, a decision, although lacking absolute consensus, might still be regarded as ethically superior for having been reached through discursive processes carried out with a genuine com-mitment to the principles of Habermasian communicative action. Even if those decision-making processes have not attained Habermasian perfection, and even if their eventual outcome fails to achieve the support of every participant, that decision is still preferable, in intersubjectively ethical terms, to one that has eschewed such processes. Even if the pole of intersubjectivist perfection is often beyond reach, it can still offer a magnetic orientation point against which leaders can align their moral compasses.

Of course, to present intersubjective purity as a pole to aim at rather than as a standard to achieve might be regarded as a cop-out. Diluting the criteria of intersubjectivist legitimacy in this way might offer a justification for leaders to drop the processual cloak of ideal speech whenever it suits their agenda to do so, whilst still claiming intersubjectivist legitimacy for that agenda. However, such contingent manipulation would not be immune to challenge. Although organizational leaders may be tempted to slip in and out of intersubjective fealty according to its congruence with non-intersubjectively defined aims, there is nothing to stop other parties from challenging the legitimacy of such a tactic. And receptivity to such challenge is a fundamental condition of inter-subjectivist legitimacy: for leaders to repeatedly rebuff critique of their fealty to the principles of ideal speech would be to pull the rug from beneath their own claims to intersubjectivist legitimacy.

Consensus and Majoritarianism

But the elusiveness of consensus does not exhaust the challenges that it presents for intersubjective legitimation. Some critics have suggested that preoccupation with consensus may actually encourage authoritarian manipulation and the repression of difference as those in authority seek to achieve that ethically legitimizing end point (Kellner, 1989). Furthermore, Carol Gould goes as far as to suggest that the quest for consensus may be inherently suppressive of difference: 'the telos of the discourse, what characterizes its aim and method, is agreement. Difference is something to be gotten past.... Diversity may be the original condition of polyvocal discourse but univocity is its normative principle.' (1996: 172). This, once again, echoes the concerns with transformational leadership's celebration of shared agendas, which were discussed in chapter 1. Leaders' desire to build commitment to a manufactured consensus might encourage them to marginalize discrepant voices, leading to a form of organizational majoritarianism in which minority perspectives are silenced by a cacophony of well-meaning unanimity.

Concerns such as these accentuate the desirability of a wide range of discursive fora, including an assortment of the safe havens of which Fraser (1992), Honig (1996), and Mansbridge (1996) speak. Not only might these splinter fora offer a bulwark against false consensus; it is also within such enclaves that separate deviations from majority positions can coalesce, gathering the necessary conviction and momentum to mount a persuasive challenge. But it may also be that Gould's argument (1996) overstates the case. There may indeed be something about the quest for consensus that seeks to establish common ground rather than illuminate difference. However, the probability of difference need not preclude the possibility of agreement. Just because people come from different backgrounds, do different jobs, have different genders and ethnicities, vote for different political parties, watch different TV programmes, and have different expectations of their working lives does not mean that they cannot move towards an enhanced understanding of one another's points of view. Nor does it preclude the possibility that they may even identify some common ground. Seyla Benhabib, calling for a variegated public sphere to support deliberative democracy at a broader political level, notes that 'heterogeneity, otherness, and difference can find expression in the multiple associations, networks, and citizens' forums, all of which constitute public life under late capitalism.' (1996: 84). If we shift Benhabib's observation from the macro level of national politics to the micro level of work organization, the presence of a variegated organizational 'public sphere' seems crucial. This underscores the need for leaders to ensure a broad sweep of discursive platforms and to put in place the necessary institutional arrangements to stop these being marginalized in the quest for consensus.

The Practical Feasibility of Intersubjectivist Leadership

Perhaps the greatest challenge to intersubjectively ethical leadership is that, notwithstanding its ethical merits, it is hopelessly idealistic in today's organizational contexts. This recalls two issues that I mentioned in chapter 1 when discussing critically inclined leadership commentaries. The first issue is that even if a facilitative leadership model were theoretically feasible in contemporary organizational settings, it is so out of tune with conventional expectations that any leaders who adopt it are unlikely to get very far. What we have come to expect of our leaders is that they overtly 'lead' the way to a better future. If we hope for transformational crusaders, we are apt to be disappointed if our leaders assume the less dramatic posture of facilitation. Furthermore, it may be that the pressures of organizational life are just too intense for a truly democratic leadership stance to work. Consultation takes time, and time is often in short supply in organizations. Any personal gratification associated with intersubjectivist ethical legitimacy may be scant consolation to erstwhile leaders who failed to sustain the tempo demanded of their role. These are significant issues which, notwithstanding its ethical merits, might seriously undermine the practical feasibility of intersubjective leadership. I will touch on these issues in chapters 5 and 6, which explore the practical application of different leadership approaches. I will also specifically discuss intersubjectivist leadership's practical ramifications during the book's concluding chapter.

Ethics Theory and Leadership: Some General Observations

In this chapter and in chapters 2 and 3 I have looked at a range of ethics theories, organized under the rubric of contrasting meta-ethical perspectives, and explored some implications that these different stances hold for leadership. In the concluding chapter of this book I will elaborate on these implications, integrating them with some insights offered in other chapters, and using this to elaborate a normative model of ethical leadership. Before moving on to Part III of the book, however, I will summarize a couple of general observations that have resulted from this discussion of ethics theory and link these to some themes highlighted in the review of leadership literature that comprised Part I.

My first observation is that, at first glance, both principle-based ethics theory and existentialism seem to offer a basis for monological ethical legitimation on the part of leaders. If ethical evaluation is all about the rational application of universal principles, then there seems no reason why leaders should not carry out this task single-handedly. Similarly, if ethicality derives from the fervour of one's moral commitment, this also seems to call upon leaders to go solo when auditing the ethicality of their decisions and actions. In this respect, principle-based ethics and existentialism resonate with the *managerialist* leadership approach described in chapter 1: the idea of morally sagacious leaders who possess the necessary technical and personal capabilities to make ethically charged decisions on behalf of their organizations. This contrasts sharply with intersubjectivism's processual legitimation of shared decision-making, outlined in this chapter, which sits more comfortably with the *critical* approaches to leadership that were also mentioned in chapter 1. Intersubjectively ethical leadership repudiates managerialist notions of hierarchical prerogative. It offers legitimation for a style of leadership that takes sincere, rather than instrumental, account of heterogeneity; that disperses the boundaries of democratic participation beyond the parameters of market-valorized expertise; and that puts everything up for discussion, rather than constraining discourse within the bounds of preset values and agendas.

However, on closer inspection neither principle-based ethics nor existentialism offers quite such a straightforward justification for moral unilateralism. As far as principle-based ethics goes, the apparent simplicity of principle-based legitimation should not disguise the difficulties that this entails. To select, interpret, and apply a moral principle to a complex organizational dilemma is no simple matter. It involves many practical and theoretical challenges. As such, to expect leaders to shoulder the burden of principle-based legitimation single-handedly on behalf of their organizations would be to ask an awful lot of them. Similarly, when considered within a leadership context, existentialism's celebration of personal choice is more equivocal than when it is viewed individualistically. Notably, the existentialist 'authenticity' of a leader needs to be balanced against the authenticity of those whom the leader leads: while monological ethical pronouncement may allow leaders' authenticity to flourish, this would be at the expense of the authenticity of their followers. So, it may be that the distinction between, on the one hand, principle-based theory and existentialism and, on the other hand, intersubjectivism, is not quite so clear-cut. When applied to the practical context of leadership, all three meta-ethical stances point to the ethical merits of consultation. All three may therefore sit more comfortably alongside critical leadership approaches than they do alongside managerial convention.

A second observation relates to a compelling challenge to principle-based theory: that it does not account for the manner in which we actually make ethically charged decisions. We do not tend to approach moral dilemmas as we would an engineering commission, rationally applying founding principles in order to derive the 'right' answer. Moral choice is a far more emotively volatile affair than that; it is more a matter of applying a moral gut feel that tells us what is right and what is wrong. In this respect, existentialism seems more in tune with what actually goes on when we make moral choices. However, two points follow from this. The first is that it should not negate the usefulness of ethical principles to moral judgement. As I mentioned at the end of chapter 2, principle-based theory can fulfil a useful role in drawing attention to aspects of a morally charged situation that we might otherwise overlook. In particular, examining a dilemma through the lenses of different principle-based theories may highlight the moral claims of parties who are less able to champion those claims themselves. Principle-based theory is thus a useful tool for illuminating nuances that we might otherwise miss. Even were existentialist-style moral conviction still the ultimate arbiter, a moral conviction that has reflected on those nuances is likely to be more sustainable than one that has not.

The second point is that if existentialism seems more in tune with how we actually make moral choices, it also alerts us to the extent to which moral sentiment can be influenced by the 'attunement' or the 'facticity' of our situation. Existentialism reminds us that we are not autonomous, neutral decision-makers, standing outside our environment and making cool-headed judgements about it. We are unavoidably embedded in social, temporal, and purposive contexts. The ethical pronouncements of a leader necessarily carry the print of that embeddedness. In particular, a leader's moral conviction will most likely be influenced by the 'facticity' of his or her social and professional context and by the expectations of that context. Nevertheless, in celebrating 'authenticity', existentialism also points to our capacity to acknowledge the embedded nature of our moral sentiment, to allow for it, and to move on. This goes for leaders as much as it goes for anyone else. Despite circumstances that may seem to impede and limit their choices, leaders are always free to decide how they respond to those circumstantial constraints. So, while existentialism calls upon leaders to be sensitive to the extent to which their convictions are determined by their social and professional context, it also highlights their freedom to reflect on such influences. Furthermore, it leaves leaders with no hiding place from the ethical commitments that are the outcome of such critical, context-sensitive reflection. And if ethical legitimation is found to lie outside the contours of managerialism then, although conventional expectations of leadership may be firmly set within those contours, existentialism emphasizes leaders' ineluctable freedom to choose to be different.

Part III
Empirical Research

Part I and Part II of this book discussed some ideas about ethics and leadership that were drawn from the leadership literature and moral philosophy. In order to elaborate a normative understanding of ethical leadership, though, it seems sensible to augment and synthesize these theoretical perspectives with empirical enquiry. Accordingly, Part III will look at what practising leaders have to say on the subject. Chapters 5, 6, and 7 will report on discussions with senior executives of UK-based organizations; people who are formally expected to demonstrate leadership in their professional lives and who might therefore be familiar with some of the ethical challenges that this involves.

My purpose in interviewing these people was not to find out how 'leaders' per se think about ethics. I was not trying to gain access to some unitary, stable leadership mindset that they all share; nor was I trying to reveal the essential nature of each particular individual's moral understanding. Rather, on the assumption that different leaders are likely to think differently about ethics, and that any one leader might think and say different things at different times, I sought to uncover some of these ideas and consider how they might enrich theoretical enquiry. Nevertheless, although my objective was to reveal neither a shared leadership mindset nor a set of discrete, individual understandings, I was alert to common themes; themes that might recur across a number of discussions and, importantly, themes upon which contrasting perspectives might be offered. I was also on the lookout for resonance with any of the theoretical currents already highlighted in this book. The relationship between those theoretical currents and empirical research should not, however, be thought of as linear. I did not begin empirical research armed with an immutable, theoretical framework upon which to hang empirical insights. Instead, the relationship between theoretical and empirical research was iterative. Although my familiarity with theory constituted an outline structure for initial empirical discussions, that structure, and thus the theoretical chapters of this book, also evolved in response to the insights afforded by those discussions.

Before embarking on this empirical report I will say a few words about the approach that I took to gathering and analysing data. I will also offer an outline of the structure of these three empirical chapters.

Overview of Empirical Research Method

The empirical research reported here comprised loosely structured interviews with sixteen 'leaders'; men and women who have occupied roles within large organizations where they were formally expected to show leadership. Twelve of these people had worked as chief executive officer (CEO) or managing director (MD). The other four had occupied substantial executive board roles: two had been finance directors and two had been HR directors with big private companies or large voluntary organizations. As well as their professional work, several respondents also undertook formal leadership duties outside their main job, either with trade associations, sports and leisure organizations, educational institutions, or charities. One had retired from full-time employment when I met him, although he still worked part-time as a director of two organizations. Four had left corporate leadership roles, either to take up leadership positions in other sectors or to pursue alternative career avenues.

My choice of interviewees was partly opportunistic (Bryman and Bell, 2003) insofar as access to some of them was facilitated by personal contacts.[1] I was then introduced to additional interview candidates by some of these early inteviewees—a snowballing (Goodman, 1961) approach by which I was able to gain access to an 'elite' through other members of that elite (Pettigrew and McNulty, 1995, cited in Bryman and Bell, 2003). However, mindful of a tendency for snowballing to throw up interviewees from similar backgrounds, I augmented this by approaching some CEOs without prior introduction. This permitted an element of purposive sampling (Patton, 1990), which partly compensated for any tendency towards homogeneity in the snowballed sample.[2] Thus, I eventually spoke with people with leadership experience in a range of industry sectors, including financial services, hospitality, travel, music, sport, food production, and health care, as well as in large public sector and voluntary organizations. Purposive sampling also gave access to more female participants than had taken part in earlier discussions. Four of the eventual sixteen were female. I should stress, however, that my intention in accessing a more heterogeneous sample was not to generate sector- or

---

[1] I was personally acquainted with two of my research participants. Eight others agreed to participate because of referrals from these two people or from other contacts from my management career. One was referred by an academic colleague.

[2] I approached eight people 'cold'. Of these, five agreed to meet me and three turned me down.

gender-based comparisons; it was only to incorporate the thoughts of a theoretically interesting cross-section of organizational leaders.

I briefed interviewees on the purpose of our discussions before meeting them, either by letter, by email, or by telephone. I told them that I was researching ethics and leadership in association with Loughborough University Business School and that I was keen to explore their ideas on this topic. I also promised to disguise their identities in my report of our discussions. Accordingly, I have changed all the names of people and companies used in these three chapters, although I have tried to give some idea of interviewees' backgrounds and of the type of organizations in which they worked.

Interviews took place mostly in interviewees' offices, although some people met me in mutually convenient locations outside their workplaces. Each interview lasted for between 1 and 2 hours. Interviews were semi-structured (Bryman and Bell, 2003). I approached each with an outline plan, applying this with sufficient flexibility to permit digression into areas that were of particular significance to interviewees. A range of 'grand-tour' and 'mini-tour' questions (Prasad, 1993, cited in Bryman and Bell, 2003) were used to evoke ethically oriented reflection and to 'probe' (Easterby-Smith et al., 1991) responses for clarification. During each interview I asked the interviewee to describe a particular moral dilemma that she or he had encountered. This 'critical-incident method' (Bryman and Bell, 2003) proved quite productive in ways that will become apparent over the next three chapters. I also encouraged interviewees more generally to offer concrete examples drawn from their personal experience to illustrate principles or concepts that they articulated.

Clearly, research of this nature throws up a number of interesting ontological and epistemological questions. For example, to what extent were the ideas expressed in interviews preformed prior to the meeting, and to what extent were they negotiated during the course of the meeting? My aim was to uncover what people thought about ethics. Consequently, I tried to encourage interviewees' self-expression without offering responses that might have shaped the nature of that expression (Easterby-Smith et al., 1991). Nevertheless, the very process of articulating one's ethical understanding is likely to evoke a degree of reflection on it. If some interviewees left our meetings with a mindset that was slightly altered as a consequence of its articulation, then this is perhaps a welcome corollary of the research exercise. However, it was not its prime objective. One technique that did prove quite useful was occasionally to summarize points made by interviewees in order to clarify and confirm my interpretation of those points. This was done, however, in such a way as to invite the interviewee's confirmation of the accuracy of my summation.

A key epistemological question concerns the extent to which a discussion with a stranger gets to the bottom of what that stranger thinks. In this respect, some interviewees may have offered manicured versions of their ethical commitments rather than telling me what they really think and what they really do. I was not too bothered about this. When recounting their real-life responses to moral dilemmas, or when reporting their ethical priorities, research participants may well have offered accounts that were judiciously modified for public consumption. However, this does not diminish the relevance of those accounts. Interviewees are unlikely to have presented themselves as more morally reprehensible than they are (if, indeed, they are morally reprehensible at all). It is more likely that any lack of candour on their part would have involved airbrushing their accounts in order to present themselves and their organizations as more, rather than less, morally praiseworthy. In such cases then, what they have told me is not what they actually think and do, but what they believe would have been a morally correct thing for them to think and do. Thus, they have offered me an insight into the way that they think about ethics. And since this is what I was seeking to access, the content of these articulations is the most important thing for the purposes of this research.

All interviews were audiotaped and verbatim transcripts were subsequently compiled. Around 130,000 words were eventually transcribed. A grounded approach (Strauss and Corbin, 1990) was taken to the collection and analysis of data. Theoretical exploration had provided a tentative structure for empirical research, which comprised a number of *themes* that seemed to hold resonance for the research topic. By themes, I mean headings that had emerged through theoretical research as being of particular interest. However, these themes evolved considerably during empirical enquiry. Furthermore, additional themes emerged, waxed, and/or waned as the research progressed. Therefore, the relationship between theoretical and empirical research was highly iterative throughout.

I roughly followed the stages of *coding* suggested by Bryman and Bell (2003), where open coding is understood as the 'process of breaking down, examining, comparing, conceptualizing, and categorizing data' (Strauss and Corbin, 1990, cited in Bryman and Bell, 2003: 429). Three stages of coding led to the preparation of *concept cards* (Bryman and Bell, 2003). These concept cards were under continuous review: new cards were added as additional themes emerged during ongoing analysis; cards were also withdrawn as multiple themes were sometimes combined onto one card. Twice during my research I carried out a major review of coding: after three interviews and after eleven interviews. This included the creation of 'secondary order cards' (Prasad, 1993, cited in Bryman and Bell, 2003: 430), which consolidated the earlier concept cards in the light of relationships that were emerging between different themes. Subsequent interviews were then conducted against the framework of these consolidated themes, which were subsequently augmented and shaped in response to new data.

Throughout this coding process I tried to remain vigilant to the hazard of decontextualization (Coffey and Atkinson, 1996, cited in Bryman and Bell, 2003) and misappropriation, which are a corollary of extracting passages from transcripts and thus considering fragments of data apart from their narrative context. I sought to ameliorate this difficulty by frequently referencing sections of data back to their original context. In this respect I found it particularly helpful to re-read passages that had been extracted from transcripts whilst simultaneously listening to original recordings of interviews.

Overview of Empirical Report

By this method I arrived at the categorization of data that is discussed in the next three chapters. Chapters 5 and 6 relate to the meta-ethical perspectives reviewed in chapters 2, 3, and 4. In chapter 5 I will introduce three contrasting 'ideal-type' ways of thinking about leadership ethics; ideal types which correspond in some respects to those three meta-ethical perspectives. I will draw on discussions with three particular leaders in order to illustrate these ideal types. Then, in chapter 6, I will expand on this discussion by considering one particular tension associated with each ideal type, drawing upon interviews with other leaders in order to illuminate these tensions. Chapter 7 takes a slightly different tack, moving away from this threefold, ideal-type classification. It follows, instead, the structure of the review of the leadership literature in chapter 1, elaborating on the two particular concerns that were discussed in that chapter. It begins by exploring some ways of thinking about the ethicality of leadership agendas. It then considers some contrasting ways of thinking about leadership in relation to suppressing and facilitating agency.

Before embarking on this report I will mention one last issue. This is that by inviting only leaders to participate in empirical research, I have precluded contributions from other people in organizations. The research does not, therefore, embrace the views of those people who bear the consequences of the ethically charged decisions made by leaders; those whose material and emotional well-being may have been affected by those decisions and who might therefore have as much to say about their ethicality as the leaders themselves. This is a significant omission. However, by accessing and drawing uniquely upon the discourse of organizational leaders I am not honouring that discourse with the tag of normative legitimacy. Indeed, the whole purpose of synthesizing these empirical accounts with theoretical perspectives is to expose them to critique. I do concede, though, that empirical research amongst 'followers' could make a useful addition to the ideas developed here.

5

Identifying Three Ideal Types

This chapter will consider the role of a leader in relation to setting the moral tone of an organization. I propose to draw on the discourse of three particular people in order to illustrate three contrasting approaches. I have selected these specific individuals for several reasons. Firstly, each is especially expressive of his[1] moral understanding. All of the leaders who participated in my research showed an interest in ethics; indeed their willingness to participate might be taken as an indication of the seriousness with which they take this aspect of their leadership roles. However, I gained the impression that some were more preoccupied with that aspect than others. The three people that I will discuss in this chapter are amongst that group.

But a more important reason to focus on these three individuals is that each articulated a very different understanding of his role in setting and implementing his organization's moral agenda. I thus hold up the discourse of each as exemplifying a separate, *ideal-type* understanding. I use the term 'ideal-type' to refer to a heuristic classification, which highlights idiosyncratic features of distinctive versions of a particular phenomenon; in this case, distinctive ways of thinking about the leader's role in relation to ethics. These ideal types are stereotypical depictions. In presenting them I will emphasize certain aspects of these leaders' discourses; aspects which illuminate the distinctiveness of each ideal type. By emphasizing these distinctive characteristics I hope to draw attention to contentious aspects of these different ways of thinking about the leader's role in relation to morality, particularly when taken to extremes.

A final reason why these particular individuals merit special attention is that the understanding articulated by each resonates in some respects with one of the meta-ethical perspectives discussed in Part II. I pointed out, when discussing these meta-ethical perspectives, some implications that each holds for

[1] Although some female leaders took part in my research, the three discussed in this particular chapter are men.

leadership. It will become apparent as this chapter progresses that each ideal-type personification corresponds in significant respects to a meta-ethical counterpart. Consequently, the narratives of these three individuals offer a useful platform for further reflection on the implications of those meta-ethical stances.

A Company Advocate

David works as Managing Director of the UK Division of Rutherford, a global, family-owned business. Rutherford is one of the world's largest privately owned corporations, and its founding family continues to exercise a firm influence over its affairs. I met David in his office at Rutherford's main, UK manufacturing and processing depot. During our meeting, David seemed particularly keen to orientate our conversation towards Rutherford, its management systems, and its values, rather than dwelling on his own views about morality. I was immediately struck by his pride in the company and his loyalty to it. In short, David came across very strongly as an *advocate* for his company. Furthermore, David seemed very comfortable operating within Rutherford's value systems. He began the meeting by describing, with a lot of pride, the high profile that morality occupies within the company's decision-making processes:

> *Is ethics something you spend time thinking about, David?*
>
> Well that's a good [question] actually because the answer is yes. And this is where you can't avoid the culture of the corporation...because one of Rutherford's fundamental values and one of its building blocks to work with in this organization...is its ethics. Rutherford have very strong ethical values and ensure that the employees understand those...As [the company] has got bigger and bigger and more global, we have a set of behaviours that we all sign up to as employees. And what it says is that even though we are a global company—eighty countries, all that kind of stuff—here is a set of values that this business is going to operate by...So, to be fair, ethics...it's not a bolt-on. It's more endemic as one of the core cultural behaviours of Rutherford, I would say. Probably more so than a lot of organizations. A lot of organizations talk about ethics; I've never really seen it so consistently applied as it is in Rutherford. It is quite amazing really...And the right of it is, if you cut to the chase, if I make a big mistake that costs this business a million pounds, I'll be forgiven, quite frankly. If I do something unethical, I'll be sacked.

David went on to describe how Rutherford's values are established from the centre, by the Rutherford family. He also related the steps that the company had recently taken to formalize and communicate its ethical code and to ensure that its members adhere to that code:

You mentioned there that it is very important that all the employees understand [the company's] values. But where do those values come from in the first place?

The reality of it is, from Rutherford. They are passed down from generation to generation. Rutherford is a family-owned business so the family determine: this is what we are about; this is what we are; yes, it's different to everybody else, but this is what makes us. That gets passed through the organization through very well-communicated briefings, documentation, just reinforcement . . . Some of those values were implied for many, many years; they've been implied and they've been passed down . . . About ten years ago [Rutherford] actually formalised some of those values and made a much, much better job of saying actually, you know, we are on a big growth strategy; that means that we acquire businesses. That means that people need to understand that when we acquire them and when we do our due diligence: . . . yes, we look at numbers; yes, we look at plants. But we also look at the culture; we look at the ethical values; we look at the safety; we look at their past history on environmental [matters]. I mean we put a lot more emphasis on those kind of things . . . you know: what's your level of safety; what's the culture like; do people tell lies; have we got outstanding issues with local governments, with regulatory bodies? . . . [Rutherford] tends to be very, very, you know, very, very open and transparent about those things.

And because we have a big growth strategy as Rutherford world-wide, it needed to be more formalised to give people boundaries to operate in . . . When we bought businesses, people needed to know what they were letting themselves in for regarding the way Rutherford does business. So that was much more formalised about ten years ago. And programmes were set up within Rutherford to really explain to people what Rutherford's culture is and what it wants to be, what its ethical values stand for, what its leadership responsibilities are, what the behaviours that we would like to see in our culture, [what] the expected behaviours are and that kind of thing.

Ok. So the impression I'm getting is that the values are something which are shaped from the top of the organization. And then anybody that comes in for any form of relationship with the organization, whether it be another company which you bring in . . . whether it's an employee, they will be expected to conform to those values.

Absolutely . . . We all sign documents every year to say we are going to conform to certain levels, standards, and ethics.

David seems very happy, then, to judge the ethicality of his own behaviour in relation to the company's moral code. But where does his confidence in the moral probity of Rutherford's values derive from? Why is he so convinced that they offer a sound template for his own conduct? The answer to this question seems to relate partly to the seriousness with which the company treats ethics. That it cares enough to have formalized a set of behavioural principles and that it invests resources to ensure adherence to them seems, for David, to convey legitimacy upon those principles: that his organization is ethically sensitized guarantees the moral probity of its actions. However, David also offered slightly different, although related, reasons to explain his confidence in Rutherford's moral code when I specifically asked him about this:

> *So how can people be sure that the values that Rutherford stands for are the right values morally?*
>
> I think it's, I mean, they're not rocket science, to be fair, they are pretty basic; they are not exactly rocket science.

David's observation that Rutherford's values are 'not rocket science' illustrates a fairly straightforward approach to morality. It implies that fundamental principles of right and wrong are easily discernible through the application of common sense and that an ethical business is one that follows these self-evident principles, instead of allowing other considerations to stand in their way. So, its preoccupation with ethics necessarily makes Rutherford an ethical business. Furthermore, by leading in a manner that is congruent with these self-evidently right values, David can be confident that he will be leading ethically.

A further interesting aspect of David's discourse was his frequent reference to the importance of consistency—a subject to which he returned several times during our conversation. There are several interrelated strands to the way that David spoke about consistency. Firstly, he suggested that people expect leaders to show consistent fealty to altruistically tinged principles, even when those principles conflict with self-interest or organizational performance:

> And it's just like watching on TV all the politicians; why do people get pissed off with the politicians? Because they are not consistent. You know, what people consider to be good, strong, core values; they expect certain people to operate within that parameter. And when they are not consistent that's when they lose trust... I think if you are consistent, if the people think you are looking after their interests, not just the interests of yourself or the organization, if you do what you say you are going to do... well, I think people are going to trust you. And I think that whole issue about are you looking after their interests as much as looking after your own interests is a big part of it.

David also dwelt on the importance of consistency when asked about the part played by employees in the definition of corporate values. He suggested that, for employees, it is more important that corporate values are consistently implemented than that they have the opportunity to contribute to the definition of those values:

> *Do [employees] get an opportunity to contribute? You mention that the values have evolved to a certain extent; do people in the organization get the opportunity to contribute to that evolution?*
>
> Well, it is Rutherford that sits right up there and it says: 'this is what, these are the behaviours we want around the world'... But based on our experience here,

this word consistency crops up a lot whenever I [conduct employee feedback] and talk to our employees. Because above all they want to be consistent:... the feedback we get is 'we don't care if you are as tough as old boots and we don't care if you are as nice as pie. But please be consistent because what we can't handle is when one week you are nice to Jo and the next week you are bad to Bill. We don't know where you are coming from'. So that inconsistency then allows people to play games, it allows management to do different things and what you can't have is inconsistency regarding the values of the management and the values of the supervisors.

Yes. So I'm getting the impression that the employees, for them, it is more important that, whatever values the company has, they are consistently applied than that they get the opportunity to contribute to the evolution of those values.

Absolutely... I think it's important that it doesn't matter where you sit in the organization, I think you need to know what is and is not acceptable.

The way that David speaks about employees' participation in the definition of company values concurs with the idea that moral rectitude is self-evident: if corporate values are so obviously right, why should employees want to be involved in their definition? Their only concern would be that those abundantly obvious standards of moral rectitude are consistently applied by management. They would expect different managers in different parts of the organization to treat different people consistently. They would also expect consistency in the conduct of any particular manager. And in both respects, those who occupy leadership roles have an important part to play: their consistent application of the organization's moral code is critical to its perpetuation:

In my view you can pass down whatever memos you want from the top, it means Jack Shit unless the living organisms of the company; the bosses, the managers, the employees within it, unless you actually—people just mimic behaviour. So if you've got a boss who says one thing and does another you are going to have chaos. If you have a boss who lives certain values, no matter what they are, whether it's, you know; we'll do we what we say, whether we'll treat people properly, whether we'll have recognition processes, whether we're consistent in how we manage people, you know, some of the core values I stand for, people see them and say: 'is he consistent in the application of those values?'

David's discourse, then, points towards a mutually supportive relationship between organizational values and organizational leadership: on the one hand, the values offer a template of moral rectitude for leaders within the organization to follow; on the other hand, the perpetuation of those values demands their consistent exemplification in the behaviour of the organization's leaders. The values support the leaders and the leaders support the values. The result of this mutually supportive relationship is a virtuous spiral of moral probity.

I will sum up some features of the Company Advocate ideal type illustrated by David's discourse before moving on to the second ideal type. The first point is that, such is his confidence in his organization and its moral code that David seems happy to orientate his moral compass in accordance with that code. Secondly, the importance with which Rutherford treats ethics reassures David of the moral probity of its values. As he sees it, since the apprehension of moral rightness is a relatively straightforward matter, an organization that permits this self-evident moral template to direct its decision-making is likely to be an ethical company. Consistent application of an ethically responsive company's moral agenda therefore offers a dependable template for ethical leadership. A third characteristic of David's discourse is that it portrays consistency as, in itself, a virtue. Consistent application of commonly shared, behavioural principles, particularly in the face of competing self-interested or commercial imperatives, is therefore an important part of ethical leadership. A fourth feature, which follows from the self-evident nature of morality, is that there is little need for a company to engage in internal debate about ethics. If the definition of appropriate values is, as David suggests, 'not rocket science', then organizations that aspire to ethicality need to devote few resources to moral soul-searching. Furthermore, there is little need to involve employees in the definition of the organization's moral agenda. Since moral probity is a relatively straightforward matter, organizations should not bother too much about consultation around ethics. Instead, they should focus their efforts on communicating and enforcing the code of conduct that instantiates those self-evident moral truths.

A Moral Crusader

James runs the UK division of a multinational company. At the time of our meeting he had been in this post for just over a year. He had previously worked in a number of other managing directorship and board roles. I discussed leadership ethics with James over lunch and at a subsequent meeting in his office. James stated at the beginning of our conversation that he does not tend to think explicitly about morality but that it nevertheless plays a big part in the way in which he fulfils his leadership responsibilities:

> I've realised that a lot of, I guess, my values, a lot of what I try and do in terms of my style and what I try to bring to the business, is about [morality] but I have never thought about that as 'okay, this is my morality bit' because it's not a word I would necessarily always use. But the elements of it, and there are many, many elements of it, would all be things that are probably very important to me and are probably a lot of the values that I know I have brought to this business in the last year relative

to my predecessors. So, yeah, I don't sort of package it like that but it's a part, I guess, [of] what things are important.

The core message of this statement was reinforced throughout our conversation. This is that James attaches a great deal of importance to morality and, although he may not conceptualize it in theoretical terms, he takes the ethical dimension of his leadership role very seriously. His willingness to assist with my research seemed to derive from a genuine interest in how ethics relates to his job. He was keen to share his reflections and experiences in a frank and open manner. James also expressed a great deal of faith in his own moral judgement and seemed to have few qualms about implementing that judgement. In this respect, James' discourse struck me as that of a *Moral Crusader*: assured of his own moral conviction and keen to encourage others' conformity to it. This came across in the way that he talked about the definition and implementation of corporate values. Like David, James spoke of the importance of a shared moral code. However, whereas David emphasized the role of the company's founding family in shaping that code, James dwelt on the part that a leader could play:

Who decides what's important? Who should decide what is important morally for businesses? Who should be making those decisions about which are the morally significant subjects?

I think the leadership of the company. I am not just on about the individual and myself, there is also a team responsibility in terms of the Senior Board. And it is, I think, in any company it is absolutely the style of the leader and it's then the style of the leadership team that definitely influences and creates a culture across the business. And so it is incredibly important that, as a team, you recognise that and I always say to my [senior management] team, you know: 'it's about the shadow that we create...The leadership team is responsible for it'.

I returned to this theme a little later in our conversation. Again, James emphasized the role played by leaders in shaping the moral tone of an organization. Although he suggested that junior employees might play a small part, he depicted those at the top as the principal moral architects:

What I am getting the impression of is a fairly top-down management approach. You know, the role of the leadership is to define the moral agendas and to define the responses that we should be taking in those moral agendas. Is that the way that you tend to run the business? Is that your general approach?

No, I'm not autocratic in that sense...I think a lot of what you are asking about, though, does come from the top. You know, the personality of a business: you can often see where it comes from by looking at the leader of the company. And that can be in a very small company [where] you can see it much more visibly. Or it can be a large company.... There is a top-down [effect] which is that if you behave like that, you instil a style that you hope that people like and they respond to that and then they try and do it. It cascades down . . . . And coming up from the bottom there is an element; but a lot of it, a lot of it has to come from the top, particularly on this [moral] agenda.

James offered two examples of the significance of leadership in shaping an organization's moral tone. Firstly, he contrasted the moral climate that he had developed since his arrival with that permitted by his predecessor. Such is the moral potency of leadership that, even in a relatively short time, James had been able to drive some fundamental changes:

> We'd been a sleeping giant for about five years in this company and it was, if you looked at the manager, the MD who was here, you could understand why because he's a bit of a sleeper and it's just his style and everything about him; he has absolutely zero energy or motivational dynamism or whatever else; he hadn't really had control of his team. The standards therefore had fallen . . . . There had been a bit of a drinking culture going on with some of the senior team and some people were definitely abusing trips we get offered by airlines and so on: it was always the same people with their wives going away. Well, we stopped all of that and we've injected a momentum and a belief and a different culture in our business.

A second example is James' description of someone he holds out as a role model of ethical leadership. His account is notable for its depiction of Stuart Rose [who was, at the time of our meeting, CEO of Marks and Spencer] as having unilaterally defined and imposed Marks and Spencer's environmental policy:

> Stuart Rose of Marks and Spencer announced recently that they were going to go carbon-neutral and that would mean a dramatic change in everything that they did. He was very honest about it. It was shortly after the Stern Report had come out and he said, 'I read the Stern Report and I read the news and I heard it on the radio and everything else' and he said, 'I felt that I had a responsibility because I could influence it. I had a responsibility and we in our business . . . have a responsibility to do what we can about this. So that is what we are doing'.

James' own determination to implement his personal values is illustrated by an account of his summary treatment of a moral transgressor. This case involved a senior manager who had behaved in a chauvinistic and drunken manner towards some of his female colleagues during a residential business event; conduct which conflicted sharply with James' standards:

> I've fired two directors this year. One . . . he went to a . . . team meeting and did an overnight. He had too much to drink and was fairly abusive to some of the women on the team. I fired him for it because I said 'that is unacceptable behaviour. That is not how we behave. That is just not the culture of this company. I don't want you around'. Clearly, and he was terribly apologetic, he recognised that he made an

error and I said 'no, actually it's more than an error. You have a different set of values than I have and that we have so: bye-bye'.

These passages suggest that, for James, the leader is and ought to be the most significant shaper of an organization's moral tone. Although he mentioned the need for a 'leadership team' of senior managers to buy in to that tone, the initiative should come from the top. The leader, whether it is James in his organization or Stuart Rose at Marks and Spencer, should be the one to set the moral direction. Furthermore, James spoke of his ease in fulfilling the roles of moral author and moral enforcer on behalf of his organization. But from where does the legitimacy of a leader's moral legislation derive; how can the leader be sure that his or her moral appraisal is accurate? I posed that question to James:

> *Is there a danger that, if the moral agenda is being set by the person at the top and the way that that moral agenda should be handled is being set by the person at the top, you may be missing out on some things and some responses to those things which are, morally, quite important? Can you necessarily assume that the person on the top has that sort of moral perspicacity to be able to see what is important and how we should respond to those things?*
>
> No, you can't . . . that person could be pretty immoral . . . you know this actually affirms the influence of the role. You can have somebody pretty immoral at the top and that would very quickly drive a pretty immoral culture because the style of that person would run that through the team. . . . You can see how I sort of, if you like, laid down the culture and style around those issues. Somebody else might come in with a very different agenda. They might be quite an immoral person and before you know it, they might be dishonest in their dealings. They might go to a client and actually look a client in the eye and lie to them; you know, promise them that we can do something that we can't do in order to win the business. You don't do that. Because I don't believe in that and therefore I am trying to create and develop a culture around, if you like, values that I think are important. But it is dangerous because I might miss some things, but it's equally dangerous that somebody in my position could have a very adverse effect because I like to think things I am doing are fairly positive, but somebody could have an incredibly negative effect if you got the wrong person in the role.

Later in the conversation, I returned to this issue. James had just recounted a period of a year or so when he had been unemployed. This, he suggested, had helped him to appreciate the point of view of other people who were in a similar situation; to see the view from the 'other side of the tracks':

> *So is there a danger then, given the importance of seeing things from the point of view of the 'other side of the tracks', is there a danger in the moral agendas of the business and the way that we respond to those agendas being driven primarily by senior management who presumably are seeing things mostly from one side of the tracks?*

...Yes there is a danger because you know it can be a positive or negative influence on a business. The responsibility, if you like, then comes at every level of the company in terms of the recruitment, to try and recruit leaders and managers at every level so this does apply all the way down. What we are talking about is where I am sitting in the company but you can equally have a conversation with the [chief finance officer] and look down from there or you could have a conversation with someone who is running our service centre of one hundred people and they would have the same view because they have got a team, and so at every level and every layer these things apply...At every layer we have got a responsibility to try and recruit people who have sufficient maturity and experience and the right value-fit so they will do the right things.

So, James acknowledges the danger of investing so much moral responsibility in the people at the top, but he proposed that this hazard can be avoided if the right people—that is, people of the requisite moral fibre, who will do the 'right' thing—are appointed to leadership roles throughout the organization.

The way that James speaks of ethics implies that it is a straightforward matter; that right and wrong are readily apparent, at least to those who have reasonably well formed moral judgement. Moral leadership, therefore, consists of ensuring that members of the organization pursue self-evidently, morally desirable imperatives, rather than subordinating those imperatives to considerations such as the unbridled pursuit of profit or the personal foibles for which James has dismissed senior executives. A further task of leadership is to appoint, to subordinate leadership roles, people who share the leader's moral acumen and integrity. If immoral leadership occurs, it is most probably because a person who is either unethical or beset with moral torpidity has somehow attained a leadership role. It is less likely that a morally well-meaning leader would be misguided in his moral appraisal.

It would be misleading to present James as offering an unbridled endorsement of moral autocracy. As I will relate in chapter 7, he articulated some sensitivity to the expectations of his employees and also spoke of the need to respond to the ethical demands of his customers. Nevertheless, the overwhelming message contained within his discourse is that the difference between moral leadership and immoral leadership lies, firstly, in the extent to which a leader is willing to promote a self-evident moral agenda over other considerations and, secondly, in the vigour with which that person reinforces that agenda throughout the organization.

To summarize, James articulated an understanding of moral leadership that differs notably from that expressed by David. Whereas David presented moral leadership as being deeply embedded in the values that have sustained his organization over many generations, James accentuated the part that a leader can play in shaping those values. David emphasized the need for a leader to apply a predetermined and well-established moral agenda in a consistent manner. James, on the other hand, focused on the leader's role in defining that agenda, which may involve changing established behaviour patterns and introducing new priorities. For David, moral leadership is measured in accordance with the template offered by his organization's traditions; for James, moral leadership involves shaping organizational behaviour around the leader's apprehension of moral probity.

Despite these differences, though, David's and James' discourses share some common ground. In particular, both depict the apprehension of moral probity as a relatively straightforward matter. This common stance might be paraphrased as: 'we all know what's right and wrong; it is just that some of us act on our apprehension of moral rightness while others choose to ignore it'. Therefore, if organizations and leaders care enough about ethics to privilege it in their decision-making processes, they will be ethical. Although David tended to focus on the organization while James focused on the leader, in both cases there seems to be an assumption that moral sensitization engenders moral probity.

A further common feature of their respective discourses is that neither David nor James had much to say about junior employees participating in the development of his organizations' moral agenda. As far as David was concerned, junior employees have little interest in such matters; they just want that agenda to be consistently applied. From James' point of view, the people at the top of the organization are the ones who are influential in shaping its behaviour; therefore, responsibility for setting its moral tone should reside with them. And although the senior management team is expected to exemplify the organization's moral code, the key role in its definition lies with the leader. Such appraisals of junior players' capability and willingness to contribute to an organization's moral direction contrast sharply with the approach that I will outline next.

A Mediator of Communication

When I met Roger he was working as CEO of a large, public-sector organization. A long career in the public sector had included CEO roles in several similar organizations. Roger had been in his role for ten years and was due to retire during the following year. Like David and James, Roger suggested that it is important for an organization to have a shared moral code. In response to my opening question about the ethical dimension of leadership, he reflected on the need for a clearly defined set of values and described some steps that he had taken to enhance clarity within his own organization:

I wasn't satisfied that the core values [in this organization] were clear enough—we did have a set of core values but they were too long, and they were too wordy, and therefore people were able to interpret them. So instead of them becoming a set of organizational values they became a set of individual values, still in the right areas but people could place there own interpretation on the bits that they were less comfortable with, and I think that can then give confusing messages around leadership. So we've only recently, actually, very much simplified our core values . . . So we looked quite carefully at some of the subtle distinctions that there are in that set of values.

However, despite this common endorsement of a shared moral code, Roger expressed an understanding of ethics and leadership that differed in some fundamental ways from those articulated by David and James. The first point of departure is that Roger presented morality as a more nuanced affair than did either David or James. David, the Company Advocate, spoke of the importance of consistent application of the corporate code throughout the organization, suggesting that the content of that code is 'not rocket science'. Meanwhile, James, the Moral Crusader, articulated a steely resolve to encourage conformity to his own apprehension of moral probity. But both spoke about the identification of moral rectitude as if it were a straightforward matter. Roger, on the other hand, left space for ambivalence. In particular, he reflected on the possibility of tension between, on the one hand, the personal values of organizational members, and even of organizational leaders, and, on the other hand, the moral code of the organization. Nevertheless, he suggested that there ought to be some shared ground between the values of a leader and those of the organization that he or she leads:

The way we put it in the debate is: we can have different core values in relation to our personal lives. So we are not an exact match for what we might live out personally because we'll feel stronger about some aspects. But I think when you come to work you sort of put on a hat saying: 'what's the minimum value that will actually make me wonder whether I wanted to put my name to leading this organization?' So I think there are two different—there's actually a separation between your own personal values, which might be better or worse but will almost certainly be more detailed, and some will be significantly different from those that you are required to adopt in an organization.

Roger's suggestion that 'we can have different core values in relation to our personal lives' and that these 'will almost certainly be more detailed and some will be significantly different from those that you are required to adopt in an organization' implies a far less straightforward meta-ethical stance than that articulated by either David or James. Roger's discourse leaves space for conflicting ethical positions, which seems to contradict the presupposition, implicit in David's and James' discourses, that the apprehension of moral probity is straightforward.

A second difference between Roger's stance and those expressed by David and James is that, although he believes that leaders play a key role in shaping and upholding organizational values, Roger also spoke of involving other members of the organization, including junior members, in the definition of its moral code:

> *... the core values of the organization: where do they actually come from ...?*

We had this debate, and it's a fascinating debate: you have to allow discussion around them. But I also think that it's a function of leadership, I was going to use the word to 'impose' those core values and that's too strong a word. But it is a function of leadership, at the end of the day, to take a clear view on what the core values of the organization are. But I don't think you should deny the organization the opportunity to feed into that process ... We had a debate in the corporate management board to start with around some of the thoughts. We then put them out to the outer service group, the senior managers. We then had a series of groups to which people could volunteer to feed in their views. And they were refined as a result of that. And I think they were improved as a result of that, actually. But they are still held and they are still owned in leadership terms. I think that's absolutely vital. So it's interesting that we had actually been through that.

> *So that process of engagement, how deep down into the organization did that go? Did that stay at a fairly senior level?*

No. We certainly wanted to take the view of the senior managers in the organization so we ran it through ... a tier immediately below Directors. We run with a very small management team of five directors and myself and then we have about another sixteen people who are heading up individual functions. And then we have a tier then of people who are in a management capacity of one form or another, and that's probably around about the ninety mark. So anybody who is managing a team in any shape or form will be included in that senior management. And they participated. We then had a series of focus groups which was sliced through the organization. So we'd have people from the top to the bottom of the organization working as interest groups to feed into that.

> *Those managers that took part in that process; were they also expected to engage with their respective teams?*

Yes. We had quite a bit of effort in the communication strategy around that so that people [could participate]. There was a website so people could participate individually as well.

So, although leaders have an important role to play in defining and supporting the organization's moral agenda—'it is a function of leadership, at the end of the day, to take a clear view on what the core values of the organization are' and those values 'are still held and they are still owned in leadership terms'— Roger also envisages a role for junior employees. Although managers seem to have played the more substantial part in the process of value definition, focus groups and the intranet have also enabled contributions from junior levels. Furthermore, Roger's observation that the outcomes 'were improved as a result of that' implies his approbation of this consultative undertaking. I therefore refer to the ideal type illustrated by Roger's discourse as that of a *Mediator of Communication*. Whereas David, the Company Advocate, described how the organization's founding family defines its values, and James, the Moral Crusader, dwelt on his own contribution to the organization's moral agenda, Roger placed a lot more emphasis on the role that a leader might play as a facilitator of dialogue concerning morality.

During our discussion, Roger spoke a lot about consulting with others and encouraging participation. But this presents a potential difficulty: what are leaders to do if a democratically derived ethical agenda, which they have facilitated, conflicts with their own moral convictions? By relinquishing his grip on the organization's moral tiller, Roger must confront the possibility that it might steer a course with which he is personally uncomfortable. This tension would be of little concern to either a Company Advocate or a Moral Crusader. In the case of the former, consistent application of the self-evident standards of probity that are enshrined within an organization's moral code offers a dependable and stable reference point for personal conduct. In the Moral Crusader's case, self-assurance of the probity of the leader's own ethical commitments legitimizes their imposition over and above any alternatives. Such certitude is not possible for leaders who adopt the consultative style articulated by Roger. Facilitators of intersubjectively agreed moral agendas must face the possibility that the consultative processes that they mediate may reach conclusions with which they radically disagree. Roger's discourse is interesting for his reflections on how he negotiates such tension. Consider, for example, the following two passages. Each offers a specific example to illustrate a tactic that Roger adopts when chairing public meetings on behalf of his organization:

> I do a significant number of public meetings and I can probably illustrate it in two ways because there are two messages that come out. We don't meet a cross-section of the community, I think it's important I say that, but predominantly people will say 'if only we exterminated young people the whole world would be a better place: because young people commit crime and young people drink; young people smoke drugs; young people make a lot of noise and drop litter; young people congregate in groups and frighten us'. An incredibly powerful message [is] coming from the public at large. Now if I weren't to offer some challenge and some leadership in those circumstances, people will go away from those meetings reinforced in their view that if we got rid of young people the world would be a better place. But I do fairly simple things in leadership terms which I think, again, come back to what I think is a set of core values that I want to espouse. And I say 'look there are the same number of good, bad and indifferent young people as

there are of good, bad and indifferent people of any age group; the same good, bad and indifferent policemen as there are people'. And those are some of the things I think that you sometimes have to be prepared to do. And you have to do it quite sharply because people won't respond otherwise, they will just fudge it.

And the second example:

Let me try and give you an example … We've had a very significant influx of Eastern European workers [in the local area], predominantly young, predominantly quite bright young people, working in areas that are poorly paid. So they are augmenting our existing work force. They haven't posed a threat locally in terms of jobs because we've got virtually full employment locally. And one of the early challenges, actually championed by [a local celebrity] because he got very involved in this, started a little bit of a hare running about: you know: 'lock up your daughters, the Eastern Europeans are coming' … And I did actually say at a public meeting 'look we need to wake up to the fact and actually we need to be blunt about it: these young people are coming from societies that are actually far less sexually promiscuous than our own'. Now that's a value that I feel very strongly about: treating people equally. It's something that I would be very forceful about in my personal life. But I am probably getting quite close to the margins of where I ought to be going in terms of challenging locally because I am exhibiting what is a very strong personal value to me … it's about equality and that sort of thing. But there is a limit to how far your role permits you to go in there and I think that example, I've been ok, I got away with it, it was taken in the spirit it was intended. But you've got to be careful how far you push that sort of line.

In these simple examples, Roger relates how, as a leader, he is well placed to encourage reflection amongst the group to which he is expected to provide leadership. In each case, Roger describes interaction with external stakeholders rather than the internal groups that have been the focus of attention in my discussion so far. Nevertheless, this distinction need not preclude the broader relevance of Roger's facilitative tactics. As CEO of his organization, these external stakeholders look to him for leadership. Furthermore, his description of the measures that he has taken to provide that leadership may be apposite to other leadership contexts. Rather than directly imposing his own convictions on the group, Roger speaks of encouraging group members to think critically about the implications of their own perspectives and to reflect upon the presuppositions upon which those perspectives are based. He thus portrays a compromise between, on the one hand, leadership as moral autocracy and, on the other hand, laissez-faire, relativist tolerance. By encouraging critical reflection, and by offering insights that might broaden the scope of that reflection, a leader can point a group in a direction that he or she believes to be morally correct without demanding that they follow that direction. Notably, Roger articulates sensitivity to the potency of his position and to the impositional propensity that it entails. Roger's circumspection in offering his own views in these meetings does not derive from personal ambivalence about those views; rather, it derives from his awareness of the undue weight that his leadership status might give to them.

Notwithstanding the effectiveness of this tactic in the particular instances reported by Roger, Mediators of Communication must still come to terms with the possibility of rupture between their own convictions and those of the group that they lead. Roger's persuasive attempts to encourage critical reflection may not eventuate in a consultative outcome with which he is comfortable; there is always a chance that a facilitated intersubjective conclusion will conflict with the views of its facilitator. In such instances, Roger indicated some readiness to temper his personal views in order to bring them in line with those of the organization. In the following passage he speaks of the onus that rests upon leaders to observe fealty to democratically defined, organizational agendas, even where those agendas may clash in small ways with their own moral sensitivities:

> So I think it does get more complex and I think some of my personal values are probably still simpler and stronger than the values that I bring to the organization ... [which] are more subject to the compromise of everyday practical experience than some of the personal values that I would hold very, very strongly in my personal life, when I feel much freer to deal with it. You deal with the consequences in your personal life in a different way. You are not carrying responsibility for an organization. You know you can ... be freer in terms of the values that you would espouse as an individual than you can be with those you would espouse on behalf of an organization. I don't think it's going to be huge, I think it would be worrying psychologically if there was a huge mismatch between the two.
>
> *Yes. Is it a difference in values or is it similar values applied in different contexts with slightly different outcomes?*
>
> I'm not going to allow it to be as easy as that. I think what you are saying is partly right. The challenge back, I think if the fundamental values were to be different again I think you would be worried. I think it's about, you know, feeling free to be more extreme sometimes in the way that you express them, in the way that you would apply them if you are exercising personal freedom. You know you might take some more radical action against elements of society that you are more uncomfortable with in a personal capacity than you know you can afford to take in a political environment and leading an organization that is democratically elected and which is trying to combine different views.

So, for Roger, taking on a leadership role in a democratically accountable organization entails a duty to observe the outcomes of its consultative processes, even when these outcomes conflict with his own moral convictions. Roger suggested, however, that there are limits to the extent to which he would be prepared to compromise his own moral convictions to consultatively defined outcomes. I asked if he could envisage a situation in which the chasm between a democratically agreed organizational agenda and his own perspective was so wide that such compromise was impossible:

> That's a very difficult question because, you know, if you are a democrat you believe in democracy. I think the way I'd answer it, which is a bit of a cop out, is that I think that the decision that you have to make as a leader is: are you prepared to go in and fight against that democratic process? ... My line would probably be to say that I shouldn't accept an appointment in those circumstances because it is not my role as an appointed officer to challenge the democratically elected organization.

Roger's response, then, is that where the rift between the democratically elected stance of an organization and his own values is too great, he would decline appointment to a leadership role with that organization. This, of course, leaves unanswered the thorny question of what Mediators of Communication would do if the consultative outcomes that they facilitate once in post became significantly out of kilter with their own values.

One final question that I explored with Roger is whether his commitment to facilitating consultation conflicts with what is expected of him as a 'leader'. Are the stakeholders in his organization happy for him to consult around issues or do they expect him, as the leader, to 'lead'; that is, to impose his own convictions on the organization:

> *Does the fact that you are formally expected to provide leadership; does it reduce the amount that you can be a mediator as opposed to an imposer of values?*
>
> No, I don't think it does. I mean it's a question you would have to put to other people in a sense, because I think there is always a danger in trying to answer that one yourself. I think, you know, I've been here now for ten years and people will understand that in the way that I exercise leadership: that I am anxious to engage with other people; that I am not going to close the door to those ideas; that those ideas genuinely and importantly influence my outlook on running the organization. And I think it is wrong to see that as negating leadership. I mean actually what you are doing is you are enhancing your ability to lead by listening and creating a climate in which people aren't afraid to contribute their views.

Roger's suggestion that 'it's a question that you would need to put to other people' may indicate a personal ontology of intersubjective constructivism that extends even beyond his understanding of moral leadership. Most importantly, though, for the present discussion, his response indicates that, in his view, a commitment to consultation need not undermine the effectiveness of leadership; indeed, it can enhance that effectiveness.

To summarize, in my conversation with Roger he expressed a more consultative and more nuanced understanding of the relationship between ethics and leadership than did either David or James. Whereas these two located authorship of the organization's moral agenda either in its traditional values or in the judgement of the leader, Roger spoke of involving other stakeholders in ongoing processes of value definition. The desirability of such consultative processes seemed to be partly dependent upon the complex and diverse nature of moral judgement. Whereas David and James implied that ethical evaluation is a straightforward matter, Roger suggested that different people might legitimately hold different moral views to his own. Roger's discourse is particularly interesting for its account of how he negotiates the tensions that such an understanding entails. The most apparent tension is that between his desire to be true to his own convictions and his perceived responsibility to facilitate a democratically responsive outcome. The response offered by Roger emphasizes the role that a leader might play as a facilitator; not just as a facilitator of consultation but also as a facilitator of critical reflection on the part of those whom he consults. As well as mediating democratic processes, he proposes that leaders might encourage people to reflect on their convictions. If the outcomes of such facilitated, reflective processes were to differ markedly from their personal convictions, Mediators of Communication would have to choose whether to overrule those outcomes and impose their own heartfelt convictions, or to respect the democratic process and support its outcomes. Roger gave the impression that he would generally favour the latter course. Furthermore, he would carefully vet the leadership roles that he took on to avoid putting himself in a situation where the chasm between personal conviction and democratically constituted values was too wide for comfort.

General Observations

In this chapter I have highlighted aspects of the discourses of three leaders in order to present three very different ways of thinking about organizational leadership and ethics. Certain parallels are apparent between these three ideal-type discourses and the three meta-ethical stances that I reviewed earlier, although it would be misleading to overstate the extent to which the views expressed by these particular individuals fit neatly into meta-ethical boxes. Thus, Company Advocate David's emphasis on consistent application of predefined moral standards is redolent of a principle-based meta-ethic. Furthermore, his tacit assumption of self-evident moral rightness hints at the objectivist, universalist moral ontology that underpins a lot of principle-based theories. However, apart from his evocation of a utilitarian-style rationale to justify redundancies (which I will discuss in chapter 7), David did not draw explicitly on theoretical rationales to explain his moral commitments. Indeed, his commitment to the established values of the organizational community seems more evocative of conservative (as opposed to intersubjective) versions of virtue ethics than it is of a principle-based understanding.

Meanwhile, the confidence expressed by James, the Moral Crusader, in his own moral judgement, along with his willingness to implement his own ethical choices, is redolent of the 'authenticity' that is enjoined by existentialism. James' readiness to assume the role of moral author on behalf of his organization is notably devoid of the 'anguish' which existentialists suggest may attend apprehension, on the part of the 'inauthentic', of their moral autonomy. On the contrary, the fervour with which James brandishes the sword of moral execution reverberates with a Kierkegaardian celebration of personal conviction. On the other hand, some aspects of James' moral understanding do not fit with existentialism. He, like David, offered a utilitarian-style justification for making people redundant (see chapter 7); he articulated some sensitivity to the moral expectations of stakeholders (which I will also discuss in chapter 7); and, like David, he sometimes placed a virtue-style emphasis on conformity to shared values. A particular departure from existentialist meta-theory is James' apparent assumption that the values that he upholds can claim some sort of self-evident moral probity; a seemingly objectivist, universalist understanding that is at odds with existentialism. James' insistence that others share his moral agenda also contrasts with the relativist tolerance that permeates some strands of existentialist thought.

Of the three, the discourse of Roger, the Mediator of Communication, seems to offer the closest match to meta-ethical type. Throughout my conversation with Roger I was struck by the extent to which he articulated an intersubjectivist understanding of his leadership responsibilities; by his presentation of his role as that of a facilitator rather than an imposer of values. Nevertheless, even he departed from the intersubjectivism presented in chapter 4 in his occasional references to seemingly universal standards of moral rightness.

However, despite these departures from meta-ethical purity, each of these ideal-type depictions sits close enough to his meta-ethical counterpart to offer a useful platform for illuminating those three meta-ethical perspectives and for exploring some tensions associated with them when applied to leadership. In chapter 6 I will build upon this platform by recounting the extent to which the other leaders whom I met echoed the understandings articulated by David, James, and Roger, and by exploring some corresponding tensions. But first I will round off this chapter with a few words about organizational context and a couple of observations about the discourses reviewed in this chapter.

Clearly, it is possible that the way in which David, James, and Roger think and speak about ethics is shaped to some extent by the respective organizational contexts within which they lead. David, the Company Advocate, has spent a number of years working with a well-established, privately owned organization. His company was set up in the nineteenth century by its founding family, some present members of which are still involved in its governance. This entrenched governance context might partly explain David's reverence for the organization and its traditional values. Furthermore, recent media interest in some of Rutherford's activities may have encouraged the corporate centre to pay particular attention to its ethical profile. This might account for its current preoccupation with a unified corporate response. In contrast, James, the Moral Crusader, had recently taken over as the leader of a national division of a publicly quoted corporation that trades within a fast-moving industry sector. The company claims a long heritage, but its history is complicated by frequent mergers, demergers, and acquisitions. The leader whom James had recently replaced had apparently permitted morally lax practices, particularly amongst the company's senior managers. This dynamic organizational context and the moral torpor of his predecessor may account for James' eagerness to exercise moral authorship. On the other hand, Roger, the Mediator of Communication, leads a public-sector organization that has an explicitly democratic mandate. This, along with his accountability to formally empowered, external stakeholders, may have ingrained Roger's consultative disposition.

That David, James, and Roger express the moral responsibilities of their respective roles as they do is therefore unsurprising. Furthermore, the language used by each may also be symptomatic of contrasting organizational circumstances. It is possible that the way in which each represents what he does and how he thinks serves to accentuate any contrasts between the three: maybe David, James, and Roger are not so different as their discourses suggest; it is just that the nature of those discourses is itself shaped by the expectations of their respective work environments. I will briefly revisit this question of context dependency in this book's concluding chapter. However, it is not something that I intend to make too much of because, interesting though the question of context dependency is, of even greater interest is whether an approach to ethics that is articulated within a particular context may have wider relevance to the moral legitimation of leadership in other contexts. In this respect, my priority now is not to identify causal factors or to make sectoral comparisons but to explore the ramifications of different ways of thinking about ethics.

I will finish this chapter with a couple of tentative observations concerning the empirical material that I have reviewed so far. The first point is that the moral care manifested by all three people discussed here must say something positive about the ethicality of their leadership. Caring about ethics and being prepared to prioritize moral considerations over other imperatives ought to give leaders a head start along the road to ethicality. To be sure, ethical concern should not be taken as synonymous with ethical conduct. For one thing, it may be that some leaders who never spare a thought for ethics just happen to do the right things; there may just be a happy congruence between their natural inclinations and ethicality (however the latter might be conceived). The relationship between moral sentiment and ethical conduct is a vexed one, to which I will return later.

Of more interest to the present discussion, though, is another way in which there may not be a perfect fit between ethical care and ethical conduct. This is that the moral judgement of an ethically caring leader, or an ethically caring company, may be contestable. For Company Advocates and Moral Crusaders, moral judgement is cut and dried: David takes for granted the probity of his company's moral code; James articulates confidence in his own moral perspicacity. Neither seems to entertain the possibility that the moral furrow he ploughs with such vigour may be offline. Consequently, neither says much about the need for moral reflection or about the desirability of involving other people in moral decision-making. But such moral certainty seems overly optimistic. Indeed, the very persistence of moral dilemmas is testimony to the complexity of the topic. So, to invest such trust in the moral acumen of, in David's case, his company's founding family and, in James case, an individual leader, seems risky. Roger's more measured stance seems to offer a more adequate response to the intricacies of moral deliberation. For Roger, there is space for equivocation. Furthermore, by envisaging a style of moral decision-making that embraces the views of others, Roger puts less of an onus on the moral acumen of either key individuals or narrowly circumscribed groups. While Roger's discourse may lack either the reassuring stability of Company Advocacy or the exuberance of Moral Crusading, and while it may perhaps constitute a leadership style that is less attuned to conventional, managerialist expectations, it seems to have something important to say to leadership ethics.

6

Exploring Consistency, Authenticity, and Facilitation

Chapter 5 outlined three different 'ideal-type' ways of thinking about leadership ethics, illustrating each with the discourse of a specific leader. I drew attention to congruence between these ideal types and the different meta-ethical perspectives discussed earlier. David, the Company Advocate, told how his leadership agenda leans on the established values of his organization and spoke of the importance of consistent application of those values; a stance which corresponds in some respects to a principle-based approach to ethics. James, the Moral Crusader, eagerly embraced moral authorship, which has overtones of existentialist 'authenticity'. Meanwhile, Roger, the Mediator of Communication, dwelt on the merits of democratic participation; an approach which is redolent of an intersubjectivist meta-ethic.

This chapter will expand on these ideal types. It will draw upon discussions with other leaders to illuminate a particular characteristic of each ideal type and to highlight a specific challenge associated with that characteristic. In the case of the Company Advocate, I will focus on the importance that David places on consistent application of principle. I will also explore the extent to which acting on principle may challenge a leader's emotional commitments. As far as the Moral Crusader ideal type is concerned, I propose to elaborate on the existentialist notion of authenticity that is manifested so clearly in James' discourse. I will also look at the challenge that pressures to conform to the imperatives of a particular community may present to authenticity. My discussion of the third ideal type, the Mediator of Communication, will consider the extent to which other leaders share Roger's advocacy of intersubjective facilitation. It will also investigate the temptation to seek moral succour within a supportive community, and the extent to which this may shut off leaders from perspectives that differ from their own.

Consistent Application of Principle: An Emotionally Challenging Undertaking

My discussion of principle-based ethics in chapter 2 drew attention to the breadth and diversity of principle-based theories. I mentioned the expedient flexibility that this breadth and diversity offers to those who seek a convenient ethical justification for a chosen course of action: such is the range of available moral rationales that, whatever organizational leaders may wish to do, they can probably find a suitable principle-based justification if they look hard enough and apply it with sufficient imagination. I suggested that to avoid the charge of expediency, leaders who aspire to principle-based legitimacy ought at least to show consistent fealty to a particular set of principles and apply them in a consistent manner. Otherwise, principle-based ethical justification becomes a pretty meaningless exercise.

I have already elaborated on the emphasis that David, the Company Advocate, places on consistent, principled application of corporate values. David is not alone in this respect. Quite a few of the leaders I met talked of the ethical merits of applying principle in a consistent manner. However, to varying degrees, some also reflected on the need to set aside emotional attachment in order to do so. In particular, consistent application of principle may require leaders to overcome feelings of loyalty towards certain groups. More generally, it may be necessary to silence the inner voice of compassion. It seems, therfore, that principled leadership can be an emotionally challenging undertaking.

Some interviewees expressed greater comittment to consistent, principled action than others. Ray, CEO of a nationwide retail chain, suggested that there should be little space for personal affiliation in business transactions. Ray recounted his dismay at being asked by a company chairman, earlier in his career, to take long-standing relationships into account when awarding supply contracts. For Ray, contracts should be awarded in accordance with a 'fair tender process', which precludes such partiality:

> I'd decided that one of the suppliers, who had a hundred percent exclusive contract, was doing a very bad job. And I decided that I needed to find some new suppliers. I went through a tender process and out of that tender process the supplier who had hundred percent exclusivity didn't actually end up getting any part of the new contract. And I got a phone call from the Chairman of the business and I was told: 'you've got to give them some of the business'. And I remember feeling at the time: you know, that's wrong; a fair tender process, they didn't succeed in the process, they're out...
>
> *What was the basis for giving them the business then? Is there an implication of a back-hander going on?*
>
> I don't know. I think it was probably more of the fact that they'd had a hundred percent of the business and they were going to go to nil percent. And that they'd

been, in the early days of this business, they'd been very supportive of the business and the chairman, I think, felt he owed them some ongoing loyalty. I don't think there was any back-handers; but I think there was some favouritism.

Mark, who has worked in a range of industry sectors, also reflected on the need to uphold principle. He recounted a situation in which he had dismissed some long-standing employees for malpractice even though what they had been doing was, so they claimed, accepted custom. Unlike Ray, Mark expressed some compassion for the recipients of his severity, describing this particular instance of principled action as the greatest dilemma that he had faced as a leader. Nevertheless, Mark did what he felt, as a leader, he had to do. Indeed, so committed was he to stick to his principles that he resisted, during an ensuing industrial tribunal, overtures on behalf of the claimants to settle out of court, even though such a settlement seemed at the time to be in the best interests of Mark's company:

> There was a time in one of my businesses that I was running where I had to dismiss an entire department. Now I'm not saying I had to, but I believed on consideration that that was the only route. That involved five individuals with, between them, something like 110 years service. They were stocktakers and they were accepting what could be construed as bribes. Now, 'it was custom and practice', they said in their defence; 'it's always happened therefore it's [acceptable]'. I had just come into the job and the fact that it always happened, from my point of view, is irrelevant. It clearly wasn't [acceptable] for them, in their position, to do this sort of thing. Cutting a long story short ... we went to an industrial tribunal and it lasted for weeks and weeks ... but at the end of the day they came to us at the eleventh hour and said 'would you do a deal'; you know 'we're willing to settle out of court because we think you're going to lose' ... And of course the [company] by this stage were paranoid because, in those days, tribunals were, you know, get-thee-behind-me-Satan sort of stuff, and really they were seen as being always biased towards the employee ... and they said 'we'll do a deal' and I said 'well no, how can we do a deal on something this basic'. ... my immediate line boss thought we should settle because he was of that mind. Anyway, I said 'you can't do that in a business because everyone then loses confidence in your judgement and your ability and frankly you're undermining everything we're trying to do', so I said 'I just won't do it'. So, anyway, we stood by our guns and of course we won ... it's about fairness ... If you've got a sense of principles and a real balanced view of what fairness is, you'll probably win in the end, in fact invariably you'll win in the end even if it looks pretty dire when you're staring it in the face.

So, when confronted with a moral dilemma, Mark stuck to his principles, even when this may have seemed overly harsh, even when his boss advised other-wise, and even when his principled stance seemed, at the time, to be pragmatically risky. A more emotional account of the application of principle was offered by Sarah. Reflecting on her experience as director of a small travel

company, Sarah described a redundancy scenario that she felt morally compelled to implement for the greater good of the organization. In order to apply
this principle, she had to overcome feelings of affiliation and loyalty towards
members of her own work team:

> I guess that was a personally difficult decision because I had a personal affection
> for, an attachment to, the team of people, the individuals, but I had to step back
> from that . . . . There is an element of: 'try and detach myself; think of myself in my
> professional capacity and think I'm doing this because the organization needs
> it' . . . If I do become too embroiled in the emotional side of some of the decisions,
> then I'm not sure I'd ever make them. You have to step back a bit . . . just step back
> and say: 'I know this to be right for the organization, therefore this is what I feel
> has to be done'.

For Ray, Mark, and Sarah, then, feelings of partiality have to be set aside
when implementing principles in a fair and consistent manner. In all three
cases, the narrators describe having overcome varying degrees of compunc-
tion about the consequences of their actions in order to act on principle.
Ultimately, each regards it as his or her moral duty to set aside sentimental
misgivings and to apply principle in a consistent and impartial manner. This
advocacy of consistent, principled action in the face of countermanding
emotions featured quite prominently in my research discussions. It emerged
most strongly in discussions of redundancy scenarios, which I will discuss
more fully in chapter 7. Interviewees spoke frequently of the need to overcome sentiment in order to do what they felt they had to do. Sympathy for
the unfortunate victims of corporate restructuring was most often subsumed
by fealty to a rule-utilitarian-type imperative of organizational maximization: the greater good of the organization trumped any feelings of compassion towards particular individuals or groups. As with the discussions
reviewed in this section, leaders saw no legitimate place in their moral toolkit
for emotions such as partiality, sympathy, or loyalty.

Existentialist Authenticity: The Pressure to Conform

In relating my discussion with James, the Moral Crusader, in chapter 5, I
highlighted James' confidence in his own moral judgement and his readiness
to shape the ethical tone of his organization. James' discourse was evocative of
the existentialist notion of 'authenticity' in several ways. Firstly, he did not
conceptualize his ethical sensitivities in terms of theoretical principles; rather,
he spoke of following his moral intuition. Secondly, he does not seem to shirk
tough decisions. He described his readiness to impose his own version of
moral probity, even when this involved hardship for others. While he may

have regretted the harsh consequences of his decisions, and while he may have tried to ameliorate those consequences for the unfortunate recipients of his moral fortitude, he showed no remorse at having taken those decisions. Furthermore, James suggested that such self-assurance is a key aspect of moral leadership: he proposed that the person at the top can and should set the organization's moral agenda.

James was not alone in stressing the link between ethical leadership and moral authorship. An equally emphatic statement of the role of the leader in establishing organizational values was offered by Ray, the CEO of a retail chain whom I mentioned a short while ago:

I'm a great believer that a business should be very clear about what its values are...those values should be the values of the Chief Executive or certainly the leaders of the business. I don't believe that values can come up through a business. They have to come from the top....

You don't feel there's a place for involving subordinates in the evolution of those values at all?

No. No. Because if at the end of the day if the values aren't lived by the leadership of the business then they can't survive.... So if they don't see the leadership of the business living the values, they won't live the values.

Is it not feasible for the values that the leadership of the business lives to be developed in consultation with subordinates?

Oh, it can be developed, but the way I would put it is that the leadership needs to be really clear these are *our* values.... How that is then communicated, and the behaviours that are encouraged to reflect the values, that needs to be worked out. If the leader says: 'these are the four or five things that are really important', you then have to involve the rest of the business and say: 'well, how do these four things manifest themselves in what I do as a job, whether I'm a check-out girl or I'm a buyer or I'm in the supply chain somewhere; what does that mean to me?'...So there's an iterative process to actually turn those values into behaviours and into the language that the average person in the business can understand because the leaders may say: 'well these are my values', but they may be in [such] a language that the vast majority of the people can't relate to what he's on about, so there [needs to be] a translation.

Ray's observation that 'if the values aren't lived by the leadership of the business then they can't survive' is interesting. His rationale seems to be that the preservation of organizational values depends upon leaders' fealty to them: if leaders do not observe corporate values, then junior employees can hardly be expected to do so. And since leaders are only likely to observe values that emanate from their own moral conviction, it follows that the values of the organization must be those of the leader. This offers a strikingly autocratic understanding of moral authorship—one which limits input from junior employees to discussion about how they are to put those leader-defined values into practice.

In order to adopt the role of moral authorship with such alacrity, leaders need to be very comfortable with their own moral acumen. There is no space for the 'anguish' that existentialist theorists see as a likely response to the realization of one's moral autonomy. This moral self-assurance is illustrated by Gareth's description of a corporate restructuring process. When I met Gareth, he had been retired for several years. Nevertheless, he was keen to reflect on the many years he had spent running various business units with a large conglomerate. Of particular relevance to the present discussion was Gareth's apparent readiness to accept ownership for his moral decision-making, along with his retrospective ease with the decisions that he had taken. Like James, when reflecting on moral dilemmas, Gareth did not try to hedge responsibility for the hardships that his moral resoluteness may have occasioned. He did not try to absolve himself of accountability for unpleasant decisions. He did not dwell on circumstantial constraints, nor did he mention the need to respond to the expectations of powerful stakeholders. He presented his decisions as his, and his alone. One particular story illustrates this. Gareth told me of a situation in which he had been asked to take control of a subsidiary that had returned poor commercial results for some time. His brief was to make radical changes in order to improve performance; changes that were to include substantial job cuts. Gareth described a dilemma that he encountered when trimming the workforce. The dilemma was whether to tell his new employees of their impending redundancy. Gareth showed no qualms about claiming personal ownership for the decision that he took in that situation. Twelve years later, he remained comfortable with his actions:

> I suppose the biggest dilemma was always with how honest are you with your business plan when the business plan involves restructuring and when the business plan involves trying to cut costs out of the business? That's the only dilemma I've ever really had. The difficulty of: should you tell people everything or should you—because to some extent, I mean, there are business plans that you come up with where I suppose we felt that you had to keep a bit back....
>
> ...*can you think of any particular instances there; can you give me any tangible examples?*
>
> Well I knew when I went up to [a subsidiary company] that I was going to get rid of the whole board and I was going to make, of the office staff, maybe forty percent redundant. That's not what I told them. What I did say was I got up there and immediately told them that they had been unsuccessful for three or four years and that there would be changes, but I wouldn't have gone up and told them that I was going to change everything which I felt was necessary. I didn't do that.
>
> *And what were the principles at play there; why did you choose to take that course of action?*

I think it's because the one thing you don't want is people to be panicking that they're going to lose their jobs any earlier than it needs to happen because you lose the momentum and you lose focus . . . I always felt that four or five months' loss of focus would cost you and you wouldn't get it back . . .

But you had already made the decision that you were going to take that action but you were just shielding the people from it.

Yes, yes . . . .

And was that something that caused you any discomfort; did you have to think about whether that was the right move?

I would always mull it over or maybe agonize about [the decision]. But going up to [that company]; I'd known them all very well . . . but I mull it over for two or three weeks and then I do the decision very quickly: I have people in; I tell them that's it and to go and then when they've thought about it come back and see me any time, but exit interviews for me never took more than five minutes. Having worried and agonized over it I would not have a discussion on it, ever. If people ask me why I say: 'that's the decision I've made' . . . I'd always agonize over it and worry about it but then do it very quick.

And that decision to go into [the subsidiary] and not to inform them that you were going to be making some fairly drastic changes five months down the road, was that a decision which you were at liberty to take or were you influenced in taking that decision?

. . . I simply discussed it with my then boss at the time and it was a done deal, carte blanche . . .

Whether or not to make those redundancies, and whether or not to share the fact that you were going to make those redundancies with the people, that was all decisions you were at liberty at take?

Absolutely, completely my choice, absolutely . . .

So this was twelve years ago. Were you in that same position now, would you make exactly the same decision?

I think I would, yes.

Would you go about things differently?

I don't think I would. No, funnily enough, I don't think I would.

In relating this tale, and more generally in our discussion, Gareth adopted a somewhat different tone from James, the Moral Crusader discussed in chapter 5. Insofar as the discourse of both leaders manifested existentialist authenticity, that authenticity was of a slightly different nature. Whereas James alluded to ethical decisions as if they were clear-cut, Gareth offered a more nuanced understanding. Despite his moral self-assurance, Gareth did not present ethical choice as a straightforward matter. He struck me as a reflective individual who had thought deeply about the ethical dilemmas that he had encountered. Nevertheless, despite acknowledging their complexity, Gareth seemed unlikely to lose sleep over his decisions once he had made them. I gained the impression that whereas James fires his ethical six-shooter from the hip, Gareth carefully evaluates his target. Nevertheless, once the target has been selected, Gareth is equally ruthless in his aim and just as unlikely to show contrition for any casualties.

In contrast to Gareth's account, Max offered a very different story from early in his leadership career. In Max's case, he described how, in response to pressure from the chairman of the business of which he was CEO, he had made what he considered to be the wrong decision: he had done what was expected of him rather than what he had believed to be right. As such, Max's account might be interpreted as a retrospective acknowledgement of his own 'inauthenticity'. The background to Max's story revolves around his promotion from London-based MD of the European division of an American company to the role of CEO, based in its head office in the United States. Once in place as CEO, Max was called upon to close down parts of the business that seemed to be underperforming. This included closing down a brand in London that he had helped to set up. Max believed that this was the wrong thing to do. Nevertheless, he took this action, even though it was against his better judgement, because his chairman expected it:

> I clearly remember putting a lot of emotion and energy into setting up a [brand] in London, in the early nineties, with a guy who was, you know, quite a close friend. And I felt a huge amount of pressure [later when I became CEO], because it wasn't working, to make it work. I felt I was put under unfair pressure by [the chairman], who was my boss, because...in the meantime I'd moved from London to [head office in the USA] and had had to close down a lot of things that weren't working there. And I believe that [the chairman] then sort of looked at this ineptness that I was behind and put a huge amount of pressure on me to close [the London brand]...A huge amount of pressure on me, which you know, clearly it's my job to absorb and to think about objectively. I think I rushed closing it because of that. And I had a big impact on the office in London, who'd put a huge amount of resources, not just money but a lot of time and effort. And they were very, very committed to the product.
>
> That, I think, was a huge clash of your loyalties and your judgements and, actually, I think that I didn't do the right thing; I made a mistake...I wanted to be seen to be fair and equitable. And I think when you're closing things down you have to be objective, right...So I felt that because I had more emotional attachment and maybe to an extent obligation to what I had set up, I didn't want to feel it was compromising people's view of my objectivity, right. So I wasn't strong enough to say: 'it wasn't', [although] it clearly wasn't...
>
> *So because you'd set up the London business you didn't want anybody to feel that you were showing any favour towards it?*
>
> Yes, absolutely. I was shutting down these things and it could look [as if] I was shutting down things that hadn't got my stamp on it. And that wasn't the case, but I felt it looked that way. And therefore in the interests of being fair and equitable I was unfair to the guys who had—I was over-hard on them. I guess it's a bit like, you know, the bit about you can be tougher on the people that are closest

to you in many ways. And that was something that—it was a huge dilemma for me at the time.

In his eagerness to do what other people perceived as 'being fair and equitable', Max had therefore acted in a manner that was unfair according to his own judgement. His observation that 'I didn't want to feel it was compromising people's view of my objectivity, right. So I wasn't strong enough to say: "it wasn't"' might be interpreted as a cry of Heideggerian 'anxiety' at his own existentialist 'inauthenticity'.

Of course, authenticity might turn out to be a tough road for those who are embroiled in establishment expectations that are out of tune with their own moral convictions. Acting in accordance with one's moral commitment might not always be the best career move. James and Gareth described how they had been true to their own moral agendas without detriment to their personal circumstances. However, authentically ethical leadership may not always be so simple, and it is easy to sympathize with Max's decision to privilege his chairman's version of fairness over his own. Indeed, organizational leaders who aspire to moral authenticity might have to face up to some significant career sacrifices. In this respect, I found several of the leaders I met particularly interesting. These were people who had occupied leadership roles in corporate environments but who had chosen to leave those roles to pursue alternative career avenues. The first of these 'leavers', George, was most emphatic about his reasons for career change. After spending ten years in HR directorships with various companies, George had encountered a takeover scenario that presented him with a new job opportunity. However, he was unhappy with the employment ethics of his potential new employer, so he turned down a lucrative board role, choosing instead to work for a while in the private sector before eventually running his own, small, tourism business. George described this scenario as follows:

> The first question is to decide whether you want to be a part of what it is that you're serving . . . For instance, [a large multi-national] took over [my company], then merged with [another company]. [This other company] were given the sort of whipping hand in the integration. The process they followed was to get two directors together—[for instance,] marketing, finance, HR—and give them a set of objectives in terms of how the business was to be reshaped and save huge amounts of money at the same time, and a short timescale to agree to it all, and then report back to the European head office. So the pressure was incredible, because everybody realised that only one of them would have a job at the end of it. Well, my response to that was to say: 'well, thank you, it's not for me'. They actually offered me the Vice Presidency of Europe for HR and I told them to shove it up their arse. And I took some pleasure in doing that. Because it wasn't an environment I wanted to be a part of.

Dennis was a lot more circumspect than George in describing his move from an executive seat on the main board of an international financial services provider to self-employment. Dennis diplomatically deflected my attempts to explore his views of corporate ethics in a large plc. Nevertheless, it became apparent that a key reason for switching to self-employment was that it affords him greater freedom to veto the value systems alongside which he works. He was particularly critical of the investment banking industry, and explained why he avoided taking clients from that sector:

> *With reference to [your current consultancy business], you mention that you especially enjoy working with people who want to make a difference. How do you understand 'making a difference'?*
>
> Well, people who want to feel they've left things in a better shape, in a better place, than when they started.
>
> *In a better shape, in a better place in what respect?*
>
> Well, not purely in commercial terms, if that's behind your question, with some of these other sets in mind, so it's more robust, more sustainable environment than previously.
>
> *And do you find that your clients are generally open to that perspective, or do they tend to view things in more instrumental terms?*
>
> By and large the answer to that is yes, although some people have narrower fields of vision than others obviously, as you would expect. I don't like working with investment bankers and I feel entirely confident that the reason is that they subordinate, insofar as they have those instincts, the ones that I've come across, tend to subordinate them to earning lots of money. I've got nothing wrong with earning lots of money but I don't like the subordination of value systems to capital employment.

A third 'leaver', Gill, had been a director with several nationwide retail companies. She chose to leave the corporate world to set up her own small business in a completely different field. Gill's dissatisfaction with the values of the corporate world pervaded our discussion. She expressed particular frustration with the masculine, short-term, commercially driven culture that she had encountered, in which people came second to profit:

> It's a very difficult, macho business to make a difference in—very macho, very male, talking about feelings and so on was just not on, you know, it didn't even appear in the dictionary... ultimately what do the guys want, what do shareholders want, what do the owners want? They want profit. They're not particularly interested actually in the welfare of the people in the business.

The accounts of different leaders, then, illustrate contrasting ways of affirming their own authenticity. Those differences have a lot to do with the extent to which a leader's ethical commitments are in harmony with the imperatives that imbue her or his organizational context. Some leaders can remain true to their own convictions without rocking the boat of organizational expectation. Other leaders, who do not share so readily those imperatives, may find it necessary to explore new organizational contexts in order to sustain their authenticity.

As a postscript to this discussion of authenticity, I will briefly reflect on contrasting attitudes to the role of the leader in facilitating followers' authenticity. In this respect, Gill's discourse is interesting. She is one of the 'leavers' referred to above. She used the word 'authenticity' several times to describe her experiences. I do not know if she is familiar with the use of this term in existentialist philosophy, but it seems to figure prominently in her understanding of ethical leadership. What is particularly significant about Gill's discourse, and what differentiates it most strikingly from that of James and Ray, is that she did not only valorize leaders' authenticity; she also expressed concern for the authenticity of those who looked to her for leadership. For Gill, helping others to be true to themselves is a key ingredient in ethical leadership:

> I think it comes back to, through my own behaviour and therefore the knock-on effect, to be honest and straightforward and courageous and to be myself. Because only by that can you actually ask others to do that . . . And authenticity I believe is absolutely fundamental to being a good leader. It isn't necessarily, interestingly, what I think businesses want. I don't think they want authentic leaders because authentic leaders are a little bit difficult; they're a bit more hard to manage and to fit in . . . So, I think in terms of responsibility to the employees, I think it is to behave in way which you're asking them to behave and to create an environment in which it is safe for them to be themselves.

Authenticity, then, can take different forms, ranging from the self-assured moral autocracy articulated by the likes of James, Ray, and Gareth, to the moral empowerment that Gill sees as a key aspect of leadership. Whereas the former emphasizes both the inevitability and legitimacy of leaders imposing their version of moral probity on their organizations, the latter stresses the capacity of leaders to enable authenticity in those whom they lead.

Mediating Communication or Taking Refuge in Supportive Homogeneity

Chapter 4 of this book discussed intersubjective ethics. It focused on the philosophy of Jürgen Habermas and outlined some implications that Habermas' work holds for leadership. Despite the seeming incongruity between Habermasian theory and received notions of 'leadership', I suggested that there is a place for leadership within the framework of intersubjectivist ethics.

That intersubjectively ethical version of leadership would comprise mediation of Habermasian 'communicative action'. I have already described how Roger's discourse conforms quite closely to the Mediator of Communication ideal type that is congruent with that version. Roger emphasized the part that a leader can play in mediating reflective communication amongst those internal and external stakeholders to whom he is expected to provide leadership. This section will discuss the extent to which other leaders articulated similar commitment to facilitating dialogue. On the other hand, it will also explore the tendency to turn to a supportive community; one which is more likely to offer confirmation of a leader's own moral conviction than to offer any challenge to it. I will also consider the extent to which a consultative approach to leadership might thrive in organizational settings that do not share the formal democratic expectations of Roger's public-sector context.

If Roger's advocacy of democratic participation is partly a consequence of his public-sector background, then it should come as no surprise that another leader from what might be described as a 'quasi-public' environment also spoke of the need for organizational values to embrace the views of employees. When I met Alison she was working as CEO of a regional, business-support network. As did quite a few interviewees, Alison responded to my opening query about ethics and leadership by stressing the importance of shared values to her organization. Unlike some others, however, she went on to describe the consultative processes that she has put in place to generate those values:

> Everybody in the organization went away [to facilitated 'away days']. It wasn't just management team; everybody. And some of the values...some of them aren't necessarily ones that I would have put down...[for example] people wanted 'to have fun'. I'm not sure that I would have put that one, but they felt that they should come to work and have fun...And there was another one that they wanted to put in and that was that they [should] treat each other as they would treat external customers. Because what we were finding was that we presented a wonderful face to the outside world but we didn't present that face to each other within the organization. So that was another one...
>
> In this very diverse world in which we live, I would find it very difficult to take on board an external creed and force people into it...And what we did, we had an away day, where I tried to get people to tell me what they felt. Not what they thought, because I employ intelligent people and they tell me what they think all the time...but getting people to really tell you what they feel is very—that's where they live, it's much more difficult. And we used [another] organization to get to the bottom of some of those things and some of those values that they wanted this organization to hold close.
>
> ...And I learned a lesson that you need to listen more and speak less, if you're going to get the values—and that's when we then did the values thing, you see. It's

more about encouraging people to tell you what they feel. And it's a very fine line because having got those core values, occasionally you need to tell people what to do. And you can do all of the consultation you want but, at the end of the day, I will listen to everybody and then I will say 'this is the way we're going'... I think I consult: the values of the organization are consultative; the vision and mission of the organizations are consultative; and then directed.

Alison's discourse is interesting not just because of the importance that she places on gathering the views of others, but also because of the way that she speaks about using non-conventional communication media in order to do so. Her observation that 'I employ intelligent people and they tell me what they think all the time... but getting people to really tell you what they feel is very—that's where they live, it's much more difficult' resonates with the point made in chapter 4 about the limitations of conventional modes of discourse for accessing diverse perspectives. Alison also offered an observation on the value of listening to discrepant voices; an observation which might be interpreted as an explicit endorsement of pluralism:

I think you don't listen to the spiky ones at your peril. I've got a very disparate management team; they're not all clones of me. And the quiet ones or the spiky ones who don't want to do it your way, don't think it makes any sense, if you don't listen to them, you don't learn.

However, support for the consultative definition of organizational values was not unique to public-sector and quasi-public-sector organizations such as those within which Roger and Alison worked. Several leaders from private corporations also spoke about encouraging others to participate in setting their companies' moral agendas. For example, Nigel, who is CEO of a building society, also spoke of the need for consultation around values:

Ultimately, in this role you do things alone because you are in charge. And there are some decisions that you know you just need to draw in yourself. I guess I am a democrat by nature in terms of the role... I don't tend to keep much to myself that I don't share with other people and I think the value of debate in terms of the final judgement is key. So I'm not an autocrat. I don't sit here and say 'that's how it's going to be'. But ultimately I am paid to make decisions.

And how deep down through the organization does that sort of democratic process go? You know, if you have to make a decision to what extent would you –?

Well again, it depends, because you can't have six hundred people in the core business being involved in every decision. So what we do is—in terms of alignment, hearts and minds, personal credibility, direction, all of that stuff—once a year we will kick off; we'll get everybody in from the top team through to the maintenance guy and all of those people. And we will say: 'this is the picture for the next twelve months' or 'three years'—whichever picture we are trying to paint. We will have sessions then, as part of those six days we do each year, where there's a: 'well, give us your view' you know; 'take an hour out on your table and discuss this and come back up and tell the rest of the group what you think.' So I think you can engage and align. But ultimately, you can't have six hundred people making one decision.

The views expressed here by Alison and Nigel share a common characteristic. This is that both leaders, while alluding to the merits of consultation and while reflecting on their role in facilitating it, also mention different ways in which a mediatory role might be reconciled with a directive one. As Alison put it: 'at the end of the day, I will listen to everybody and then I will say "this is the way we're going"'; 'the values of the organization are consultative; the vision and mission of the organizations are consultative; and then directed'. For Alison, leadership entails calling time on intersubjective dialogue; making the final decision and then ensuring organizational commitment to that decision. Meanwhile, although Nigel is keen to invite participation from all levels of the organizational hierarchy at periodic communication events (and also to permit what the deliberative democracy theorists discussed in chapter 4 might call 'sheltered enclaves', in which less confident employees can debate and develop their responses), he sometimes has to take the initiative: 'ultimately I am paid to make decisions'; 'ultimately, you can't have six hundred people making one decision'.

So, Alison and Nigel, speaking from the contexts of business support and a building society, attribute normative significance to consultation. They also outline alternative ways in which leaders might intervene in intersubjective processes without necessarily undermining them. Alison alluded to the role of the leader as chairperson and enforcer. Nigel reflected on the need for the leader, on occasions, to take unilateral decisions and then to build support for those decisions. Whereas Roger's discourse draws attention to the part that a leader can play in enhancing the quality of processes of intersubjective engagement by encouraging critical reflection, these other participants dwelt on the need for the leader to sometimes cut short or shape the outcome of those processes.

But if Alison and Nigel envisaged such constraints on the genesis of inter-subjective decision-making processes, other leaders spoke of a more stringent form of restriction. The type of intersubjective responsiveness that was described most frequently in my research discussions involved consulting within a narrowly circumscribed group of professional and social peers. For example, Robert, who is MD of a large sports venue, described how, when he confronts a moral dilemma, his first inclination is to canvass the views of his senior colleagues:

Where do you, if you confront something which you find a bit challenging on a moral level, you know something that you feel a bit morally uncomfortable about, how do you go about resolving that? What sort of intellectual processes would you go through?

Well obviously you've got to give it a bit of your own thought and put your own intellect into it. But I'd discuss it with HR and I'd certainly discuss it with my legal director and get their opinions of what's going on . . . it depends on the nature of the beast really. But then I would probably discuss it with the senior management team generally. So I would rarely these days—I mean I'm not saying I wouldn't in the past ever make these mistakes—but I think rarely would I have a moral situation that I would just keep to myself. I think that's about right. I actually think whoever you are . . . you see things the way you see them and you are incapable of seeing them from another perspective, and you need another perspective.

Robert, then, acknowledges the limitations to his own moral perspicacity. But the intersubjective court of appeal to which he turns to compensate for those limitations is restricted to senior managers and directors. In a similar vein, Mark described how he depends upon fellow directors when confronting a moral dilemma:

You've talked about how you like to have firm principles and you stick by your principles . . . have you found there's a bit of a grey area outside those rules where you feel a little uncomfortable?

Yes, I think there are grey areas and I think, inevitably, when you're sitting on a board you will come across those grey areas. There isn't a simple answer and there very rarely is. There's usually, if you've got good experience and good principles around the board table, a way through all of those and that is best course. There's no right or wrong but you can, at the end of it, agree that, 'yep that's within my principles, it's within everyone's principles; [it's] probably the right way to go' . . . that's how a good board works I think. But equally, you've got to have diversity on a board as well. If you have a lot of people who think—I mean you've got a religious sect haven't you, in a business sense. That wouldn't be much good I wouldn't have thought.

Mark also suggested that he may augment input from fellow directors with contributions from mentors and consultants:

Given that type of situation where you have a moral dilemma, you mentioned that you discussed it with your mentor. Is that something that you're prone to do, to talk things through?

Yes. I've been very lucky. [During] my time [in a former role] I had a very good mentor and I also had some very good friends [he mentions two other MD/CEO figures with whom he had previously worked] and I think you need to be able to talk to people . . . The other mentor I had was when I went to [a major retail consortium]. I was there for ten years and I had a mentor, again one of the senior directors, a lady this time, and she remains a mentor now and has been in [the] company that I've just left. I think they are very important and the reason for it is just to be able to talk something through and have someone listen. They rarely make decisions for you, in fact virtually never if they're good. But they will ask questions that you've already asked yourself but they'll put it in a different way and make you think and make you argue it through. I found that very helpful...

Would you discuss with those mentors value-based issues as well as strictly business issues?

Yes I would. I also was fortunate to find a couple of people—consultants if you will—one took as a principal foundation of his teachings this thing of 'positive mental attitude'. I've always found that a very attractive and very positive way of looking at things generally. The other is a lady who also has done a lot of work on building teams and leadership and devolving leadership and actually dealing with emotional intelligence...and she is particularly good at discussing things on a broader scale.

Max, who has worked in several different industry sectors, also reflected on the desirability of consulting peers when he confronts a moral dilemma. However, he also spoke of the value of talking things through with close family members and with friends from outside the business:

So what was the process, what sort of processes, thought processes, did you go through in reaching the decision [to make some people redundant]?

I talked to quite a lot of people... Anyone that I felt needed to judge whether the decision was right. So some of them were my colleagues, some of them were—one of them was [the owner of the business]... And I always talk things through with [my wife], you know, someone from afar. Sometimes I had reference points of friends who I respect.

Such accounts might be interpreted as endorsements of diversity; of the value of getting a broad range of inputs to moral decision-making. However, an alternative interpretation is that they reveal an inclination to reference moral decision-making against a value system that is likely to deliver a reassuringly homogeneous response. These leaders seemed to value advice from within a kindred circle of colleagues, friends, and relatives. However, they had little to say about engaging with perspectives that might offer fresh insights. Junior employees are accorded a particularly low profile in their accounts. Robert alluded to one possible explanation for this. He described some steps that he has taken to encourage various stakeholders to engage with him. However, he suggested that contributions from junior employees were limited by reticence on their part:

I have a sort of a policy. For instance, I am the sort of manager that has an open-door policy...so I like to be involved with the employees...And I think that's quite important in management that you are as fairly open as you can be. You can't always be. But I think you need to be as open as you can...

Yes, ok. What you refer to as an open-door policy; can you give me an idea, any example, of how that actually operates in terms of employees?

In terms of employees, I mean I have structured meetings during the day but I have periods in my day where the door is left open for people to come in and interact with me on a regular basis. I also, rather than just them having to come in here, I walk around the building at least three times a day and just go to every department and just make sure that they can see me ... And I think it's better to try and encourage them to have some dialogue with you and not be intimidated and think you're part of the team as well as they are and everybody's necessary. You know, I mean, I'm just a necessary evil that controls the whole thing.

But it's a tough thing to do for a junior employee to walk in here and feel –

Well they don't tend to walk in here. What happens then is, if I'm walking round the building then they, you know, that sort of thing. But we do, you know, I do encourage, if I sense there's areas in the business that aren't quite right, I go back to HR and say 'well I think that person isn't quite right', so I sense there is something wrong ...

So does it tend to be more managers that come in and talk to you than –

Yes it would tend to be more the middle managers and senior managers that would come in here and talk to me. From a general point of view then it would be the senior managers.

So, despite Robert's consultative aspirations, intersubjective participation is limited by employees' inhibitions. Robert also remarked that junior employees are disinclined to contribute to substantial, commercial topics during formal meetings, restricting their input to 'housekeeping' issues. He reflected on why this might be so:

Because at an employee-forum level they actually talk about issues that are important to them. That could be: 'the fridge hasn't been cleaned out for a long time'; or 'why do we have to pay for our coffee?' ... things like that; 'we always have to go to Tesco for our sandwiches because the catering is disgusting'; or something. Those sorts of things you get from the employees, you know, and they are normal human things.

Yes, sort of housekeeping things.

Yes, more sort of housekeeping things, but very important to them ...

Yes. Do you think the employees feed in to that commercial debate with their managers?

I think some do ... They all have their own characters and some people are more able to express themselves better and some people want to express themselves better, and they will engage with their managers or they might engage with me, you know. And other people are very quiet and don't communicate particularly well and don't feel they would be listened to if they did, and those people are a bit of a problem.

Robert's suggestion that junior employees' inhibitions may derive from their sense that they 'don't feel they would be listened to if they did' is an interesting point. It suggests that an open ear on the part of a leader is not the only prerequisite to consultative engagement; leaders may also need to think creatively about how they may overcome potential barriers to communication if they are to encourage otherwise marginalized groups to contribute to consultative fora.

Two of the leaders I spoke with offered explicit observations on the homogeneity of the world inhabited by organizational leaders. It is perhaps significant that both of these people were amongst the 'leavers' whom I referred to in the previous section; that is, people who have stepped out for their corporate leadership roles: one to take up a board role with a major charitable organization and one to work as a self-employed consultant. Thus, Sarah reflected on her former role with a travel company, suggesting that the uniform profile of senior-management groups has a homogenizing effect on debate:

> Again, since [working for a charity] I've been able to look back at [a former employer], for example, where the senior finance team was the most undiverse, if that's a word, team that I've ever been part of. I think I was the only female in the senior finance team [as] the group finance director, and the profile of them was all practically identical: all male, all roughly between the ages of thirty-five and forty-five; all straight; married with two children. Just absolutely clones of one another. I hadn't ever really questioned in my mind whether...there's any weakness in that or the strength that diversity can bring...there wasn't even a female member of the executive board—there were a couple of female non-exec directors, I think—let alone anybody from any form of ethnic minority or sexuality, whatever.

Dennis also suggested that the rarefied circles within which they move tend to cut corporate leaders off from 'ordinary' voices—a factor which may prevent exposure to views that differ from their own:

> I don't come across many people in my walk of life who I would think are, you know, the forces of evil and darkness. Most people I come across and talk to... seem to be pretty decent people with their hearts in the right place and a value system that seems by and large to be very honourable...I think the difficulty...of people who have influence...then reverts to: how open do they remain, once they get to these positions of power and influence, to a whole range of influence from fairly ordinary people? And my experience...is that they don't remain very open to that, not because they don't wish to but because they just move in some very rarefied circles. You can only spend your time once, and they're quite used to spending it with movers and shakers—people who have influence—in very protected environments. And the impact of day-to-day drudgery and the ordinary lives are, sort of, taken away by flunkies and money.

General Observations

This chapter has drawn on discussions with leaders to illuminate three specific challenges associated with the three ideal-type approaches outlined in chapter 5. I began by discussing how the consistent application of principle sometimes presents leaders with significant emotional challenges. Nevertheless, a number of the leaders I spoke to suggested that it is their duty to suppress such unruly distractions of the heart. For these people, the leader's task is to apply principle in a rationally consistent manner. Sentiments of loyalty and partiality should not be permitted to get in the way. This raises important questions about the part played by emotion and rationality in ethical decision-making. I will return to this theme in the concluding chapter, asking whether emotional responses to principled action may actually have something important to say about the ethicality of that action; whether, by ignoring their hearts, these leaders may be disregarding some important cues concerning the moral quality of their conduct.

I then expanded on the issue of existentialist authenticity. Some of the people whom I interviewed suggested that willingness to make ethical judgements on behalf of their organizations is a key part of leadership. Thus, some sustain their own authenticity by adopting the role of moral author for their organizations. The way that leaders negotiate a pathway between their own moral commitments and the value systems within which their organizations are embedded is interesting. In this respect, some of the leaders discussed here seemed able to preserve their authenticity, acting in a manner that is true to their own convictions, without compromising tenure of their leadership roles. Harmony between their personal convictions and the imperatives of twenty-first century market capitalism may account for this. However, others had not been so fortunate. I outlined the choices that several erstwhile corporate leaders had made to exchange their former roles for career paths that were more in line with their personal values. In existentialist terms, these people might be described as having made career moves in order to preserve their authenticity. Clearly, authenticity may not always be consistent with traditional notions of career progression within commercial organizations.

In the final section I explored the extent to which other leaders that I interviewed shared Roger's endorsement of mediation. Some, from private as well as public-sector organizations, described decision-making styles that resonate with Roger's account. Furthermore, some described different ways in which a pathway between imposition and facilitation might be negotiated. Thus, for facilitative leaders to proffer their own views need not undermine intersubjective legitimacy, as long as those views are not imposed. And for a leader to rally support for a particular agenda within a dialogical forum is considerably less erosive of intersubjective credibility than foisting that agenda upon followers without debate. Moreover, there seems no reason why leaders who aspire to intersubjective legitimacy should not pick up the referee's whistle from time to time. That way, they can signal when debate has run its course as well as ensuring that democratically agreed 'laws of the game' are observed by all the players.

However, most of the leaders I spoke with offered exclusive notions of intersubjective engagement, precluding contributions from outside the leader's social and professional peer group. Whatever consultation does take place under such circumstances is unlikely to offer a platform to diverse perspectives. Notwithstanding the occasional appreciative mention of diversity around a board table, it is questionable whether the range of views accessed through consultation with fellow directors, mentors, business consultants, and close family members will introduce radically new insights to the leader's ethical horizon. Such forums, by admitting only those who are singing enthusiastically from the senior management hymn sheet, are unlikely to offer much assistance to leaders who wish to be informed by dialogical interplay of moral perspectives.

So, three points stand out from this chapter. The first is that consistent application of principle has something going for it. For leaders to apply principle in a consistent, dutiful manner, rather than allowing caprice to govern their decision-making, seems ethically meritorious. However, in order to do what principle says must be done, it is often necessary to suppress powerful emotional responses. And it may be that these countervailing sentiments are telling leaders that, sometimes at least, principle is not everything. Secondly, authenticity also has much to recommend it in an organizational leadership context. It seems right that leaders should have the moral courage to stand up for their convictions. But, in order to realize their own authenticity, leaders may have to stand against conventional expectations that imbue the establishments within which they lead. Despite the self-assured fervour with which some leaders articulate their moral conviction, it is not always easy to tell whether that conviction is an expression of individual authenticity or just a convenient rationalization of an institutional status quo. Furthermore, leaders who crusade to sustain their own authenticity should also spare a thought for that of their followers. The third point is that for leaders to expose their moral convictions to the rigours of intersubjective debate is likely to enable more reflective, better-informed decisions. But if that debate is restricted to an homogeneous community that thinks as the leader thinks and does as the leader does, it is unlikely to realize its morally uplifting potential.

I will say more about each of these points in the concluding chapter of this book. Before doing so, chapter 7 will consider empirical data from a slightly different perspective. Rather than viewing it through the lens of three ideal types and their corresponding meta-ethical perspectives, the chapter will organize data within the framework of chapter 1's review of leadership theory. Accordingly, it will draw on empirical research to consider two particular challenges that were discussed in that review: the ethicality of leadership agendas, and leadership's inherently suppressive connotations.

7

Considering some Moral Concerns
with Leadership

Chapters 5 and 6 have synthesized empirical research findings with the three chapters on ethics theory that comprised Part II, using the prism of ideal types to illuminate the meta-ethical stances reviewed in those chapters and to consider some corresponding tensions. This chapter will look at empirical data from a different direction. Here, I will use my discussions with leaders to illuminate the two specific challenges associated with leadership that were explored in chapter 1. I will begin by discussing how the people I interviewed evaluate the ethicality of their actions and decisions. This discussion will draw attention, firstly, to the way that these leaders accord moral primacy to their employees, and secondly, to how they associate the interests of those employees with the survival and prosperity of their organizations. In the process I propose to highlight some distinctions between different ways of thinking about stakeholders: how stakeholders might be classified according to either their intrinsic significance or their instrumental significance; and how they might be considered in relation to either dependency or affect. The chapter will then consider the second concern discussed in chapter 1: that leadership may be an intrinsically suppressive undertaking. It will look at contrasting ways of thinking about followers' interests and aspirations, suggesting that one way is more likely than the other to ameliorate that concern. I will finish by saying a few words about leaders' agency. This will involve revisiting the three individuals discussed in chapter 5—this time considering how they articulate contrasting ways of thinking about their own agency.

The Moral Probity of Leadership Agendas

Chapter 1 began by exploring some responses offered in the leadership literature to the following question: how can we tell that leaders are applying their exceptional influencing skills to bring about morally desirable ends, rather than morally undesirable ends? In other words, how do we judge the ethicality of the outcomes of leadership? This section will also start with this question, considering some criteria of ethicality that were offered during my research interviews. I will begin by saying something about leaders' *universes of moral relevance*. In other words, I will identify the individuals and groups to whom these leaders accorded relevance when they spoke about morality. I will go on to discuss the basis upon which moral relevance was attributed to those specific groups. This will permit the identification of a particular rationale that was frequently offered as a justification for morally challenging decisions. However, not all of the people I spoke to offered this rationale all of the time. Some stepped outside it to consider the broader consequences of their actions. In undertaking such broader consideration, contrasting approaches are apparent: one monological; the other dialogical. I will round off this discussion with some reflections on how these contrasting approaches relate to the theoretical perspectives reviewed in chapter 1.

Defining the Universe of Moral Relevance: Who Matters?

One way to find out who leaders consider to be morally relevant is to ask them if they think that their leadership role entails responsibilities to anyone in particular. When I specifically posed this question, responses tended to focus on employees. For example, Mark, reflecting on some time that he had spent in the pub trade, told me that his most deeply felt responsibility is to:

> Employees of the business . . . you have just as much responsibility to the cleaner in that pub as you have anyone else . . . I think that is a big responsibility and in fact if anything that's the one I pay most attention to, rather like Richard Branson. I think the major stakeholders in any business in that sense are the people who work in it.

But perhaps a more spontaneous expression of interviewees' sense of responsibility towards various people was offered in the context of general discussion. In this discursive context, the group that cropped up most frequently was, again, employees. For instance, while discussing his feelings towards his employees, David, upon whose discourse I drew to illustrate the Company Advocate ideal type in chapter 5, noted that:

> You feel responsible for them. That's point number one. So every single employee that I have, whether it's in Holland, because we've got factories in Holland, in France, in the UK, in Ireland, you feel responsible. And that responsibility can also bring a burden. I talk a lot about the burdens of leadership because everybody aspires to be the boss, but that carries a huge amount of burden with it.

While specific questions and general discussion offer a glimpse of intervie-wees' universes of moral relevance, perhaps the most revealing insights come from their accounts of moral dilemmas. I asked each interviewee whether any specific scenarios stood out in their leadership careers as being particularly challenging from a moral perspective. I asked them to describe these dilem-mas, to relate the processes they had gone through in resolving them, and to describe how they had justified their decisions from a moral point of view. With very few exceptions, the responses that were offered revolved around making people redundant. And the justifications that were offered for redun-dancy indicated that the ultimate reference point for moral decision-making is the survival and prosperity of the organization. When these leaders recounted hard choices, the good of the organization was most often held up as the weathervane of moral probity. So, despite the high profile given to employees in interviewees' universes of moral relevance, when it came to conflicts between the interests of particular groups of employees and the good of the organization, the organization came first. For example, Jane, who is MD of a drinks company, described how, when she confronts such a dilemma, the right course is clear to her:

> You know, making people redundant is quite a difficult thing. And the moral dilemma there is you're giving someone the sack as such. So to them it's really terrible because their livelihood is going to go by the wayside... But then you've also got a bigger picture to look after. So if you don't do that you're not going to save, you know, the rest of the business. So those are the sorts of things which are difficult. And you have to be right, you have to be sure that you are doing it for the right reasons... [that is] what it is you're here to do... to keep the business going.

However, it would be misleading to suggest that the prosperity of the organization was thus offered as a *categorical* good. These leaders did not tend to privilege the good of the organization as, in itself, an overriding criterion of moral evaluation. More usually, the survival and prosperity of the organization was accorded value insofar as it promotes the interests of those people who depend upon it. Thus, Sarah, reflecting on her experiences as a director of a small travel business, offered the greater good of the 'wider group' as a justification for the trauma associated with a redundancy programme:

> That was the first time that I'd ever gone through a redundancy programme at all in my career and I found that horrifically difficult... What makes me do it?... Well, again, I look at the other stakeholders. I think there were about thirty-odd engineers in that instance, and I talk about it easily now but at the time I was in pieces; I found it personally extremely difficult. We had guys in their mid-fifties in tears and it's incredibly difficult... but I have to look at the wider group.

Here, Sarah presents the interests of 'the wider group' of employees as her rationale for making job cuts: she describes the moral reassurance that she draws from her belief that these measures are necessary if she is to ensure the survival of the organization and if she is thus to secure the interests of that wider group. Therefore, although the organization takes priority over any particular group of employees in her moral decision-making, this is because the interests of the wider group of employees are equated with the survival of the organization: 'the many' is thus accorded precedence over 'the few' in a utilitarian-style moral calculation. The leader's responsibility is to maximize the good for the greatest number of morally relevant people. And maximizing the good of the organization is the best way to achieve this.

However, the survival of the organization need not be directly at issue for this utilitarian-style rationale to apply. Even when its survival is not threatened, the prosperity of the organization, and thus the interests of the majority of its employees, was sometimes advanced as a moral justification for efficiency measures. James, reflecting on a situation in which he had made some people redundant, alluded to his responsibility to maximize efficiency, specifically reflecting on how, in the long run, this serves the interests of the majority of his employees:

> It's also validated by the responsibility you have to everybody because if you compromise on those decisions, the company doesn't perform so well, you might then have to make some [more] people redundant. If you make the right decision, you are being more responsible to everybody else in the business because you are doing the best for the business, which is then doing the best for them. So you are doing the best for the majority in effect, but at the cost of some individual.

So, behind even these leaders' ethical concern for the survival and prosperity of their organizations, there generally sits a preoccupation with the interests of their employees. Employees thus remain at the centre of their universes of moral relevance. To be sure, employees were by no means the only group to be accorded value. Other stakeholders, such as long-standing suppliers and customers, were also mentioned from time to time. Some even spoke of the ethical significance of shareholders, although this tended to be in grudging terms or as an afterthought. However, despite these occasional references to other stakeholder groups, employees came across throughout my research discussions as the most ethically significant constituency. The rationale offered by nearly all these leaders was that employees are morally important and that the survival and prosperity of the organization is the ethical Holy Grail because this ensures the interests of the majority of those employees. This might be characterized as a *rule-utilitarian* rationale: these leaders privilege the moral rule that they should maximize the survival and prosperity of the organization—the *rule of organizational maximization*—in the belief that this will bring about the greatest good for the greatest number of morally relevant people. And the people who are accorded most moral relevance are the organization's employees.

It is significant that the moral dilemmas upon which these leaders dwelt nearly always involved harm to small groups of employees; those very people who are privileged by this rule-utilitarian rationale. The ethically challenging scenarios described by leaders, either spontaneously or in response to my specific request to identify a moral dilemma, generally concerned situations in which groups of employees had lost out. Although those scenarios usually involved redundancy, this was not always the case. For example, Alison offered an account in which she presented the survival of her organization, and thus the greater good of the majority of employees and their families, as a moral justification for 'dissembling' on her part. In this conversation, she had just reflected on the vagaries of funding decisions for the business-support organization of which she was CEO; a discussion which initiated the following exchange:

Have you encountered any situations where, for example, you know that the project is going to run out of funding in six months time, this project is extremely important, results continue to be extremely important for that six-month period? [Where] the people who are involved in that project don't know that the funding is coming to an end? Where you've had to wrestle with –

Dissemble?

Well, when you've had to make the decision as to whether to tell them or not?

That's a very tricky one . . . The first thing that I would say is [that] it's happened a couple of times. And subsequently to that, because it has been difficult, it's been a problem I've wrestled over . . . But yes, I have dissembled. And I told one individual because I thought they were resilient enough to cope. And I didn't tell another individual until three months before the end of the contract . . . I didn't see his long-term future with the organization. And I knew that if he'd been told his results would have gone out of the window.

. . . On what basis; why did you do that? What was the motivation to do that?

The health of the organization supports currently one-hundred-and-twenty-eight families. You've only got to see the Christmas party, where suddenly your responsibilities are clear. When you see four hundred people who depend on you getting it right. And at the end of the day, the health of the many support the decisions you make about the few.

Alison's story, although it does not revolve around redundancy, involves dissembling to an employee. It thus concerns harm to an employee insofar as Alison describes keeping her true intentions from that employee. This feature characterized all but one of my research discussions. Almost every participant told me of a dilemma whose perplexity stemmed from its detrimental impact on a small group of employees, either through redundancy or through some other form of perceived harm. This further underlines the moral weight accorded to employees by these leaders: not only are employees morally relevant as the potential beneficiaries of the organizational maximization that these leaders seek to promote; the most ethically troubling decisions that they describe owe their moral perplexity to their injurious consequences for small groups of employees.

To summarize, the basis of moral evaluation that featured most strikingly in my research discussions was the prosperity of the organization. This, in turn, was valued insofar as it promotes the interests of those who depend upon it. The rule of organizational maximization was thus offered as proxy for the maximization of the well-being of morally relevant people. Particular emphasis was placed on the employees who stand to lose or gain from changes in the organization's fortunes. Although some leaders spoke of duties to other stakeholders, employees were mentioned most frequently as the ethically relevant beneficiaries of the organization's survival and prosperity. The moral significance of employees is further underlined by the regularity with which they featured as the losers in interviewees' accounts of moral dilemmas: it is the harm caused to employees that makes those scenarios morally problematic.

Why do these People Matter?

It is also instructive to consider why particular groups, especially employees, are accorded moral relevance: why should these people matter so much to leaders? In particular, it is helpful to differentiate *intrinsic* significance from *instrumental* significance; in other words, to distinguish between according intrinsic moral significance to people and according significance to them insofar as they contribute towards the achievement of some overarching moral imperative. I often encountered ambivalence on this issue: the leaders that I spoke to were sometimes uncertain whether stakeholders carry moral significance in their own right, or whether they are only important because keeping them happy helps the leader to achieve a further moral purpose. I will illustrate this point with a passage from my discussion with Ray, CEO of a nationwide retail chain. Consider the way that Ray speaks about his responsibility towards his customers:

> *Are you conscious of any particular responsibilities to any groups, any individuals?*
> ... there's two groups that I think you're responsible to: one is your customers, primarily, because I fundamentally believe that customers pay your wages, and then your employees and colleagues ...
>
> *Just coming back to that first group that you mentioned there, customers, what is that responsibility?*

Well, to give them what they want. You know, they, customers are very canny people, no matter where they're from, who they are, what sex they are. In my experience customers are very intuitive and your responsibility to them is to give them what they want, when they want it and to anticipate what they're going to want in the future...And certainly, as a retailer, your job is to try and work out what it is they're going to want in eighteen months time and provide it for them, and that's a responsibility.

And you feel that that is a moral duty rather than just a pragmatic duty which contributes to the commercial success of the business?

Well...it's probably more of the latter than the former. I'm not sure it's a moral—I mean, morally, do I have any responsibility to my customers? It's difficult; I mean, if I'm not looking after my customers, they're not going to look after me, and therefore the business will suffer. So it could be described as a moral responsibility, but it's also practical, it is also pragmatic, and it's also, you know, financially essential.

In this passage it is not altogether clear whether Ray's sense of duty towards his customers accords intrinsic significance to them or whether he just wants to keep them happy because this will help him to achieve a further, morally valorized purpose. Ray was not alone in this respect; several other interviewees offered similarly ambivalent responses to this type of question. The source of that ambivalence seems to be that these leaders were offering *instrumental normative* responses to what I intended to be *intrinsic normative* questions. In other words, my efforts to find out who is *intrinsically* important to their moral decision-making elicited observations about who is *instrumentally* important to the realization of their moral objectives. Ray was not articulating an intrinsic normative valorization of his customers; he was describing instrumental normative responsibilities: how it is important for him to look after these people because doing so will promote the prosperity of his organization, which, in turn, will help him to fulfil his intrinsic responsibilities to those who depend upon that prosperity.

It is important to note that whether the sense of responsibility Ray articulates is intrinsic or instrumental does not necessarily impact on its moral worth. In either case, the sense of responsibility ultimately derives from a moral concern. Although Ray's responsibility to his customers accords intrinsic value not to those customers but to those who stand to gain from their support, his is nevertheless an expression of moral responsibility towards that latter group. Both senses of responsibility can be described as *normative* insofar as they are both, ultimately, driven by a moral regard. An *instrumental normative* understanding of one's responsibilities towards stakeholders is no less morally charged than an *intrinsic normative* understanding. The people to whom Ray articulates a sense of responsibility might thus be referred to as *instrumental normative stakeholders*. That is, they are stakeholders whose importance derives from their instrumental significance to an ethically valorized objective. They can thus be distinguished from *intrinsic normative stakeholders*; that is, groups to whom a leader feels a responsibility irrespective of any instrumental relationship.

As well as illustrating the distinction between intrinsic normative stakeholders and instrumental normative stakeholders, this discussion also points towards another important distinction: this time, between two different notions of intrinsic normative stakeholder. This distinction is between people who are *affected by* the activities of the organization, and thus by the decisions of a leader, and those people who *depend upon* the prosperity of the organization. To illustrate this difference I will draw on an example offered by Jane, who is MD of a drinks company. Like most interviewees, Jane spoke of her responsibility towards her employees. However, she also included other stakeholders in her universe of moral relevance. But the point I would like to focus on here is not so much the target of Jane's intrinsic responsibilities as one particular characteristic of those responsibilities:

> It's not only us, it's all our employees, all our local farmers. Their main crop now is [fruit that goes into our drinks]. We're not only looking after us as shareholders, as directors, but we've got the employees, we've got our suppliers. There's a huge knock-on effect...so I need to keep the company sound and that would be looking after everybody that's involved with the business. So whether it's a shareholder, whether it's an employee, whether it's a supplier or whether it's a customer.

Jane's account focuses on those stakeholders who *depend* upon her organization's ongoing prosperity. This includes the shareholders and creditors who depend on the organization for a return on their capital. She also mentions her employees, who depend on the organization for an income and for all the other benefits associated with employment. Local farmers are also dependent on her organization, for they would have to find another outlet for their crop if it went out of business. She could have added other members of the local community, who also have a dependency relationship with her company: for instance, other local businesses, as well as those stakeholders who depend upon them, would suffer were Jane's company to fail. It could even be argued that the retailers and pubs who buy drinks from Jane's company depend, to some extent, on her organization's survival and prosperity. Although these outlets could source their drinks elsewhere in the event of the company's demise, this would probably entail switching costs on their part.

What Jane does not refer to in this passage are any stakeholders who may not have a *dependency* relationship with her organization but who may nevertheless be *affected* by its activities. Take a hypothetical example: Jane's company might choose to market its alcoholic drinks aggressively to young people. The company might do this because it enhances commercial performance and thus promotes the interests of all those dependent stakeholders that Jane lists. However, encouraging teenagers to drink strong alcohol may incur a range of social and economic costs that would have to be borne by other members of society: those people who may be directly affected by the actions of binge drunk teenagers; or those who may find their own demands for medical and police services curtailed because the providers of those services are dealing with the repercussions of teenage drunkenness. All of these people are *affected stakeholders*. However, they are not dependent in any way on the survival and prosperity of Jane's business. The environmental effects of Jane's business are also potentially significant. She may choose to cut corners in matters such as waste disposal, thus enhancing profitability and protecting the interests of her dependent stakeholders. However, other stakeholders who may be affected by consequent environmental degradation would pick up the tab for such ecological inattention.

Now, I am not suggesting for one moment that Jane would sanction such socially or environmentally damaging actions. Indeed, it seemed to me that her company takes its social and environmental responsibilities very seriously indeed. Nevertheless, to focus uniquely on responsibilities to dependent stakeholders may serve to marginalize, or even obscure, the broader social and environmental consequences of an organization's activities. Prioritizing the intrinsic moral significance of *dependent stakeholders* may thus deflect attention from the consequences of the organization's activities for its *affected stakeholders*.

It is helpful, therefore, to make a further distinction to that already made between *intrinsic normative stakeholders* and *instrumental normative stakeholders*. This is to differentiate two types of intrinsic normative stakeholder. On the one hand, there are what might be called *dependent intrinsic normative stakeholders*; that is, groups who are accorded intrinsic importance within a leader's universe of moral relevance and who depend upon the organization's survival in some way. On the other hand, there are an organization's *affected intrinsic normative stakeholders*. These are stakeholders who are in some way affected by an organization's activities but who do not necessarily have a dependency relationship with it. Clearly, there will quite a lot of crossover between these two groups. Indeed, all dependent intrinsic normative stakeholders will also fall into the category of affected intrinsic normative stakeholder since, by definition, their dependency relationship with the organization entails an affect relationship. But the key point is that there will usually be some affected intrinsic normative stakeholders who do not fall into the category of dependent intrinsic normative stakeholder. And the interests of these people will not be included in the moral calculus of leaders who focus uniquely on their responsibilities to instrumental normative stakeholders and dependent intrinsic normative stakeholders.

Evaluating Wider Social and Environmental Effect

However, to suggest that the leaders I met focussed uniquely on their responsibilities to their dependent intrinsic normative stakeholders, with no regard for affected stakeholders, would be misleading. Despite their preoccupation with the former, and particularly with their employees, several also spoke of wider social and environmental considerations. I will draw on three examples to illustrate contrasting ways of thinking about that wider social and environmental effect. These examples are drawn from my conversations with Gareth, Roger, and James, each of whom I have already introduced. I do not offer these sections of discourse as exemplifications of the understanding expressed more generally by these three in my conversations with them; indeed, the statements I reproduce here contrast in some ways with what James, in particular, said elsewhere. Rather, I offer these three short statements to illustrate different ways in which broader effect might be evaluated. I will start with Gareth's unilateralist expression before describing how Roger and James articulate, in slightly different ways, greater responsiveness to the ethical expectations of other people. Gareth, who worked for many years for a pub-owning company, reflected on the capacity of the pub trade to play a positive role in society:

> The pub business I've always been so proud of...there are vast tracts of this country, those '50s and '60s housing estates, where, if there wasn't a pub there, there would be no social infrastructure; there would be nothing at all. And the good that a well-run pub in a [housing] estate does can be fantastic. The purpose in other places is to provide an atmosphere where you can do the most important things in life, which is to eat and drink in a convivial and pleasant manner. So I've always felt that the industry I've worked for was a force for good; always, always ...My happiest memories are always associated with pubs, as most people's are, you know: the birth of your child, you go and have a beer; you have a beer at your wedding.

I will recount Roger's statement before considering how it differs from Gareth's. Roger, remember, is CEO of a large, public-sector organization.

> There is a principle...an issue about 'social morality'...it is something that joins those issues together...if you believe as I believe, not in a fluffy way, about an ethos of public service. And it's quite easy in an area like this, because...if you serve an area like [this one], to use European terms and not party political terms, even though we have a wide variety of representation, the community we serve is effectively social democrat. So they are not going to let old people die, they are not

going to fail to educate young people, and they wouldn't want to be biased against young people from different backgrounds or people with different disabilities. So if you start from that base in terms of the society that we serve—and, obviously, that's a huge generalisation; I am not suggesting every member of the community comes into that category—but there's a broad consensus out there around the core. That's how we ought to be managing the area. That's a strength in the community which we then need to reflect in the way that we add to that.

Ok, so there's a sense that because of the political, in a constitutional sense, nature of the organization that you represent in the community, the values that you adhere to need to be reflective of the values of those people.

Yes.

A notable contrast between these two sections of discourse is that the source of moral legitimation provided here by Gareth is personal. In this instance he offers a personal assessment of what is in the best interests of the public; an assessment upon which he bases his estimation of the beneficial social impact of his industry. Thus, Gareth takes the beneficent role of pubs in everyone's life for granted and, from that premise, he deduces the morally beneficent impact of the pub trade. However, Gareth's contention is contestable. It is unlikely that his estimation of pubs' positive social impact would meet with universal agreement. Some people might even suggest that pubs do more harm than good to individuals and to communities. Roger offers a different model of legitimation; one which is built upon responsiveness to a very different court of moral appeal. Rather than depending on his own sense of right and wrong, Roger speaks of the need to respond to the moral expectations of the community that he serves. Therefore, it is that community, not Roger, which provides the standards by which he judges the ethical legitimacy of his organization's agenda.

Now, it might be suggested that this difference in emphasis reflects the respective governance contexts to which Roger and Gareth are accustomed. Roger is accountable to a democratically elected political body, whereas Gareth has spent most of his career within commercial organizations. While it is appropriate for a public-sector organization to respond to the expectations of the community that it serves, leaders of privately funded organizations may be permitted a more unilateral stance on ethical evaluation. This is where James' observations are of interest. James, like Gareth, has spent his career in the private sector. But like Roger, he speaks in the following passage of the need to respond to the moral expectations of his organization's stakeholders. James reflects here on the recent increase in environmental consciousness. Since James' company is a significant purchaser of air transport, this has important implications for him:

I mentioned to you CSR, which we talk about day in and day out in our business because corporate social responsibility is such a huge thing...that it's affecting our business and that is everything to do with the health and safety of people. But also it's becoming so much broader and the environmental piece is a big part of that. We are doing a huge amount on the environmental side, which I feel, not just from a business point of view, we should do certainly, but morally and from a personal responsibility point of view we should do.

In this passage, James speaks of two reasons for taking environmentalism seriously. One is the business case: the 'business point of view'. If influential stakeholders care about the environment, then it makes good business sense for James to care about the environment. In other words, he is responding to the expectations of his *instrumental normative stakeholders*. However, James also believes that there is an intrinsic case for corporate environmental care: 'morally and from a personal responsibility point of view we should do'. Here, then, he is alluding to a responsibility to *affected intrinsic normative stake-holders*; those people who, ultimately, will be affected by the environmental degradation caused by air travel. What is particularly interesting about James environmental rationale, though, is expressed in the following passage:

About a year ago there was a lot of hype being generated about 'green' and everyone was suddenly talking about it...Now people are talking about it really seriously...And my point is that, people at home, our people in this company... at home they are increasingly being exposed to recycling. They are getting more keen on doing their piece; they are looking at how much tax they pay on the car because of carbon emissions; they are going to be buying food in Tesco's, Sains-bury's and other things with carbon labels on them, and whether they are flown into the country or not, and it's becoming a part of peoples lives. When they go to work, they don't expect that to be a different world. When they go to work, they expect the company to be responsible about recycling paper and those things;... about plastic cups at the vending machine. Increasingly this affects us. They expect the company to be responsible about the hotel they book them into, and the airline that they book them onto, because those things are also now becoming key factors. So the company, our company, and all the companies that we deal with, have a sort of push-and-pull thing going on. You have your people that are increasingly going to demand things of you and saying, 'well why aren't we being responsible at work?' and we have a responsibility to them to do that.

What I find especially significant about this passage is James' suggestion that it is important for his business to reflect, in the way that it conducts itself, the values and preoccupations of the community within which it sits. Thus, he articulates, from the perspective of the private sector, an attitude that is quite similar to Roger's. Now, clearly, there is an instrumental need for a business to respond to the expectations of its influential stakeholders—in this case, James speaks in particular of the need to meet the expectations of his employees—so his statement could be interpreted as just another expression of the need to meet the expectations of instrumental normative stakeholders. Indeed, there is a sense in which the commercial requirement to respond to the moral expectations of instrumental stakeholders necessarily injects an element of intersubjective moral responsiveness into any business's strategic decision-making. But there seems to be more going on in this statement than that. That James is expressing more than just an instrumental need is apparent from the last sentence of this passage: 'we have a responsibility to them to do that'. So, James seems to be hinting at more than an instrumental need here; he is alluding to an intrinsic normative responsibility to ensure that the working environment that his employees inhabit is congruent with their moral sensitivities.

I will offer two observations on the above. The first is that this expression of intersubjective responsiveness on James' part belies his more frequently articulated view that leaders should set the moral tone for their organizations. Perhaps James is not quite such a moral autocrat after all! But the second observation hinges on a slight difference in emphasis between Roger's and James' statements. In meeting the expectations of the community that he serves, Roger is responding to the expectations of his *affected intrinsic normative stakeholders* since, for the most part, that community comprises the extent of his affected stakeholders: the scope of his organization's activities is predominantly local. On the other hand, in attributing normative significance to the community within which *his* business resides, James leaves many of his affected stakeholders unrepresented. For the effects of James' business, activities are far more geographically dispersed than are those of Roger's organization.

So, perhaps this second observation says something about the respective moral sensitivity of locally embedded and geographically dispersed organizations. If intersubjective engagement with affected stakeholders enhances the ethical credibility of an organization's agenda, and if such engagement is easier for an organization with local scope than it is for one that is globally dispersed, then there seems to be something intrinsically more ethical about the former. But, on the other hand, if the geographic scope of organizations is to continue to expand—and there seems no reason to expect otherwise—then perhaps this underlines the moral desirability of institutions that can represent the perspectives of those who are too far away, or who lack the necessary resources, to speak for themselves. And if this offers a resounding endorsement of the normative importance of institutions such as non-governmental organizations and other pressure groups in the contemporary organizational landscape, it also underpins the need for global corporations who aspire to moral legitimacy to listen to them.

Some General Comments

I have emphasized several points during this discussion. The first is that the leaders whom I met tended to privilege dependent intrinsic normative stakeholders when speaking of ethically charged decisions, with a particular emphasis on employees. However, the principle of organizational maximization featured prominently in my interviews as a rule-utilitarian style proxy for the well-being of those dependent intrinsic normative stakeholders. In other words, interviewees tended to put the good of the organization above other considerations because this will, in the long term, be best for the organization's dependent intrinsic normative stakeholders, amongst whom employees comprise the most significant group.

This resonates with chapter 1's discussion of the ethicality of leadership agendas. In that chapter, I pointed out how some leadership commentators judge ethicality in relation to altruism. These theorists present ethical leaders as those who prioritize the interests of their followers, contrasting them to unethical egotists. Most of the leaders discussed here articulated a similar understanding of ethicality. They spoke of a moral responsibility to do what is best for their people; to promote the interests of those people who depend upon them; that is, their dependent intrinsic normative stakeholders. On the one hand, this rationale holds a great deal of intuitive appeal. It seems right that ethical leaders should look after their people and that they should put collective well-being before self-interest. But, on the other hand, to place too much weight on altruistic regard for dependent stakeholders runs the risk of limiting leaders' ethical purview. Just as focusing on altruistic regard for followers may occlude broader considerations, so might prioritizing the interests of dependent stakeholders marginalize other affected stakeholders. Given the far-reaching effects of organizational leaders' decisions, this is a worrying limitation of focus.

For this reason it is reassuring that some of the leaders I spoke to also reflected on the broader social and environmental consequences of their organizations' activities. And, as with the theoretical stances reviewed in chapter 1, their responses can be located in relation to managerialist and critical perspectives. On the one hand, monological assessments of the ethical desirability of an organization's social and environmental impact strike a resoundingly managerialist chord. On the other hand, a stakeholder-responsive discourse resonates in some respects with a critical stance. However, it is important to be clear about just whose expectations are being valorized by any particular stakeholder-responsive discourse. For, by offering a seat at the table of discourse only to local instrumental and dependent stakeholders, leaders may preclude other, geographically dispersed voices that may have something important to say about the ethical quality of their organizations' agendas.

Leadership and Agency

This section will consider the second of the two questions explored in chapter 1's discussion of the leadership literature: that is, the extent to which leadership tends to be intrinsically suppressive of the agency of those who are 'led'. I will start by outlining contrasting ways of evaluating the interests of followers, one of which amplifies this concern while the other alleviates it. I will then round off the chapter by moving away from the issue of followers' agency and considering that of leaders.

Who is to Say What is Best for People?

The leaders I met tended to dwell on the personal satisfaction that they take from releasing potential in their people. Given the moral significance that they accord to their employees, which I have already emphasized in this chapter, it is unsurprising that these leaders should speak so enthusiastically about helping their people to develop. Take the following example from my conversation with Mark. When I asked Mark about the things that gave him satisfaction in his work, he was quick to reflect on the pleasure that he derives from helping his people develop, offering an example to illustrate the kind of employee development that he has in mind:

> *What would be the things that have given you a great deal of satisfaction in your business career; what sort of thing gives you satisfaction as a leader of business organizations?*
> ... What gives me most pleasure in it quite apart from results, because results do give me pleasure, is the people, particularly in terms of those who are there when you arrive in a business and who you are able to, through whatever minor skills you may have in this area, develop so they can come through the business. To give you a good example: when I was first a director with [a brewery], I was a retail office director in a region of the country running a few hundred managed houses and there was one pub... the one thing that gave me a lot of pleasure was one of the cleaners there had been cleaning in the pub for years, and of course a great cleaner, very proud of the work she did... She had a daughter who also used to do some part-time cleaning and that daughter was really very impressive just in terms of personality. She worked behind the bar then and then she became, over a few years, an area manager and worked up to that and then she became a director and the last I heard of [her] she was actually working for [the brewery] as one of their two major retail directors. Now that is a good example of things that give you a real pleasure in business.

In this instance, Mark describes a developmental intervention on his part that most would consider to be worthwhile. Mark clearly considers this person's subsequent progress to be in her best interests and it is unlikely that she would disagree. Indeed, so obvious is the beneficent nature of this development that Mark does not consider here the possibility that she may think otherwise; that perhaps she may reflect back on her career with the brewery and wish that she had followed a different career path. However, Mark expressed elsewhere a somewhat more contentious appraisal of the best interests of his employees. Having described his sense of responsibility to do the best for his people, he then adopted a surprisingly paternalistic tone in suggesting that there may even be times when it is in an employee's best interests to show them the door:

> It might be your responsibility is to explain to that person that they would really hate it there in future and therefore their best interests are served [by] being somewhere else.

A subtly different approach from Mark's is apparent in the following account. This is taken from my conversation with Dennis, who had spent most of his career working in financial services:

> *What I'd like to begin with Dennis, is just to get some understanding of what are the sort of things that have given you personal satisfaction in your business career?*
>
> To a degree, they've been really about seeing other people take off, as it happens...
>
> *Can you give me any tangible examples of any particular events that have given you particular satisfaction?*
>
> Early in my career, I think it was successfully leading and running a process that involved substantial operational change and building a good team and helping that happen. I think in my middle career it was seeing people that had felt they couldn't break through to the levels and perhaps positions they aspired [to], to sort of work with them; to find experiences that enabled them to do that. And I am particularly thinking of one occasion where... somebody that led a very old-fashioned work-measurement team converted [it] completely into a group of people that added enormous value to the operation, into the customer service units and the rest of it... Those kind of things give me a certain kind of pleasure.
>
> *So, looking at that last example, what is it in that situation that you found particularly satisfying?*
>
> I think at the root of it is, it's a combination of two kinds of things. Firstly [for] the key individuals: building their self-belief and being able to express it in a way they find meaningful and motivational and fulfilling; and at the same time doing something that lends a value, which the team that they work for, or people outside the business—people who buy and sell [their services]—also find [to be of] value. And I think a further experience of that kind which is later in my corporate career, where we mobilised the entire front-end team of an insurance business to reinvent, over a very short timescale, the proposition to the consumer, which involved working differently with each other, breaking some of the rules that they felt existed, resolving those constraints, working completely differently with suppliers ...and showing what they could do as a team of people, which completely

transformed our customers' experience . . . Another example of people changing forever on the basis of an experience they had and making change happen and doing things that they believed were right but they felt were constrained by the way they thought the organization wanted them to work.

So there seem to be two threads coming through there. The first is the development of peoples' potential, helping people to realise and achieve their potential, and secondly there's something about the quality of the offering, the actual outcome of the process.

Yes, I think so. The quality of the outcome having two bearings. The first, how it's measured by the outside world, the recipients, so people might have a view about what they get. But also that the people delivering it thinking that what they're now doing is right or righter than it was, so there's a sense in which I now believe that what I deliver, my day job, is now much more fulfilling because I think I now deliver something that I'm proud of, that other people respect and like, whereas before I didn't.

A notable feature of Dennis' description is the emphasis that it places on other people's estimation of the development that Dennis has enabled. In contrast to Mark's personally derived approach to evaluation, Dennis adopts a subject-centred stance. That subject-centred quality is particularly apparent in Dennis' reference to people 'making change happen and doing things that they believed were right but they felt were constrained by the way they thought the organization wanted them to work'. It is also explicit in the second of the 'two bearings' which he mentions in the last paragraph of this narrative: projecting himself into the changed person's perspective, Dennis suggests that 'there's a sense in which *I* now believe that what I deliver, my day job, is now much more fulfilling because *I* think I now deliver something that *I'm* proud of, that other people respect and like, whereas before I didn't.'

The distinction that I have drawn here resonates with that which I drew in the previous section between managerialist, unilateral pronouncements of social and environmental effect and critically inclined, intersubjective responsiveness. Just as some of those accounts articulated greater responsiveness to the views and expectations of those who are affected by organizational activity, so does the approach illustrated by Dennis' discourse demonstrate greater sensitivity to the aspirations of the recipients of leaders' developmental endeavours. In other words, both distinctions centre on the contrast between a monological and a dialogical approach. This distinction seems significant to the issue of suppressed agency. If leaders use their influencing skills to bring about changes in people that are valued by those people on their own terms, then concerns about suppressed agency ought at least to be diminished. On the other hand, if the sole arbiter of the desirability of change is the leader, who also happens to wield exceptional influence over those people, then the threat of suppressed agency looms larger. It is understandable that leaders should seek to enhance people's contribution to the performance of their organizations and that they should use this as a yardstick to appraise and evaluate those people's personal development. It may sometimes be hard to distinguish instrumental motivation of this kind from intrinsic care about people; nor should these two imperatives necessarily conflict. But if some attention is also paid to individuals' opinions of what constitutes desirable personal change, then a more genuine harmonization between employees' interests and organizational contribution seems likely.

Contrasting Responses to Leaders' Agentic Responsibility

Having discussed the agency of followers, I will now consider a slightly different topic: the agency of leaders, along with the extent to which leaders might avow or repudiate that agency. To do so, I will draw again on the three research participants whose perspectives I described in chapter 5. Remember that David was described as a Company Advocate, who is happy to work within the values set by his organization; James was portrayed as a Moral Crusader, who privileges his own apprehension of moral probity; and Roger's willingness to encourage and respond to intersubjective processes evoked the Mediator of Communication ideal type.

I will draw here on selected passages from the discourses of David and James to illustrate one way of thinking about a leader's agency. I will then highlight an aspect of Roger's discourse to demonstrate a rather different approach. Interestingly, these sections of discourse gainsay, in some respects, the ideal-type caricatures that emerged in my earlier discussion. I will discuss this apparent contradiction in a little more detail once I have presented the contrasting perspectives. The passages that I have chosen to illustrate these differences centre, once again, on the issue of redundancy that featured so prominently throughout my empirical research. David identified redundancy decisions as the most morally challenging situations he faces as a leader:

> *Can you think of any situations where that feeling of responsibility for those people has conflicted with what is expected of you as the person who is in charge of this organization?*
>
> Oh, many I guess. I guess if you are going through a rationalisation programme where you may have to make people redundant: that hurts; that hurts.
>
> *Ok, so how do you come to terms with that?*
>
> I don't think you do. If I am really honest, I don't think you do. I mean, you try and blank it out, but it's painful.
>
> *But presumably you morally justify that.*
>
> I think, from my point of view, one [reason] is you know you have to give a return. So, you know, it sounds callous but, you know, do you sacrifice a hundred to save the thousand? And sometimes you've got to make those decisions to be honest. It's no different from when you are in the army, I guess, making those decisions. But sometimes if we've got a business that's dragging the whole down, you know, do you get rid of that business in order to make sure the whole is ok?

James also spoke of redundancy as presenting his greatest moral challenge:

Can you think back to any ... particular moral dilemmas that you have had to deal with in a leadership role that you would be comfortable telling me about?

I suppose the sort of examples that immediately spring to mind where I am always most uncomfortable is when you have to make people redundant.

Ok. Why is that particularly uncomfortable?

Because you know what it is doing to the person ... And it's hard, you know, because if you think, where it's hard and where it's relevant to your question, is where it potentially is a marginal decision. Sometimes it is really clear-cut: you just say 'look those roles don't exist; most people are going to go'. Other times you have really got to try and hit your budget. You have really got to try and make sure that you are running as efficiently as possible but there is somebody that you quite like, they are doing a sort of comfortable job, they are not going to change the world but they have been there for years and it's a comfortable environment. When you go into a company there are always those people around. And some of them you keep because you value the knowledge that they have got; and you put them into industry relations or industry affairs or something like that, you know the sort of thing I mean. And there are others [about] who you say, 'well actually we can't afford to carry you anymore'. But you know that they are so committed to the company. They love it and their social world is around it, and they have got a family with children, and they might be approaching an age where they are ten years from retirement but if you make them redundant now they are going to struggle finding another job. What do you do? And at the end of the day, you have to do what is right for the business. That is the dilemma. Because you are paid ... you at the end of the day are paid by the shareholders to do what is right for the business. And if it's the right thing for the business, however much you would like to go with the comfortable route, you have got to do what is right and you have got to lose them.

A common feature of the above accounts is that both David and James present the redundancy decision as a necessary task, which it is their unfortunate duty to perform. They did not dwell, in these passages or elsewhere in our conversations, on the possibility that they might have averted the need for redundancy or even that they, as leaders of their organizations, may have contributed in some way to it. The redundancy scenario is, for both, a done deal. The only personal participation that either envisages is the enforcement of the inevitable, organizational maximizing decision. A somewhat different approach is apparent in the following description from Roger:

One of the greatest challenges in leadership is those difficult situations you face when you have to balance the interests of the individual against the interest of the organization. And where, ultimately, you know the right answer must be that it's the organization that must triumph in those circumstances ... There is always a sense of failure I think in those situations where you find yourself in a situation of having to take a decision against an individual in the interests of the organization. And the first question I tend to ask myself in those circumstances is 'how did I create this problem? What role did I have in creating this?' Because you can't always believe that the individual or the organization has created it, because you know sometimes it's leadership that creates those situations.

Like David and James, Roger envisages scenarios in which individuals have to be sacrificed in the interests of organizational prosperity. Like David and James, he regards such situations as morally challenging and, as they do, he proposes that, in such situations, the organization must take precedence over the individual. The difference, however, lies in Roger's response to such scenarios. David and James speak of redundancy as the inevitable outcome of structural and agentic forces that are beyond their control. Roger, on the other hand, reflects on the role that *he* may have played in bringing about such predicaments, to consider what *he* might have done to avoid the need for redundancy, and to learn from the experience.

To some extent, these accounts contrast with the ideal-type characterizations that I attributed earlier to David, James, and Roger. That David understates his own agency in the face of corporate strategy is perhaps understandable given his eagerness to harmonize his own agenda with that of his organization. In James' case, though, it is surprising that he does not dwell on his own contribution to the situation whose resolution he describes. This seems to conflict with his general eagerness to take ownership for what happens in his company. In Roger's case, his willingness to reflect on the part that he has played in bringing about the need for redundancy indicates a degree of personal authorship that may be at odds with his generally consultative mien.

Perhaps, in these cases, contextual circumstances are more elucidative of these differences in approach than are the personal styles of the respective leaders. The transient nature of James's career to date, along with his recent appointment to his present role, might account for this uncharacteristic repudiation of ownership. On the other hand, Roger had been in post for ten years, which, along with similarly lengthy tenure in prior leadership roles, may have encouraged ownership of the unpleasant situations that he has had to resolve. If this is so, then perhaps it says something about the moral desirability of transient leadership appointments: if leaders change so frequently that each spends his or her time mopping up the moral spillage of his or her predecessors, then ethically sensitive behaviour seems less likely. On the other hand, if leaders stick around long enough to confront the moral downsides of their own leadership actions, rather than leaving a successor to pick up the pieces as they move swiftly on to their next leadership challenge, then they may be more sensitive to the moral repercussions of those actions.

To recap, this section has highlighted two distinctions concerning agency. The first contrasts a monological, leader-centred approach to the evaluation of followers' personal development with a subject-centred approach. I have suggested that a subject-centred stance may diminish the challenge that leadership presents to the agency of followers. On the other hand, a leader-centred approach seems less likely to do so. I then distinguished between leaders who are inclined to overlook any part they might have played in creating moral dilemmas and those who reflect on their contribution and learn from it. I suggested that leaders might be more inclined to acknowledge their agentic responsibilities if they remain in leadership roles long enough to confront the moral detritus of their own earlier decisions. This raises the question of whether transient leadership career patterns may be inherently suppressive of moral agency in leaders, and whether more stable leadership contexts might encourage it.

General Observations

Several points that have arisen in this chapter seem particularly relevant to the development of a normative model of ethical leadership. The first is that leaders' enthusiasm for looking after their people must surely be ethically praiseworthy. It seems intuitively right for leaders of organizations to use some of the power and influence at their disposal to protect dependents, particularly those who are most vulnerable. However, if altruistic care for their people goes too far, it may blind leaders to the wider moral ramifications of organizational activity. An understandable desire to minister to the needs of *dependent* stakeholders should not eclipse the plight of *affected* stakeholders. Secondly, there may be times when the letter of a rule-utilitarian principle is so discordant with its spirit that its efficacy is undermined. The adoption of a simple, rule-utilitarian principle of organizational maximization may indeed offer a pragmatic response to the burden of continual utilitarian calculation, but leaders should remain alert to the pernicious possibility that rule-utilitarian principles may end up burying their intended beneficiaries. A third point is that the enthusiasm shown by some leaders for promoting the personal development of their employees is heart-warming. However, for such enthusiasm to ameliorate concerns about suppressed agency, it seems reasonable to expect followers to have a say in what sort of development is good for them. And lastly, leaders may be more inclined to take ownership of the moral devastation that their decisions engender if their career trajectories permit them to stay in any one place for long enough to confront that devastation.

Conclusion

In the introduction to this book I outlined two aims. The first was to explore a range of different ideas about leadership ethics and to draw out some of their implications. In the process I intended to illuminate tensions that infuse these various ideas and to highlight some prominent themes contained within them. This is what I have attempted to do in the preceding chapters. Each chapter has explored the ethics of organizational leadership from a different direction, and each has drawn attention to themes that seem pertinent to that exploration. A characteristic of these themes is that each has something positive to say about leadership ethicality, but that each also offers grounds for disquiet. The second aim to which the book addressed itself was to elaborate a normative model of ethical leadership; to develop an understanding of what ethical leadership in organizations might consist of. I suggested that fulfilling the book's first aim would offer a platform from which this second, normative aim could be achieved. Accordingly, this concluding chapter will pull together and expand on some of the insights already discussed in order to address the book's normative aim.

One thing that I hope has become apparent throughout this study is that ethicality in relation to organizational leadership is no simple matter. I do not think that ethicality can be located in single-minded attentiveness to any one criterion, because the ethical merits of each of the various themes that have been considered here are contestable: although each has something going for it, each is also potentially troubling. Rather, I suggest that ethicality lies in a nuanced response to that contestability. In order to work out what such a response might look like, the first part of this concluding chapter will discuss some of the themes that have figured most prominently in the preceding chapters. This discussion will draw attention to the morally generative and morally troubling aspects of each of these themes. I will then offer some observations about a normative model that is most likely to reap the moral benefits of these themes while avoiding their respective pitfalls. This is a facilitative style of leadership; a style which resonates with the intersubjectivist meta-ethic outlined in chapter 4 and which is personified by the Mediator of Communication ideal type described in chapter 5. I will go on to discuss how this facilitative style departs in one way or another from the discourse of most of the leaders I met during my research, as well as how it conflicts with conventional, managerialist expectations of leadership. The chapter will end with some suggestions concerning what it might take for this facilitative style to catch on in contemporary organizational contexts.

Some Prominent Themes

Moral Sensitization as a Guarantor of Moral Leadership

Many commentators speak of the amoralization of work organizations. Drawing on Weber's depiction (1968 [1911–1920]) of a rationalization process that defines late modernity, they note that organizational environments are generally perceived by those who work within them, and especially by those who occupy their most influential roles, as contexts in which measures of effectiveness ought to prevail. For example, Alasdair MacIntyre, commenting on the pervasive influence of managers in the contemporary scene, notes that they tend to 'conceive of themselves as morally neutral characters whose skills enable them to devise the most efficient means of achieving whatever end is proposed' (1985 [1981]: 74). MacIntyre suggests that in such an effectiveness-driven culture, there is little space for managers to reflect on the moral desirability of the ends towards which effectiveness is directed. Nor are they encouraged to agonize about the broader ramifications of single-minded application of effectiveness measures. Similarly, Zygmunt Bauman (1993) refers to the 'adiaphorization' of social organization—a process by which distancing agents from the consequences of their actions and minimizing ownership of outcomes through strict functional compartmentalization leads to a numbing of the moral impulse. The scant attention paid by leadership theorists to ethics further underlines this image of an amoral organizational world. Leadership is generally viewed by researchers as an instrumental tool—a tool that is applied in the interests of organizational success with little thought for moral considerations. A picture emerges of organizations as morality-free zones; as arenas within which ethical talk has no currency.

Contrary to this gloomy Weberian picture, my own discussions with organizational leaders offer grounds for optimism. The leaders with whom I spoke do not tend to prostrate themselves before the altar of effectiveness: each articulated an interest in morality; all considered ethics relevant to their leadership duties. For them, leadership should not be conceived as a purely instrumental undertaking that is devoid of moral significance. They readily reflected on the ethical quality of the goals towards which they lead and on the repercussions of achieving those goals. Of course, this may not be indicative of the attitude of organizational leaders in general, for this was not necessarily a representative sample. All of these leaders had explicitly agreed to participate in discussions about morality, so one might expect them to have some interest in the subject. It may well be that for each of these morally sensitized leaders there are many others who would see little point in talking about organizational leadership ethics. Nevertheless, that these people participated in my research with such enthusiasm suggests that there is at least some space in organizational life for ethical discourse.

However, while it is encouraging to know that at least some people who occupy leadership roles consider morality relevant to the performance of those roles, some contentious points emerged from my discussions. One particular issue concerns the reassurance that some of these people take from moral sensitization, either from their own moral sensitization or from that of the organizations for which they work. These leaders seemed to make a tacit assumption that moral sensitization ensures moral conduct. If leaders care enough about ethics to include moral considerations in their decision-making, it is thus assumed that decision-making will be ethically correct. Similarly, if morality is accorded a sufficiently high profile by an organization, then it is assumed that organization will conduct itself in a morally sound manner. As long as leaders and organizations care about ethics, the ethicality of their actions is taken for granted.

This faith in the uplifting power of moral sensitization is premised upon a belief that the apprehension of moral rectitude is a straightforward matter: that we all know what is right and wrong. It is just that some of us choose to do what is right while others choose not to. And since we all know what is moral, as long as leaders and organizations conform to these self-evident standards of moral probity, they will necessarily act ethically. Such is the basis of the ethical self-assurance of the Moral Crusader ideal type depicted in chapter 5. I have characterized Moral Crusaders by their existentialist authenticity, although they could equally be cast as self-acclaimed moral sages who credit themselves with an unerring vision of universal principles of right and wrong. Whichever is the case, Moral Crusaders are keen to implement the ethical agenda that is so readily apparent to them. They see little need to corroborate their personal, moral acuity. Theirs is a self-assured, top-down recipe for organizational morality. Meanwhile, the Company Advocate ideal type, also portrayed in chapter 5, is no less sure of the moral furrow that she or he ploughs. But whereas Moral Crusaders take reassurance from the infallibility of their own moral conviction, Company Advocates trust in the wisdom of the corporation's moral lawmakers. So confident are they in the probity of the tablets of stone passed down from Global Head Office that they are happy to measure the ethicality of their leadership decision-making in accordance with them. The Company Advocate, like the Moral Crusader, sees little need for critical reflection on the substance of those values and wastes no time debating the company's moral stance with junior members. That Head Office cares about ethics, and that it cares enough for ethics to shape organizational policy, is enough to guarantee the ethical quality of leadership that implements that policy.

To find morally resolute individuals in leadership roles, who are willing to challenge accepted practice and even, on occasions, to fall on their moral swords, offers a welcome antidote to Weberian visions of a morally torpid organizational world. For values to be accorded the primacy reported by my research participants also conflicts with the image of organizations as shrines to bureaucratic efficiency. And were the apprehension of right and wrong as straightforward as is suggested by the discourses of Moral Crusaders and Company Advocates, then it would be easy to share their trust in the morally uplifting force of ethical sensitization. However, things are rarely that simple. The occurrence of personal moral dilemmas and interpersonal moral disagreements, as well as the failure of over 2,000 years of moral philosophy to identify commonly agreed criteria of right and wrong, testifies to the complex and contested nature of moral judgement. Therefore, to assume that either a leader's determination to act ethically or a company's preoccupation with morality is enough to guarantee moral probity seems overly optimistic. What is more probable is that the version of moral probity favoured by the leader or by the company's key influencers will prevail over rival versions.

So, while it is encouraging to find morality treated with such reverence by leaders and their organizations, this only goes part of the way towards reassurance of the moral quality of organizational leadership. There is more than one aspect to moral leadership: that leaders care enough, and that they are allowed to care enough, about ethics for it to impact on their decision-making is of fundamental importance. But ethical solicitude needs to be augmented by some acknowledgement that moral judgement is not and never will be a simple affair, and that the manner in which morally charged decisions are reached ought to reflect their complexity. Without that qualification, there seems to be little to stop Moral Crusaders and Company Advocates from sliding down the slippery slope towards moral zealotry.

Consistent Application of Moral Principle

A key feature of the principle-based ethics theory discussed in chapter 2 is the idea that ethicality consists of applying moral principle in a consistent manner. This is accorded particular significance in Kantian ethics. Kant's first formulation of the categorical imperative (1948 [1797], 1997 [1788])—that we should only act upon those maxims that we would wish to become universalized—offers a simple and straightforward expression of the legitimating force of treating all people, including ourselves, the same. More generally, consistency is important if principle-based ethics is to avoid the charge of expedient flexibility. There are so many theories to choose from, with each pointing in different directions depending on how it is interpreted and applied, that the least we can expect of those who appeal to principle-based theory for a moral blueprint is that they apply their chosen principle consistently.

Consistency seems particularly important for leadership. It seems reasonable to expect people in positions of power to dispense that power with a degree of constancy. For leaders to treat some people differently to others would seem wrong. And for them to apply different standards at different times according to arbitrary preference also seems morally problematic. In particular, it would seem unreasonable for leaders to leverage their influence in order to privilege their own interests, or those of close colleagues, at the expense of others. It is encouraging, then, that so many of the leaders whom I met spoke of the importance of doing their duty in a principled and consistent manner; of treating different people the same; and of applying the same standards at different times. Such an approach is intuitively appealing.

However, consistent application of principle is not always as straightforward as it might seem. In particular, allowance must be made for the contestable quality of attributions of consistency, for what looks like consistent treatment to one person may not look so to another. The consistent application of principle demands that relevant similarities in various scenarios are identified and addressed. Of course, no two scenarios are identical. The key to consistent treatment is to identify those dimensions upon which similarity or dissimilarity is relevant to a particular decision. However, to make such assessments of relevance is to take a stance; to make a subjective judgement concerning which similarities matter and which do not; to make a subjective distinction between those differences between scenarios that justify contrasting responses and those that do not. This subjective quality need not undermine the ethical merits of consistency, particularly as a foil to the expedient flexibility to which principle-based ethics is prone. However, for the notion of consistency to fulfil its legitimizing function, the contestable nature of its associated attributions of relevance needs to be acknowledged. Furthermore, it seems reasonable for those attributions of relevance to be negotiated between implicated parties rather than unilaterally proclaimed by the most powerful. The legitimizing force of consistency is diminished if implicated parties consider its attribution to be haphazard, arbitrary, or just plain wrong.

So, on the one hand, the notion of consistency does seem to have something important to say to ethical leadership; it offers a morally legitimating core. In particular, it seems right that leaders ought not to use the power that attends their position to privilege their own material interests and aspirations or those of their social and professional allies. However, the assumption that leaders can stand apart from their organizational contexts, cool-headedly dispensing moral justice in accordance with the consistent application of principle, is unhelpful. Such a depiction obscures the contestable nature of attributions of consistency as well as the inevitable complexity of the organizational contexts within which those attributions are made. Given the potential for contestation, monological pronouncements of consistency on the part of leaders are likely to rest on unstable foundations. The legitimating force of consistency only works against a presupposition of multilateral agreement.

Suppressing Emotion in Order to do the Right Thing

A number of the leaders whom I interviewed dwelt on the importance of applying principle in a rational, cool-headed, and dispassionate manner. This, again, concurs with the Kantian notion of ethics described in chapter 2: that ethical conduct consists of acting dutifully in accordance with reason. According to Kant (1948 [1797], 1997 [1788]), emotions such as charity and benevolence should take second place to duties that are apprehended via the application of moral reason. For Kant, acting in response to the 'imperfect' duties indicated by moral sentiment is a frivolity that is permissible only after the main business of rational, 'perfect' duty has been dealt with. However, the accounts described in chapters 6 and 7 indicate that cool-headed, rational application of principle can be a challenging undertaking. It is not an easy thing to overlook feelings of partiality towards familiar faces, and interviewees' accounts of having to do so were tinged with sorrow. Nevertheless, leadership duty, as these people see it, is to set aside such misgivings. According to this understanding, moral leadership demands dispassionate application of principle; there is no space for sentimentality. In dealing with ethically charged issues, the heart should not be allowed to rule the head.

This valorization of rational duty, and its associated emotional discomfort, featured most prominently in accounts of redundancy scenarios. Most of the leaders I met recounted the personal distress that they had experienced when making people redundant. But such is the burden of leadership: leaders must not permit the indulgences of sentiment to intrude on their decisions. Whereas people in less exalted roles might take the soft course and listen to their heart, these leaders believe that they must avoid such temptations in order to dispense moral justice in a level-headed and even-handed manner. It is the unpleasant, but necessary, task of leaders to do what the voice of reason tells them has to be done. That is what, as more than one interviewee emphatically stated, they are 'paid to do'.

But is this really what moral judgement is all about? David Hume (1985 [1738], 1998 [1752]) alerted us over 250 years ago to the role played by passion in moral evaluation. Subsequent efforts by Enlightenment thinkers to banish this untrustworthy and unruly aspect from the field of moral debate have not been entirely successful: sentiment continues to insinuate its way into ethics theory, as is apparent from the discussion of existentialist theory in chapter 3. Thus, William Barratt (1990 [1958]) speaks of existentialism's contribution to the 'Flight from Laputa'—that world of unbridled rationality encountered by Gulliver on his fictitious travels. According to existentialist theory, Enlightenment rationality would be of little use to the leader in apprehending moral probity.

Zygmunt Bauman (1993) picks up on ideas such as these to describe how dispassionate application of moral principle detaches us from our moral sense. Drawing in particular upon the work of Emmanuel Levinas, Bauman proposes that the nature of moral commitment can only be accessed through direct, face-to-face encounters with people who are affected by our actions. Bauman observes the tendency for social organization to separate us from such encounters, or at least to suppress their impact. It thus makes redundant the moral sense, substituting it with a cruel, rational accounting that is consistent with the bureaucratic expectations of the contemporary organizational world. Martin Parker (2002) echoes Bauman's theme when he reflects on how the globally dispersed organizational form, in which electronic communication increasingly replaces face-to-face encounters, tends to undermine any sense of local responsibility amongst senior management. Parker also recounts deliberate actions taken by companies to distance senior managers from exposure to the consequences of their decisions, thus making it easier for them to 'downsize without looking employees in the eye' (2002: 85).

According to Bauman, to privilege detached, principled action, far from morally invigorating workplaces, is to denude them of moral sensitivity. By suppressing countervailing sentiments in order to conform to the expectations of rational moral law, leaders would, on this account, be cutting themselves off from the moral sense upon which ethically responsive decision-making depends. So, a leader who suppresses his contrition at withholding from close associates the news of their impending redundancy may be ignoring an important cue to the ethical legitimacy of his subterfuge. Similarly, those who silence the inner voice of remorse while cutting the jobs of loyal colleagues in the interest of minor enhancements to productivity might be denying themselves access to a key indicator of the rightness of their actions. And a leader who eschews leniency to dismiss long-serving employees on a matter of rational principle may be repressing insights that would have enabled a more morally balanced decision. These leaders may be eschewing the lifeblood of ethical decision-making. Instead of subsuming their emotional misgivings under a tide of supposedly rational, moral accounting, they might do well to recognize that those misgivings have something important to say about the moral probity of their actions. Moral sentiment sends important messages. Censoring these messages out of organizational decision-making may deprive it of the nutrients that it needs to sustain its moral vigour.

Now to suggest that in evaluating the ethicality of their actions, leaders ought to respond to the messages sent by their emotions, is not to propose unreflective sentimentality as a basis for ethical leadership. In emphasizing the part played by passions, writers from Hume to Bauman are not advocating that emotion is all there is to moral judgement. By proposing that the ultimate grounding point of any ethical decision must lie in some form of emotive response, these writers do not seek to banish cognitive processes from the field of ethics. Rather, they envisage interplay between reason and moral senti-ment; interplay in which each supports the other. Our emotional responses to situations might thus be informed by rational reflection and debate; while cognitive processes might be similarly informed by the force of sentiment. So, to draw attention to the role that moral sentiment might play in guiding leadership decision-making is not to claim hegemony for it; it is simply to appeal for it to be allowed a seat at the table of moral deliberation.

On the one hand, then, there seems to be something important in the notion that organizational leaders might need to overcome feelings of partial-ity in order to do the right thing. It is also reassuring to find leaders willing to step back from the seething turmoil of emotional immediacy in order to make considered judgements that embrace a range of perspectives. However, to present such reflection as no more than a monological exercise in rational accounting is likely to be self-defeating. The notion that a leader can stand as captain on the bridge of the ship of moral evaluation, cool-headedly directing in accordance with the principles of ethical navigation, is unhelpful. Just as any sailor depends on intimate encounters with the marine environment in order to make well-informed navigational calls, so does the ethical quality of leadership thrive on the emotional messages that attend leaders' exposure to the consequences of their decision-making.

For the Good of the Organization

In chapter 7 I drew attention to the moral significance that leaders tend to place on sustaining their organizations. In my interviews, the survival and prosperity of the organization came across as an overriding preoccupation; a preoccupation that trumps most other considerations. However, it was also apparent that the good of the organization is not accorded categorical value. Rather, its survival and prosperity is valued insofar as this promotes the interests of its stakeholders. In other words, the leaders I interviewed consider it their duty to promote the good of the organization because this will serve the interests of particular people who are morally significant to them.

It is not surprising that leaders should prioritize the organizations that they lead. Nor is it surprising that they should do so in the interests of people who are associated with those organizations. A sense of responsibility to one's organization and its stakeholders seems intuitively reasonable as a basis for moral action. Such an understanding accords with several of the theoretical justifications that have been considered in this book. For instance, it might be valorized by a rights discourse; by an assumption that their relationship with the organization confers upon certain stakeholders a 'right' to consideration. Alternatively, appeal might be made to formal or tacit contractual arrangements between leaders and groups such as shareholders, employees, suppliers, and customers; arrangements which bestow moral significance on those groups. This theme also resonates with the emphasis that the charismatic and transformational leadership theorists discussed in chapter 1 place on altruism as a moral indicator, where altruistic sentiment is focused on a particular constituency with whom the leader identifies.

However, the leaders whom I met did not tend to articulate their responsibilities to stakeholders in contractual terms or in relation to rights. Neither did they appeal to the justificatory force of altruism. The theoretical perspective that best captures the way that they spoke about the organization is a utilitarian one. Its underpinning assumption seems to be that leaders have a responsibility to maximize the well-being of certain groups of people and that they are best placed to achieve this end by maximizing the well-being of their organizations. It might thus be characterized as a *rule-utilitarian* rationale: the rule of maximizing the good of the organization is taken as proxy for maximizing the interests of its stakeholders; therefore, this is the principle that is accorded primacy in leadership decision-making. Such an approach can be contrasted with an *act-utilitarian* stance, which would call upon leaders to weigh up every single decision so as to make complex judgements about which course of action, in that particular instance, would maximize stakeholder well-being. Given the practical difficulties associated with such act-utilitarian calculations, a rule-utilitarian approach as sketched here seems sensibly pragmatic. Rather than making complex predictive and evaluative calls every time they confront a decision, leaders just need to apply the utility-maximizing rule of organizational maximization, safe in the knowledge that this, ultimately, will be best for morally relevant stakeholders. In other words, if leaders look after their organizations, they will be looking after the people who matter.

The idea of stakeholding as carrying moral significance has received quite a lot of attention in the business ethics literature (for example, Donaldson and Preston, 1995; Moore, 1999; Sternberg, 1999; Stoney and Winstanley, 2001;

Kaler, 2002; Phillips, 2003) since Freeman (1984) applied it to corporate governance theory. In efforts to clarify the 'blurred character of the stakeholder concept' (Donaldson and Preston, 1995: 66), distinctions have been made between contrasting interpretations of stakeholding, or different ways in which a person might be regarded as a stakeholder of an organization. In particular, business ethics commentators have focused on the difference between *instrumental stakeholders* and *normative stakeholders* (Donaldson and Preston, 1995). According to this distinction, instrumental stakeholders are seen as important insofar as their support is instrumental to organizational performance, whereas normative stakeholders are accorded intrinsic moral significance. While the former need to be kept happy because organizations need their support, the latter are important in their own right. According to this depiction, *normative stakeholding* is offered as a basis for opposing *shareholder theory*—the idea that executives' overriding moral responsibility is to maximize shareholder wealth—by pointing to the claims of other stakeholders to intrinsic moral consideration. In contrast, *instrumental stakeholding* is often cast as an amoral, or perhaps even an immoral perspective, which values stakeholders for no reason other than their importance to the achievement of corporate success.

Helpful though this instrumental–normative distinction is, I do not believe that it offers an adequate framework for capturing the dimension of ethical leadership that I am describing here. To distinguish so clearly between normative and instrumental stakeholders is to make too stark a contrast between, on the one hand, the amoral or shareholder-driven prioritization of commercial performance, where stakeholders are only attended to insofar as they serve that end, and on the other hand, the consideration of stakeholders as intrinsically deserving of consideration. This simple dualism overlooks the capacity of instrumental stakeholding to contain a normative element; a normative element that is not exhausted by the shareholder theory discourse. In other words, it obscures the possibility that prioritizing commercial performance may contain a moral dimension that goes beyond responding to the claims of shareholders.

The rule-utilitarian style justification that I have described here expresses that moral dimension. The preoccupation with corporate success that these leaders articulate cannot be explained as an inability or unwillingness to look beyond the iron bars of bureaucratic efficiency. Furthermore, this moral dimension is more than an endorsement of the primacy of shareholders. Indeed, those who spoke of shareholders tended to downplay or dismiss the importance of the latter in their hierarchies of moral worth. For these people, prioritizing commercial performance and thus ensuring the prosperity and survival of their organizations is a moral imperative. It is so because doing this will promote the interests of those people to whom these leaders feel morally responsible; that is, not just to the shareholders of the organization, whom they tend to talk down, but all those who depend upon it. Most importantly, sustaining the organization is important because this will promote the well-being of its employees—the group that figures most prominently in these leaders' universes of moral relevance. For this reason they feel morally justified in sometimes taking action that is detrimental to the interests of small groups of employees. The moral rationale for doing so is that this serves the interests of the majority of what I referred to in chapter 7 as the organization's *dependent intrinsic normative stakeholders*; that is, those people who depend upon the survival and prosperity of the organization. It is to these stakeholders that the leaders whom I interviewed tended to accord categorical moral significance; it is these people who are the key members of their perceived universe of moral relevance.

However, despite the undoubted ethical tone of the rule-utilitarian rationale that thus emerges, I nevertheless find that discourse problematic on two counts: one that I will outline here; the other that I will elaborate in the next section. My first concern relates to the ease with which organizational survival slides into organizational prosperity as a moral imperative. While it seems reasonable to align the survival of an organization with the interests of those who depend upon it, this association is not quite so straightforward in the case of its prosperity. Consider, for example, an organization's employees. The association between the survival of the organization and its employees' well-being is clear: if the organization goes down, they lose their livelihoods. However, it is far from clear that small enhancements to an organization's prosperity will necessarily serve the interests of its employees. Indeed, where such enhancements are achieved through efficiency measures such as 'downsizing', 'delayering', 'offshoring', or simply by keeping pay levels as low as possible, there is likely to be a tangible conflict with employee well-being.

But there are other, less obvious ways in which productivity enhancements may erode the quality of the employment experience and thus chip away at the well-being of those employees whose interests are held in such high esteem by most of the leaders that I interviewed. For instance, employees may experience intensification of risk and stress as a result of the introduction of performance-related reward structures (Heery, 2000; Winstanley, 2000) or flexible working patterns (Stanworth, 2000). Similarly, they may be asked to submit to the intrusive ramifications of ostensibly performance-enhancing, occupational-testing instruments (Baker and Cooper, 2000) or aggressive and stressful selection processes (Spence, 2000). Although innovative human resource management measures such as these are generally adopted in the belief that they will enhance organizational performance, this may come at a significant cost to employees' job security, dignity, and self-esteem.

Some of the leaders whom I met explicitly addressed the correlation of prosperity with survival by warning of the insidious creep of inefficiency. They pointed out that failure on their part to attend to opportunities for small productivity gains today may result in the collapse of the organization tomorrow. There is something in this. In the increasingly competitive organizational landscape, to which business strategy theorists are eager to alert us, it is understandable that leaders feel morally compelled to keep their organizations on their toes. However, to assume that prosperity must always be maximized in order to ensure survival is a misleading oversimplification. It overlooks the unhappy side effects that efficiency measures might have on employees; efficiency measures which may have a minimal impact on the organization's capacity to resist predation but which may nevertheless have severe repercussions for the very people who are ostensibly valorized by the moral rationale in whose name they are taken.

Therefore, the care that these leaders articulate for the good of their organizations has an undoubted moral dimension. Although that moral dimension may not fit easily into a straightforward, instrumental–normative dualism, it is present nevertheless. However, by bundling together the prosperity and the survival of the organization as equally legitimate means to the achievement of morally valorized ends, leaders may find themselves undermining those very ends. To conflate the survival of the organization with its prosperity and to offer both as equivalent imperatives for leadership decision-making is to misrepresent the congruence between incremental enhancements to organizational success and the interests of dependent stakeholders. The continued survival of the organization may indeed be in the interests of its dependent stakeholders. However, this should not vindicate every measure taken to keep the organization in a position of untrammelled competitive dominance.

Looking after the People who Matter

Despite these difficulties, the preoccupation with the well-being of stakeholders that is contained within this rule-utilitarian rationale is appealing. It seems right that leaders should bother about the impact that their organizations have on people; that they should not be driven by a morally negligent obsession with rational effectiveness; that shareholders should not be the only people who matter. The care that these interviewees articulated for normative intrinsic stakeholders is good news for anyone who believes that leaders should think about those who are touched by their actions and that the universe of moral relevance should not start and end with a company's owners. However, although this concern for people is reassuring, the way that some of these leaders defined precisely who is morally relevant is contentious. In this respect, the people generally placed on the pedestal of moral relevance by those whom I interviewed are those who *depend upon* the survival and, to a less self-evident extent, upon the prosperity of the organization. Consideration may thus be denied to those who, although not dependent upon an organization, are nevertheless *affected* by its activities. This includes all those people and communities that bear the social and environmental consequences of organizational activity. To repeat the terminology introduced in chapter 7, this is to take account of an organization's *dependent intrinsic normative stakeholders* but to deny normative significance to its *affected stakeholders*.

To limit the universe of moral relevance in this way seems particularly problematic given the types of business that some of these leaders represent. For instance, the pub trade, the travel industry, and food production have an enormous impact on society and on the environment. They therefore affect many people—geographically close and geographically remote, and present and future generations—who do not depend in any way on the survival and prosperity of those organizations. Through their influence over the activities of their organizations, leaders carry awesome power. That they exercise that power in the interests of a narrowly circumscribed group of dependent stakeholders who stand to gain today, tomorrow, and next year from their dependency relationship with the organization, without a thought for the more numerous groups who are affected by those organizations now and in the future, is troubling.

Helping Followers to Develop

Throughout my research discussions I was struck by the interest that interviewees showed in the development of their employees and in the role that they, as leaders, could play in that development. Several also spoke of the pleasure that they had derived from seeing their people progress, observing that this was the most satisfying aspect of their work. This is consistent with the general valorization of employees already mentioned. It also resonates with the emphasis that the leadership effectiveness literature places on employee development. As discussed in chapter 1, many researchers have highlighted a correlation between effective leadership and attentiveness to the development needs of followers. Transformational leadership theory offers a particularly resounding celebration of leaders' capacity to foster followers' self-actualization by encouraging participation in a common purpose (I will say more, specifically, on this subject shortly). It is therefore unsurprising to find, in leadership roles, people who value employee development so highly and who dwell so readily on their own contribution to it.

This preoccupation with developing people bestows a certain amount of intuitive moral credit upon leadership. The idea of organizational leaders ministering to the formational needs of their followers is compelling. If effective leadership entails stimulating followers' career progression whilst also evoking their self-actualization, then effective leadership seems to have a lot going for it. However, before we become too carried away by this enticing vision of organizational leaders as custodians of the material, intellectual, and emotional flourishing of their followers, it is as well to reiterate some points noted in earlier chapters which might offer cause for concern. For a start, the moral allure of employee-development focus becomes a little tarnished if that focus is switched on and off in response to pragmatic need. Our moral approbation of leaders who seem to care for their people is partly dependent on a presumption of sincerity. Situational leadership models that advocate the adoption of apposite blends of employee-related and task-focused leadership behaviours in response to contingent need are problematic in this respect. They might be read as an endorsement of instrumentally driven affectation, calling to mind Alvesson and Willmott's observation (1998) that the emancipatory and humanistic pretensions of progressive management theories may help managers to infiltrate hearts and minds, but that such approaches do little to meet people's deeper, long-term needs and aspirations. So, for leaders' care for the development of their people to carry moral worth, it seems reasonable to expect it to be heartfelt.

A further issue with leaders' preoccupation with employee development concerns the way in which some define worthwhile development. I mentioned, in chapter 7, that a few of the leaders whom I met articulated sensitivity to the views of the recipients of their employee developmental endeavours. These people spoke of the need for employees to value the development to which they have been subjected on their own terms, rather than just on the leader's terms. However, others appraised the desirability of employee enhancement according to the leader's own, monologically pronounced standards. Such well-meaning paternalism, which casts the leader as beneficent arbiter of employees' best interests, may well be morally legitimated by some of the consequentialist analyses discussed in chapter 2. Nevertheless, the practical application of such justifications to the leadership domain depends upon some highly contestable assumptions. Notably, it assumes that leaders are best placed to evaluate employee welfare, or that leaders are the best judge of what is objectively good for their employees. This seems to ask a lot of those leaders: not only must they carry all the usual paraphernalia that assures success in their role; they must also become authoritative adjudicators of employee well-being. Inviting employees to participate in the elucidation of their interests, and in the identification of developmental avenues that best serve those interests, seems a far safer option than well-intended, paternalistic meddling.

Therefore, although commitment to facilitating followers' development draws intuitive moral worth to leadership, that moral worth would be less contentious if two further conditions were met. Firstly, it is easier to applaud leaders' developmental endeavours if they are driven by a sincere interest in their direct beneficiaries than if they are motivated purely by expediency. Secondly, the involvement of those beneficiaries in the identification and evaluation of worthwhile personal development would also enhance its morally legitimating force.

Building Commitment to a Shared Vision

A lot of leadership literature emphasizes the role played by leaders in building support for a shared vision. This notion is particularly evident in transformational leadership theory, where it also acquires a moral dimension that links with the topic of employee development that I have just discussed. As far as theorists such as Burns (1978, 2003) and Bass (1985, 1990) are concerned, the fundamental, morally legitimating core of transformational leadership lies in the self-actualization that followers achieve by participating in a shared endeavour. These theorists propose that such participation raises followers above the level of self-interested, transactional exchange and evokes the real humanity within them, which can only be achieved through being part of a common purpose.

It is easy to see how generating shared commitment helps leaders to achieve organizational success. If all workers are contributing wholeheartedly to the achievement of an organization's objectives, rather than weighing up the transactional costs and benefits of each and every input, then productivity is likely to be enhanced. On the face of it, this is also a harmless enough notion from an ethical perspective. There seems to be something in the idea that it is good for people to be part of collective effort and that they may become, in some way, 'better' people through such participation. This smacks of the social understanding of humanity discussed in chapter 4, upon which various intersubjectivist rationales are premised. However, this advocacy of building commitment to a shared vision also poses a number of questions.

The first question concerns the definition of the common purpose to which a leader builds self-actualizing support. In other words, who sets the agenda? A common response to this question in the leadership literature is to place the definitional onus upon the leader. Successful leaders are not only cast as those who can build commitment to a shared undertaking; they are generally portrayed as taking the lead in conceiving that transformational vision in the first place. Whether it concerns the setting of strategic goals, the shaping of a shared culture, or the establishment of core values, leadership writers of many hues describe how leaders are able to generate visions that capture the imagination of followers and which thus take their organizations to better places. Several of the leaders whom I encountered during empirical research articulated a similar theme, reflecting on their role in establishing their organizations' common, moral agenda. Although some spoke of sharing this definitional task, the extent of intersubjective participation usually started and ended with senior management. A strong note of unilateralism is therefore apparent in relation to the setting of a shared direction, both from my research and from broader theoretical and empirical studies. I will say more about this shortly.

A further issue concerns the possible effects of their participation upon those who are embraced by leaders' transformational inclusiveness. Despite the intuitive allure of group participation, and despite the self-actualizing propensity claimed for it by transformational leadership theorists, commentators from various fields have drawn attention to its less attractive ramifications. I have already mentioned, in chapter 3, Heidegger's warning (1962 [1926]) that people might dissolve their individuality in the 'averageness' of the crowd. This, for Heidegger, is one manifestation of an 'inauthentic' form of Being. Social commentators have also highlighted some disagreeable side effects of fealty to a large collective. For example, Festinger et al. (1952) use the term *deindividuation* to describe how group participation may engender a sense of anonymity that loosens behavioural constraints. This may lead to a reduced sense of responsibility, heightened inclination to act impulsively, and an increased propensity to behaviour that, in most other contexts, would be considered antisocial. Meanwhile, Marion Hampton (1999), looking specifically at the impact of group membership in work contexts, notes its capacity to induce conformity, depress individual intelligence, and eliminate moral responsibility.

The field of identity work may also have something important to say on this topic. Identity work research seeks to illuminate ways in which individuals within organizations create and experience the subjective meanings that shape their understandings of who they are and how they ought to act (Alvesson et al., 2008). On the one hand, leadership may be presented as a benign undertaking that helps followers to negotiate a pathway between the conflicting demands of multiple personal and professional identities as they seek to respond to such questions (for example, Hill and Stephens, 2005). On the other hand, Alvesson et al. (2008) offer a more critical perspective, from which leaders' transformational endeavours to unite followers to a common agenda might be interpreted as an attempt to orchestrate identities within a managerially inspired discourse—a discourse which offers the totem of the organization as the primary source of identification and which thus marginalizes sources of identity-creation which draw on extra-organizational sources. In other words, the 'I'-as-part-of-a-particular-work-organization is accorded hegemony over other possible sources of affiliative identity, such as 'I'-as-father/mother, 'I'-as-a-member-of-a-profession, 'I'-as-citizen, or 'I'-as-self-reflexive-moral-agent. And as the work identity is accorded priority over alternative sources, so does responsibility to one's work community take precedence over family and professional responsibilities, broader notions of citizenship, and wider moral commitments.

Another problem with putting too much emphasis on shared purposes concerns those who might be excluded from such participation for one reason or another. For instance, some of those who fall under a leader's sphere of influence may not wish to commit themselves to the full gamut of emotional belongingness that is acclaimed by transformational theorists. Some may prefer, instead, to view their workplace as no more than a stage upon which to satisfy basic, material needs. That these people choose to restrict their relationship with an organization to the level of transactional exchange would be considered by transformational leadership theorists as an indictment of the leader: transformational success demands that people be 'lifted above' such self-limiting, transactional trivia. But what is to become of those who thus abjure the transformational vision? Are they to be cast aside; stigmatized; rejected as being unsuitable for organizational membership?

I mentioned in chapter 4 an insight offered by G.W.F. Hegel and elaborated by Jürgen Habermas concerning the notion of individuals indentifying themselves through participation in what Hegel calls 'universal spirit'. This insight seems particularly germane here. For Hegel, if such self-actualization is to happen, there needs to be a process of mutual adaptation between the individual and the universal spirit. In other words, not only should the individual adapt to the universal but the universal should also adapt to the individual. Only then will the necessary harmony between individual and universal be achieved; only then will a basis for self-actualization be realized. Habermas pulls this insight down from the rarefied heights of Hegelian speculative philosophy and applies it to the notion of a community of interaction—in Habermasian terms, an 'unrestricted communication community'—suggesting that the identification of individuals with such a community also needs to flow from a process of mutual adaptation. For Habermas, the achievement of shared understanding through 'communicative action' is the crucial ingredient to such mutual adaptation.

To apply this Hegelian and Habermasian idea of mutual adaptation to that of a shared purpose, as envisaged by transformational leadership theory, is to propose that followers will only find self-actualization in such shared purpose if they are permitted to contribute to its elaboration. Conversely, if the process of adaptation is cast as a one-way, linear undertaking, in which leaders attempt to rally support for a predetermined, unilaterally defined vision, opportunities for mutual adaptation will be lost. Rather than enabling the self-actualization of followers of which transformational leadership theorists speak, such processes are likely to be experienced as fundamentally alienating. Furthermore, transformational leadership's morally legitimizing potential will be severely undermined.

It seems reasonable, then, to suppose that people's experience of organizational life will be enhanced by the camaraderie and inclusiveness that comes from working towards a common goal. It is nice to be part of something, and it is heartening to know that one's efforts contribute towards an agenda that is shared by others. If leaders are able to generate that sense of togetherness and if they can facilitate agreement around a shared agenda, then their leadership seems morally meritorious. In that respect, transformational leadership theorists offer an important insight to the ethicality of leadership. However, sensitivity to the hazards presented by the leader's transformational endeavours is also called for. In particular, it is important that followers are able to contribute to the definition of shared agendas in a manner that is respectful, rather than erosive, of their independent, agentic capacity.

Towards a Normative Model of Ethical Leadership

So what does all this mean for a normative model of ethical leadership? So far, this concluding chapter has highlighted a number of themes, each of which says something about how leadership might be ethical, and each of which offers grounds upon which leadership's ethicality might be challenged. I will make two observations about a normative model in relation to these themes. The first observation is self-evident. This is that sensitivity to the potential upsides and downsides of these themes will help leaders to steer a course that embraces the former whilst avoiding the latter. The second observation is that the leadership style that is best placed to steer such a course is a style that is consultative rather than directive; one which casts leaders as mediators rather than as controllers; as facilitators of dialogical processes rather than as implementers of monological edicts. This second observation becomes apparent if we reconsider each of these themes in turn.

Firstly, moral sensitization seems to be a very good starting point for ensuring ethical leadership. It is reasonable to assume that leaders who care about morality, and who devote energy and resources to encouraging other people in their organizations to reflect on the moral implications of their actions, are more likely to lead ethically than those who do not. However, the uplifting quality of moral sensitization is undermined if ethical judgement is thought of as being straightforward and commonsensical. Unless morally sensitized leaders are alert to the inherent complexity of moral judgement, the agendas that they champion and the moral responsiveness that they evoke may inhibit, rather than enable, morally legitimate outcomes. But to expect leaders to attend to such intricacies alone would be to demand a degree of moral sagacity on their part that we have no reason to suppose they possess. Despite their undoubtedly impressive range of personal capabilities, CEOs, MDs, and company directors are not necessarily imbued with higher levels of ethical perspicacity than anyone else. So, given the potency of their decision-making, the idea that the moral implications of those decisions should be evaluated unilaterally is troubling. The intricacies of moral evaluation will surely be better catered for if leaders share the burden of judgement. Therefore, moral sensitization on the part of leaders is a great deal more reassuring if it is accompanied by a willingness to involve others in decision-making.

Consistency also seems to be a reasonable indicator of ethicality. In particular, it would seem wrong for leaders to make deliberate exceptions in order to privilege either their own self-interested agendas or those of close associates. However, the contestable nature of attributions of consistency needs to be acknowledged. What seems like consistent treatment to one person may seem arbitrary to another. The morally legitimating force of consistency rests on an assumption of agreement. If attributions of consistency are delivered monologically, without reference to those who, ostensibly, are being treated consistently, then such agreement is absent. Therefore, a dialogical leadership style, which permits negotiation around ideas of consistency, seems best placed to realize this ethically legitimating potential.

The nagging intrusion of sentiment into moral evaluation also points to the merits of consultation. On the one hand, rationality surely has a place in moral evaluation, at least as an antidote to caprice. However, the signals sent by our emotions may also tell us something important about ethics. If leaders perceive moral evaluation as a purely rational undertaking, in which they can engage with a cool head and a hard heart, then they may miss some important indicators to the moral quality of their judgements. And if sentiment is to serve as a corrective to the hubris of rationality, then it seems reasonable to listen not only to what our own sentiments tell us but also to what other people's sentiments have to say. The mutually supportive balance of emotive and cognitive processes will surely be enhanced if it embraces the perspectives, both emotive and cognitive, of other people.

There also seems to be something intuitively right about leaders taking care of the organizations that they lead and thus looking after the interests of the people who depend upon those organizations. However, this should not be to the exclusion of all else. In particular, leaders' sense of responsibility towards dependent stakeholders should not blind them to the claims of affected stakeholders. And if the ultimate benchmark of moral leadership is maximizing the interests of an organization's stakeholders, whether we are speaking of dependent or affected stakeholders, then surely leaders should canvass the views of those stakeholders when deciding what to do. Thus might the rule-utilitarian principle of organizational maximization be reigned in before it destroys the well-being of those very people whose interests it claims to uphold. Moreover, consultation might also prevent the interests of less salient, affected stakeholders from being drowned under a flood of dutiful obeisance towards those dependent stakeholders who are able to stake their claims most stridently.

Moreover, if ministration to the developmental needs of employees is morally praiseworthy, then it will surely be even more so if accompanied by a consultative demeanour. Benevolent paternalism has its merits, but it can be sorely misdirected if its putative beneficiaries are denied a say in what is good for them. And lastly, being part of a shared undertaking may well make things better for people, perhaps even to the extent that it makes them 'better people'. But this happy outcome seems far more probable if they are allowed to contribute to the definition of that common purpose and if they are given a say in how it is to be achieved.

So, across each of these dimensions, a consultative approach is more likely to achieve its moral upside whilst ameliorating any corresponding downsides. The intersubjectivist meta-ethical stance outlined in chapter 4, which emphasizes the role that leaders can play in facilitating dialogue around ethics, seems, therefore, to offer the most compelling basis for ethical leadership. Similarly, of the three ideal-type characterizations offered in chapter 5, that of the Mediator of Communication is better suited than that of either the Company Advocate or the Moral Crusader to building upon the morally appealing foundations of each of these themes without stumbling over the moral tripwires that surround it.

Given the normative attractiveness of a participative leadership style, it is comforting that most of the leaders whom I met during my research expressed their willingness to share the burden of moral authorship. Despite a general readiness to take charge, most advocated some form of collaboration in setting their organizations' moral tone and in addressing moral dilemmas. Expectations of moral sagacity on their part are thus alleviated, while, considered from an existentialist perspective, this participative mien also promises to disperse the gift of authenticity. However, lest these nods in the direction of consultation are misinterpreted as manifestations of intersubjective zeal, it is important to draw attention to the circumscribed nature of the court of moral appeal to which these leaders usually turn. As I pointed out in chapter 6, this typically includes fellow directors, senior managers, consultants, and mentors. Some interviewees mentioned that they might try to embrace the views of non-managerial employees, but this was rare. More often, either they explicitly repudiated the legitimacy of junior employee involvement or they spoke of practical barriers to broader consultation.

Given the pervasive hold of *managerialism* in organizational theory and practice (Alvesson and Willmott, 1996; Parker, 2002), it is unsurprising that participation in leadership decision-making is restricted in this way. As I suggested in chapter 1, a dominant view within Western organizations, at least amongst those who occupy their higher echelons, is that those organizations should be run by their managers. The right, indeed the duty, of managers to take the key decisions is a fundamental premise of managerialism. For, the managerial mantra goes, only managers possess the understanding and personal qualities that are needed to undertake this onerous task. It should come as no surprise, then, to find that this confidence in management expertise extends to the realm of ethical legitimation. If managers are accorded hegemony in all other decision-making contexts, then why should things be any different when ethics is on the agenda?

The implication of this managerialist commitment is that the processes of ethical legitimation thus privileged fall well short of the standards to which this book's findings point. For a start, most stakeholders are denied a voice. If, as Habermas suggests, intersubjective ethical legitimacy demands that those who are implicated in a decision are able to participate in it, then the exclusion of so many dependent and affected stakeholders is clearly erosive of that legitimacy. This would not be such a big issue were decision-making fora representative of a broad range of perspectives. But this also seems unlikely. As a number of organizational theorists have suggested (such as Kanter, 1977; Marshall, 1995; Alvesson and Willmott, 1996; Hancock and Tyler, 2001; Parker, 2002) and as a few of my interviewees observed, managers tend to be drawn from within narrow ethnic, gender, and socioeconomic groupings,[1] and the moral perspectives to which they are habitually exposed will most probably reflect that homogeneity. Moreover, it is doubtful whether interaction with mentors and consultants will expose organizational leaders to opinions that are any more diverse. A comforting chorus of affirmation of a leader's inveterate moral conviction is thus more probable than any meaningful challenge to it. Such dialogue is unlikely to evoke critical reflection or to produce startling new perspectives. Nor will it do justice to the inherent complexity of moral decision-making. Rather, ready consensus amongst groups of socioeconomically privileged white men will sustain the illusion that morality is a simple matter, perpetuating the notion that 'we all know

---

[1] In this respect it is perhaps significant that of the sixteen leaders that became involved in my research through various avenues, all were white and twelve were male. I made no attempt to access a more diverse selection, since gender and ethnic comparisons were not my aim. But neither did I intentionally target white male candidates. So, insofar as generalizations can be made from such a limited random sample, this seems to support the contention that senior managers are a pretty homogeneous bunch.

what's right' so the only task of ethical leadership is to ensure fealty to that self-evident path of moral rectitude.

It seems, then, that the leadership stance that is most likely to support ethicality differs from that adopted by most of the leaders involved in this research. Ethical legitimation calls for broad and diverse dialogue around organizational agendas; the leaders whom I met tend to restrict such dialogue to a close group of professional peers. It also contrasts markedly with the approach that is privileged by contemporary Western convention, which favours top-down, directive leadership. But perhaps this is not so in all types of organization. Readers will recall from chapter 5 that the individual who was most evocative of the Mediator of Communication ideal type was Roger, who had spent most of his career in the public sector. It may be, then, that even if the private sector favours directive or oligarchic decision-making styles, a more democratic approach is allowable in the public sector. Support for this contention might also be drawn from the fact that those other leaders who came closest to Roger in articulating intersubjective responsiveness have left their corporate leadership careers behind them in order to take up occupations that are more in keeping with their moral convictions. Maybe, then, it is only in the private sector that managerialism dominates, leaving the democratically fertile public sector to nurture consultative leaders.

Clearly, it would be hasty to draw such a conclusion from a sample of only sixteen. Furthermore, developments since my meeting with Roger might actually indicate a contrary conclusion. Six months after our meeting I read in a newspaper that he had retired slightly before the envisaged end of his tenure. This was in response to the findings of an enquiry into the management of his organization. That enquiry had found evidence of lax management of both organizational and individual performance, along with 'extensive delegation when tighter controls in some corporate areas were needed'. The report recommended that management of performance needed to be more robust, underpinned by clear policies and procedures for staff, and with discipline that held them to account. Furthermore, it found that corporate checks and balances had not been applied with sufficient vigour, concluding that senior management should have exercised a greater degree of control. It seems that Roger may have been too intersubjectively responsive for the liking of his political masters. At least in this instance, rather than public-sector organizations championing intersubjective responsiveness, the opposite seems to be the case: that the public sector is as covetous of directive, controlling leadership as is the private sector.

So where does this leave us? If even public-sector organizations are turning their back on the facilitative style of leadership whose normative merits are advocated here, what chance ethical leadership? In response to this question I will draw once more on a Hegelian insight. The assumption that underpins

Hegel's critical exploration (1977 [1807]) of various systems of thought is that if a particular way of doing something does not meet the standards that we set for it, then we must either find a different way of doing that thing or revise our standards. Applying this insight to the present discussion, we might infer that if conventional ways of doing leadership do not meet our ethical standards, then we need to either look at other ways of doing leadership or rethink those ethical standards. So, should we take this second option and repudiate the ethical presuppositions that imbue our culture? To do so would be to effect a Nietzschean 'revaluation of values'; to suggest that the moral standards that pervade our cultural presuppositions hold no legitimacy; that we should cast them aside so that managerialist visions of leadership might stand unchallenged. But, if we choose not to go down that avenue, then it seems that we must reconsider our commitment to managerialism. So, what are the chances of this happening? What prospects are there for leaders who aspire to the consultative, facilitative, mediatory style of leadership that this book enjoins? Is Habermasian leadership likely to catch on?

The Practical Feasibility of Facilitative Leadership

Clearly, anyone aspiring to lead in this intersubjectively legitimate manner must confront some significant challenges. Most notably, such a style seems to be hopelessly idealistic in today's organizational contexts. Quite apart from its incompatibility with conventional, managerialist expectations, it may be that the demands of organizational life simply do not lend themselves to consultative decision-making of the kind envisaged by intersubjectivist theory. Organizational life may be just too pressurized by time constraints for such a ponderous leadership style to work. A certain amount of consultation amongst a cabal of like-minded senior colleagues may be permissible in order to compensate for the myopia to which monological decision-making by individual leaders is prone, but if the tentacles of deliberation are allowed to reach too far into organizational machinations, then organizational paralysis will surely ensue.

On the one hand, this issue echoes Habermas' own concern (1984 [1981]) about the insidious creep of what he refers to as 'steering media' such as money and power in modern society. According to Habermas, such steering media can enable the smooth operation of economic and political systems. However, that is how they should be regarded: as enablers. Their role is analogous to that of road traffic regulations, which enable the smooth operation of a transport system. But, to continue this analogy, the overall purpose to which that transport system should be put, along with the priorities that should define its structures, is a matter for shared agreement amongst those who use it and those who are affected by it. Similarly, power and money should be regarded as rules of the road that enable the coordination of economic and political activity. But those rules of the road should be put to the service of imperatives that are agreed amongst implicated parties through dialogical processes. The problem, as Habermas sees it, is that the steering media have colonized the space of those dialogical processes; they have become an end in themselves; they have usurped their supporting role and have become an overarching preoccupation. The traffic cops have taken over the ministry of transport.

Applying Habermas' insight to organizational life, it seems fair to suggest that the dominant imperatives in organizations, both public and private, are the maximization of commercial performance and the acquisition and retention of power. Reaching shared understanding about what those organizations are for and how they should conduct themselves comes well down the list of priorities. Steering media that, according to Habermas, ought only to have instrumental importance have thus become ends in themselves. Instead of applying those steering media to the achievement of communicatively negotiated agendas, we have accorded primacy to them. We have lost sight of the 'purpose' (Solomon, 1993) of our organizations; we are no longer able to see beyond the economic goals that ought to be subservient to that purpose. Those goals have thus assumed their own overwhelming 'systemic rationality': it is 'rational' for organizations to put the pursuit of money and power above all else; to place any other imperatives above these would be 'irrational'.

However, while the contagion of systemic rationality may indeed present an obstacle to facilitative leadership in organizations, it also offers an opportunity for leaders who do adopt a facilitative style to make a significant contribution on a broader societal level. Unlike some earlier theorists (such as Weber, 1968 [1911–1920]; Adorno and Horkheimer, 1997 [1944]) who present a gloomy outlook for the future of modernity, Habermas proposes that resistance across a range of fora can lay the foundation for a reassertion of a 'communicatively negotiated lifeworld' (1987 [1981]). In other words, communicative action can fight back against those steering media that have usurped its space. Thirty years ago, Habermas was particularly interested in those 'domains of cultural reproduction, social integration, and socialization' (1987 [1981]: 392) that operate in the public sphere. He had in mind fora such as single-issue protest groups, the environmental lobby, student bodies, and the news media. Habermas believed that discursive spaces such as these held the potential for a reassertion of communicative action, for a reconnection between public agendas and shared understanding, that they could recreate the discursive space upon which a more deeply democratic society could be built.

Whether these embodiments of contemporary public sphere have realized the communicative promise envisaged by Habermas is questionable. Nevertheless, other theorists (such as Gould, 1996) have broadened Habermas' notion of the public sphere, emphasizing the part that work organizations might play in extending democratic inclusion. Given the impact of organizations on the lives of the people who work in them, on the lives of those who interact with them, and on the many stakeholders who are affected by their actions, a more consensual and participative approach to organizational decision-making might contribute significantly to a more communicatively engaged society. So, were work organizations able to shake off the shackles of managerialism, they could go a long way towards facilitating democratic emancipation on a broader front. As Habermas would have it, just as bureaucratic organizations provide a fertile terrain for systemic domination of lifeworld commitments, they also offer a possible incubator for a reassertion of communicative action. As well as offering ethical legitimation for organizational agendas, then, the intersubjectively facilitative leadership style envisaged here might also contribute to a reaffirmation of democracy on a broader societal scale.

But if such opportunities are to be grasped, there must at least be some possibility of leading facilitatively in work organizations. It is one thing to imagine the steering media of systemic rationality being put back in their box; it is quite another thing to actually put them there and shut the lid. So what grounds have we for supposing that aspirant, intersubjectively facilitative leaders might succeed in such an endeavour? Well, we might begin by focussing on the abundant sources of legitimation for a facilitative leadership style that are available inside and outside of organizations. Despite the canonical grip of managerialism within organizational theory and practice, there is no shortage of popular cultural arenas of agitation against it (Parker, 2002; Rhodes and Parker, 2008). Furthermore, recent corporate scandals and financial-services debacles can only have added to simmering discontent with managerialist convention. The conduct of senior management at companies such as Enron and WorldCom, along with the widespread economic malaise that followed the banking crisis of 2008, belies the idea that the people at the top have everyone's best interests at heart and that they know best how to realize those interests.

But, as well as these catalysts of disaffection, there are also positive sources of legitimation upon which attempts at facilitative leadership might draw. For one thing, there is the taken-for-granted endorsement of democratic principles throughout the Western world. As Habermas notes, the steering media of power and money may have stilted the flourishing of those principles, while their instantiation in political reality is often pretty shallow (Wolin, 1996; Dryzek, 2000), but there is no doubting the fervour with which freedom and democracy are publicly championed on both sides of the Atlantic. And if democracy is important enough to take to other countries 'on the wings of a tomahawk missile' (Matten and Crane, 2006: 9), then surely it is not too much to expect some of it in the workplace. That democracy's theoretical merits are taken so much for granted must offer some degree of leverage to intersubjectively facilitative leaders who seek to create their own little piece of democracy at work.

But as well as these wider cultural and political reservoirs of legitimation for facilitative leadership, there are also abundant sources specific to leadership and organization theory. I have drawn attention to the democratic tenor of a lot of leadership theory in chapter 1 of this book. These prescriptions resonate with the endorsement of consultative inclusion that features prominently within contemporary human resource management literature. To be sure, the democratic purity of these instrumental prescriptions tends to be undermined by their contingent selectiveness or their limited scope. As far as leadership is concerned, I have already highlighted the danger that a participative style will be seen as just one leadership tool amongst many, to be taken out when contingently suited to a particular leader-defined project but to be put firmly back in its box and replaced by the hammer of imposition once the moment for participation has passed. Then there is the problem that when consultation is used as a motivational gimmick, the illusion of inclusion becomes more important than its actuality: it is quite enough for people to feel that they are listened to by leaders; whether or not leaders actually take any notice of them is unimportant. Superficial, stage-managed participative practices, which are aimed purely at engendering a sense of belonging amongst employees but which have no real impact on decision-making, may thus take precedence over genuine attempts to access and respond to diverse perspectives (Alvesson and Willmott, 1996; Clayden, 2000; Dundon et al., 2004; Johnson, 2006).

Nevertheless, even if flirtations with more democratic forms of leadership and management rarely deliver much in terms of genuine involvement, they indicate an organizational landscape that, for both normative and instrumental reasons, may be ready for more sincere initiatives. Theorists who draw attention to the link between consultation and effectiveness may at least make it permissible for people in formal leadership roles who are disposed to a consultative approach to indulge their proclivity. If aspiring leaders are told by management educators that it is acceptable to involve people, then perhaps the natural facilitators will shine through. They may even make it to the very top, instead of being shuffled off into middle-management 'female ghettoes' (Marshall, 1995: 16), while the impositional, masculine crusaders take up their seats around the board table.

Perhaps the conclusion that this leaves us with is that if leadership is to be ethical, then leadership is needed in the field of ethical leadership. Leadership theorists are keen to eulogize leaders' propensity to challenge convention; to swim against the tide; to question accepted practices; to oppose the status quo. Well, in that case it seems that if leaders are to lead ethically, then they need to contest conventional expectations of leadership; they need to 'lead' leadership. Managerialist convention may well call upon leaders to make unequivocal, self-assured pronouncements of right and wrong; to stand apart from emotional engagement in order to apply principle in a cool-headed and dispassionate manner; to uphold the prosperity of their organizations as an absolute moral imperative; and to impose their monologically defined, transformational visions on their followers. But if convention demands all of these things, then leadership in the field of moral leadership calls for challenge to this conventional understanding. If convention expects a directive, impositional stance, if it calls upon leaders to consult only within a privileged elite of like-minded peers, then those who seek to 'lead' in the field of ethical leadership need to depart from that convention. They must dare to be different. If the ethical quality of leadership is, as I have suggested here, distinguished by intersubjective responsiveness, then ethical leaders need to show leadership by shrugging off conventional expectations of autocratic or oligarchic imposition in order to champion the role of intersubjective facilitator.

So, if leadership is to play a part, not just in achieving the performative outcomes that are so widely revered in the organizational world, but in actually making that world a more ethically responsive place, then perhaps what is needed is not just more of the same but a different kind of leadership; a kind of leadership which challenges the managerialist presuppositions that characterize most of the leadership literature. Maybe the clamour for leadership that envelops our society is misguided. Perhaps it is looking for the wrong thing. Instead of awaiting charismatic champions who will single-handedly show us the way to a better world, maybe we should be looking for another sort of hero altogether. Existentialist theory alerts us to the agentic capacity that resides within each of us. Principle-based ethics provides a range of perspectives that might facilitate reflection on our ethical convictions. But as intersubjectivist ethics suggests, the outcomes of such reflection can only be enhanced if it is undertaken as a communicative endeavour. So, what we need in our leaders is not assertive self-assurance but the mediation and facilitation skills that will enable that communicative endeavour.

References

Adorno, T.W. and Horkheimer, M. (1997 [1944]). *Dialectic of Enlightenment*, J. Cumming (transl.). London: Verso.

Alimo-Metcalfe, B. (1995). 'An Investigation of Female and Male Constructs of Leadership and Empowerment', *Women in Management Review*, 10/2: 3–8.

—— and Alban-Metcalfe, R.J. (2001). 'The Development of a New Transformational Leadership Questionnaire', *Journal of Occupational and Organizational Psychology*, 74/1: 1–27.

—— —— (2004). 'Leadership in Public Sector Organizations', in J. Storey (ed.), *Leadership in Organizations: Current Issues and Key Trends*. Abingdon: Routledge, 173–202.

—— —— (2005). 'Leadership: Time for a New Direction?', *Leadership*, 1/1: 51–71.

Almond, B. (1993). 'Rights', in P. Singer (ed.), *A Companion to Ethics*. Oxford: Blackwell, 259–69.

Alvesson, M. and Sveningsson, S. (2003). 'Good Visions, Bad Micro-management and Ugly Ambiguity: Contradictions of (Non-)Leadership in a Knowledge-Intensive Organization', *Organization Studies*, 24/6: 961–88.

—— and Willmott, H. (1996). *Making Sense of Management: A Critical Introduction*. London: Sage.

——, Ashcraft, K.L., and Thomas, R. (2008). 'Identity Matters: Reflections on the Construction of Identity Scholarship in Organization Studies', *Organization*, 15/1: 5–28.

Aristotle (1999 [334–322BC]). *Nicomachean Ethics*, T. Irwin (transl.). Indianapolis: Hackett.

Austin, J. (1961). *How to do Things with Words; A Revised Text of the William James Lectures Delivered in Harvard in 1955*. Oxford: Oxford University Press.

Bachrach, P. and Baratz, M.S. (2002 [1962]). 'Two Faces of Power', in M. Haugaard (ed.), *Power: A Reader*. Manchester: Manchester University Press, 28–37.

Baker, B. and Cooper, J. (2000). 'Occupational Testing and Psychometric Instruments: An Ethical Perspective', in D. Winstanley and J. Woodall (eds.), *Ethical Issues in Contemporary Human Resource Management*. Basingstoke: Palgrave MacMillan, 59–84.

Barnard, C. (1997 [1948]). 'The Nature of Leadership', in K. Grint (ed.), *Leadership: Classical, Contemporary, and Critical Approaches*. Oxford: Oxford University Press, 89–111.

Barratt, W. (1990 [1958]). *Irrational Man*. New York: Anchor.

Bass, B.M. (1985). *Leadership and Performance Beyond Expectations*. New York: The Free Press.

Bass, B.M. (1990). 'From Transactional to Transformational Leadership: Learning to Share the Vision', *Organizational Dynamics*, 18/3: 19–31.

—— (1998). 'The Ethics of Transformational Leadership', in J.B. Ciulla (ed.), *Ethics: The Heart of Leadership*. Westport: Praeger, 169–92.

—— and Avolio, B.J. (1994). *Improving Organizational Effectiveness Through Transformational Leadership*. Thousand Oaks: Sage.

—— and Steindlmeier, P. (1999). 'Ethics, Character, and Authentic Transformational Leadership Behaviour', *Leadership Quarterly*, 10/2: 181–217.

Bauman, Z. (1993). *Postmodern Ethics*. Malden: Blackwell.

Benhabib, Seyla (1996). 'Toward a Deliberative Model of Democratic Legitimacy', in S. Benhabib (ed.), *Democracy and Difference: Contesting the Boundaries of the Political*. Princeton: Princeton University Press, 67–94.

Bennis, W.G. (1989). *Why Leaders Can't Lead: The Unconscious Conspiracy Continues*. San Fransisco: Jossey Bass.

—— and Nannus, B. (1985). *Leaders: The Strategies for Taking Charge*. New York: Harper & Row.

Bentham, J. (2000 [1789]). 'An Introduction to the Principles of Morals and Legislation', in T. Griffin (ed.), *Selected Writings on Utilitarianism*. Ware: Wordsworth, 75–309.

Blake, R. and Morton, J.S. (1985). *The Managerial Grid III*. Houston: Gulf.

Bradford, L.P. (1976). *Making Meetings Work: A Guide for Leaders and Group Members*. La-Jolie: Pfeiffer Wiley.

Bryman, A. (1987). 'The Generalizability of Implicit Leadership Theory', *Journal of Social Psychology*, 127/2: 129–41.

—— (1992). *Charisma and Leadership in Organizations*. London: Sage.

—— and Bell, E. (2003). *Business Research Methods*. Oxford: Oxford University Press.

Burnham, J. (1972 [1945]). *The Managerial Revolution: What is happening in the World*. Westport: Greenwood Press.

Burns, J.M. (1978). *Leadership*. New York: Harper and Row.

—— (2003). *Transforming Leadership*. New York: Grove Press.

Burns, T.R. and Stalker, G.M. (1959). *The Management of Innovation*. Chicago: Quadrangle Books.

Cantor, D.W. and Bernay, T. (1992). *Women in Power – The Secrets of Leadership*. Boston: Houghton Mifflin.

Carroll, B. and Levy, L. (2008). 'Defaulting to Management: Leadership Defined By What It Is Not', *Organization*, 15/1: 75–96.

Chomsky, N. (1999). *Profit over People: Neoliberalism and Global Order*. New York: Seven Stories.

Ciulla, J.B. (ed.) (1998). *Ethics: The Heart of Leadership*. Westport: Praeger.

Clarke, M. (1994). 'Nietzsche's Immoralism and the Concept of Morality', in R. Schacht (ed.), *Nietzsche, Genealogy, Morality*. Los Angeles: University of California Press, 15–34.

Coffey, A. and Atkinson, P. (1996). *Making Sense of Qualitative Data: Complementary Research Strategies*. Thousand Oaks: Sage.

Coleman, J.S. and Hoffer, T. (1987). *Public and Private High Schools: Impact of Community*. New York: Basic Books.

Collins, D. (1994). 'Is Business Ethics an Oxymoron?', *Business Horizons*, September–October: 1–8.

Collinson, D. (2005). 'Dialectics of Leadership', *Human Relations*, 58/11: 1419–42.

Conger, J.A. and Kanungo, R.N. (1998). *Charismatic Leadership in Organizations*. Thousand Oaks: Sage.

Conway, N. and Briner, R.B. (2005). *Understanding Psychological Contracts at Work: A Critical Evaluation of Theory and Research*. Oxford: Oxford University Press.

Cox, G. (2006). *Sartre: A Guide for the Perplexed*. London: Continuum.

Dancy, J. (1993). 'An Ethic of Prima Facie Duties', in P. Singer (ed.), *A Companion to Ethics*. Oxford: Blackwell, 219–29.

Danto, A.C. (1975). *Sartre*. Glasgow: Fontana.

Day, D.V., Gronn, P., and Salas, E. (2004). 'Leadership Capacity in Teams', *The Leadership Quarterly*, 15: 857–80.

Donaldson, T. and Preston, L. (1995). 'The Stakeholder Theory of the Corporation: Concepts, Evidence and Implications', *Academy of Management Review*, 20–1: 65–91.

Dryzek, J.S. (2000). *Deliberative Democracy and Beyond: Liberals, Critics, Contestations*. Oxford: Oxford University Press.

Dundon, T., Wilkinson, A., Marchington, M., and Ackers, P. (2004). 'The Meanings and Purpose of Employee Voice', *International Journal of Human Resource Management*, 15/6: 1149–70.

Easterby-Smith, M., Thorpe, R., and Lowe, A. (1991). *Management Research: An Introduction*. London: Sage.

Enteman, W.F. (1993). *Managerialism: The Emergence of a New Ideology*. Madison: University of Wisconsin Press.

Feidler, F.E. (1967). *A Theory of Leadership Effectiveness*. New York: McGraw–Hill.

Festinger, L., Pepitone, A., and Newcombe, T. (1952). 'Some Consequences of Deindividuation in a Group', *Journal of Abnormal and Social Psychology*, 47: 382–9.

Foot, P. (1994). 'Nietzsche's Immoralism', in R. Schacht (ed.), *Nietzsche, Genealogy, Morality*. Los Angeles: University of California Press, 3–14.

Fournier, V. and Grey, C. (2000). 'At the Critical Moment: Conditions and Prospects for Critical Management Studies', *Human Relations*, 53/1: 7–32.

Fraser, Nancy (1992). 'Rethinking the Public Sphere', in C. Calhoun (ed.), *Habermas and the Public Sphere*. Cambridge: MIT, 109–42.

Freeman, R.E. (1984). *Strategic Management: A Stakeholder Approach*. Boston: Pitman.

Friedman, M. (1970). 'The Social Responsibility of Business is to Increase its Profits', *The New York Times Magazine*, September 13.

Fukuyama, F. (2002). 'Social Capital and Development: The Coming Agenda', *The SAIS Review of International Affairs*, 22/1: 23–37.

Galbraith, J.K. (1999 [1958]). *The Affluent Society*. St. Ives: Penguin.

Gardiner, P. (1988). *Kierkegaard*. Oxford: Oxford University Press.

Gemmill, G. and Oakley, J. (1992). 'Leadership: An Alienating Social Myth?', *Human Relations*, 45/2: 113–29.

References

Giddens, A. (1985). 'Reason Without Revolution? Habermas's Theorie des kommunikativen Handelns', in R.J. Bernstein (ed.), *Habermas and Modernity*. Cambridge: Polity, 95–121.

Gill, J. and Johnson, P. (1997). *Research Methods for Managers* (2nd edition). London: Sage.

Goodin, R. (1993). 'Utility and the Good', in P. Singer (ed.), *A Companion to Ethics*. Oxford: Blackwell, 241–8.

Goodman, L.A. (1961). 'Snowball Sampling', *Annals of Mathematical Statistics*, 32: 148–70.

Gould, C. (1996). 'Diversity and Democracy: Representing Difference', in S. Benhabib (ed.), *Democracy and Difference: Contesting the Boundaries of the Political*. Princeton: Princeton University Press, 171–86.

Grant, J. (1992). 'Women as Managers: What They can Offer Organizations', in M. Syrett and C. Hogg (eds.), *Frontiers of Leadership*. Oxford: Blackwell, 298–306.

Greenleaf, R.K. (1977). *Servant Leadership: A Journey into the Nature of Legitimate Power and Greatness*. New Jersey: Paulist Press.

Grint, K. (2000). *The Arts of Leadership*. Oxford: Oxford University Press.

Gronn, P. (2002). 'Distributed Leadership as a Unit of Analysis', *The Leadership Quarterly*, 13: 423–51.

Guest, D.E. and Conway, N. (2002). *Pressure at Work and the Psychological Contract*. London: CIPD.

Habermas, J. (1974 [1963]). *Theory and Practice*, J. Viertal (transl.). Boston: Beacon Press.

—— (1979 [1976]). *Communication and the Evolution of Society*, T. McCarthy (transl.). London: Heinemann.

—— (1984 [1981]). *The Theory of Communicative Action, Volume One: Reason and the Rationalisation of Society*, T. McCarthy (transl.). Boston: Beacon Press.

—— (1987 [1968]). *Knowledge and Human Interests*, J.J. Shapiro (transl.). Cambridge: Polity.

—— (1987 [1969]). *Towards a Rational Society*, J.J. Shapiro (transl.). Cambridge: Polity.

—— (1987 [1981]). *The Theory of Communicative Action, Volume Two: Lifeworld and System: A Critique of Functionalist Reason*, T. McCarthy (transl.). Boston: Beacon Press.

—— (1990 [1983]). *Moral Consciousness and Communicative Action*, C. Lenhardt and S.W. Nicholson (transls.). Massachusetts: MIT Press.

—— (2001 [1994]). *Justification and Application*, C.P. Cronin (transl.). Massachusetts: MIT Press.

—— (2006 [2001]). *Time of Transitions*, C. Cronin and M. Pensky (eds. and transls.). Cambridge: Polity.

—— (2006 [2004]). *The Divided West*, C. Cronin (ed. and transl.). Cambridge: Polity.

Hamilton, C. (2003). *Growth Fetish*. Crows Nest: Allen and Unwin.

Hampton, M.M. (1999). 'Work Groups', in Y. Gabriel (ed.), *Organizations in Depth: The Psychoanalysis of Organizations*. London: Sage, 112–38.

Hancock, P. and Tyler, M. (2001). *Work, Postmodernism and Organization*. London: Sage.

Handy, C. (1998). *The Hungry Spirit*. London: Arrow.

Haugaard, M. (2002). 'The Constitution of Power', in M. Haugaard (ed.), *Power: A Reader*. Manchester: Manchester University Press, 307–28.

Hayek, F.A. (1969 [1960]). 'The Corporation in a Democratic Society: In Whose Interest Ought It and Will It Be Run', in H.I. Ansoff (ed.), *Business Strategy: Selected Readings*. Harmondsworth: Penguin, 225–39.

Heery, E. (2000). 'The New Pay: Risk and Representation at Work', in D. Winstanley and J. Woodall (eds.), *Ethical Issues in Contemporary Human Resource Management*. Basingstoke: Palgrave MacMillan, 172–88.

Hegel, G.W.F. (1977 [1807]). *Phenomenology of Spirit*, A.V. Miller (transl.). Oxford: Oxford University Press.

Hegelsen, S. (1990). *The Female Advantage: Women's Ways of Leadership*. New York: Doubleday.

Heidegger, M. (1962 [1926]). *Being and Time*, J. Macquarie and E. Robinson (transl. and eds.). Oxford: Blackwell.

Hemphill, J.K. (1955). 'Leadership Behaviour Associated with the Administrative Reputations of College Departments', *Journal of Educational Psychology*, 46: 385–401.

Hersey, P. and Blanchard, K.H. (1982). *Management of Organizational Behaviour: Utilising Human Resources*. New Jersey: Prentice-Hall.

Hill, R.P. and Stephens, D.L. (2005). 'The Multiplicity of Selves and Selves Management', *Leadership*, 1: 127–40.

Hobbes, T. (1985 [1651]). *Leviathan*, C.B Macpherson (ed.), St. Ives: Penguin.

Hobsbawm, E. (1995). *The Age of Extremes*. London: Abacus.

Honig, Bonnie (1996). 'Difference, Dilemmas and the Politics of Home', in S. Benhabib (ed.), *Democracy and Difference: Contesting the Boundaries of the Political*. Princeton: Princeton University Press, 257–77.

Howell, J.M. (1988). 'Two Faces of Charisma: Socialised and Personalised Leadership in Organizations', in J.A. Conger and R.N. Kanungo (eds.), *Charismatic Leadership: The Elusive Factor in Organizational Effectiveness*. San Fransisco: Jossey-Bass, 213–36.

Hume, D. (1985 [1738]). *A Treatise of Human Nature*, E.C. Mossner (ed.), London: Penguin.

—— (1998 [1752]). *An Enquiry Concerning the Principles of Morals*, T.L. Beauchamp (ed.), Oxford: Oxford University Press.

Hutton, W. (1996). *The State We're In*. London: Vintage.

—— (1997). *Stakeholding and its Critics*. London: Institute of Economic Affairs.

Irigaray, Luce (1996). *I Love to You: Sketch of a Possible Felicity in History*, A. Martin (transl.). New York: Routledge.

Johnson, P. (1976). 'Women and Power: Towards a Theory of Effectiveness', *Journal of Social Issues*, 32/3: 99–110.

—— (2006). 'Whence Democracy? A Review and Critique of the Conceptual Dimensions and Implications of the Business Case for Organizational Democracy', *Organization*, 13/2: 245–74.

Kaler, J. (1999). 'What's the Good of Ethical Theory', *Business Ethics: A European Review*, 8/4: 206–13.

—— (2002). 'Morality and Strategy in Stakeholder Identification', *Journal of Business Ethics*, 39: 91–9.

Kant, I. (1948 [1797]). *The Moral Law: Groundwork to the Metaphysic of Morals*, H.J. Paton (trans. and ed.). London: Hutchinson.

Kant, I. (1997 [1788]). *Critique of Practical Reason*, M. Gregor (trans. and ed.). Cambridge: Cambridge University Press.

—— (2003 [1787]). *Critique of Pure Reason*, N. Kemp-Smith (trans. and ed.). Basingstoke: Palgrave MacMillan.

Kanter, R.M. (1977). *Men and Women of the Corporation*. New York: Basic Books.

Kaufmann, W. (ed.) (1956). *Existentialism from Dostoevsky to Sartre*. New York: Meridian.

Kay, J. (2003). 'The Real Economy', *Prospect*, May: 28–32.

Keeley, M. (1998). 'The Trouble with Transformational Leadership: Towards a Federalist Ethic for Organizations', in J.B. Ciulla (ed.), *Ethics: The Heart of Leadership*. Westport: Praeger, 111–44.

Kellner, D. (1989). *Critical Theory, Marxism and Modernity*. Baltimore: JH Press.

Kierkegaard, S. (1967 [1845]). *Stages on Life's Way*. New York: Schocken Books.

—— (1997a [1843]). 'Either/Or, A Fragment of Life', in H.V. Hong and E.H. Hong (eds.), *The Essential Kierkegaard*. Princeton: Princeton University Press, 37–83.

—— (1997b [1843]). 'Fear and Trembling', in H.V. Hong and E.H. Hong (eds.), *The Essential Kierkegaard*. Princeton: Princeton University Press, 93–101.

—— (1997c [1846]). 'Concluding Unscientific Postscript to Philosophical Fragments', in H.V. Hong and E.H. Hong (eds.), *The Essential Kierkegaard*. Princeton: Princeton University Press, 187–246.

Klein, N. (2001). *No Logo*. London: Harper Collins.

Kleinig, J. (1983). *Paternalism*. Manchester: Manchester University Press.

Knights, D. and Willmott, H. (1992). 'Conceptualizing Leadership Processes: A Study of Senior Managers in a Financial Services Company', *Journal of Management Studies*, 29: 761–82.

Kotter, J.P. (1990). 'What Leaders Really Do', *Harvard Business Review*, May–June: 103–11.

Langiulli, N. (1971). *The Existentialist Tradition*. New Jersey: Humanities Press.

Leiter, B. (2002). *Nietzsche on Morality*. London: Routledge.

Lewin, K. (1939). 'Field Theory and Experiment in Social Psychology: Concepts and Methods', *American Journal of Sociology*, 44: 868–96.

Lewis, G. (2000). *Mentoring Manager: Strategies for Fostering Talent and Spreading Knowledge*. Harlow: Pearson Education Ltd.

Likert, R. (1979). 'From Production- to Employee-centredness to Systems 1–4', *Journal of Management*, 5: 147–56.

Locke, J. (1988 [1690]). *Two Treatises of Government*, P. Laslett (ed.). Cambridge: Cambridge University Press.

Lukes, S. (2002 [1974]). 'Power: A Radical View', in M. Haugaard (ed.), *Power: A Reader*. Manchester: Manchester University Press, 38–57.

MacIntyre, A. (1985 [1981]). *After Virtue*. London: Duckworth.

—— (1988). *Whose Justice? Which Rationality?* London: Duckworth.

Mansbridge, Jane (1996). 'Using Power/Fighting Power: The Polity', in S. Benhabib (ed.), *Democracy and Difference: Contesting the Boundaries of the Political*. Princeton: Princeton University Press, 46–66.

Manz, C.M. and Sims, H.P. (1987). 'Leading Workers to Lead Themselves: The External Leadership of Self-Managing Work Teams', *Administrative Science Quarterly*, 32: 106–28.

Marcuse, H. (2002 [1964]). *One Dimensional Man; Studies in the Ideology of Advanced Industrial Society*. London: Routledge.

Marshall, J. (1995). *Women Managers Moving On: Exploring Career and Life Choices*. London: Routledge.

Matten, D. and Crane, A. (2006). 'What is Stakeholder Democracy? Perspectives and Issues', *Business Ethics: A European Review*, 14/1: 6–13.

Matuštík, M.B. (2001). *Jürgen Habermas: A Philosophical-Political Profile*. Maryland: Rowman and Littlefield.

Mayo, E. (1997 [1949]). 'Hawthorne and the Western Electric Company', in D. Pugh (ed.), *Organization Theory*. London: Penguin, 355–68.

Meindl, J.R. (1990). 'On Leadership: An Alternative to the Conventional Wisdom', in B.M. Staw and L.L. Cummings (eds.), *Research in Organizational Behaviour*, Vol. xii. Greenwich: JAI Press: 159–203.

Mill, J.S. (1962 [1861]). *Utilitarianism*, M. Warnock (ed.). London: Fontana.

Moore, B.V. (1927). 'The May Conference on Leadership', *Personnel Journal*, 6: 124–8.

Moore, G. (1999). 'Tinged Shareholder Theory: Or What's so Special about Stakeholders', *Business Ethics: A European Review*, 8/2: 117–27.

Musser, S.J. (1987). *The Determination of Positive and Negative Charismatic Leaders*, Unpublished manuscript. Grantham: Messiah College.

Nietzsche, F. (2003a [1883–1885]). *Thus Spoke Zarathustra*. St. Ives: Penguin Classics.

—— (2003b [1887]). *The Genealogy of Morals*. New York: Dover.

Nozick, R. (1974). *Anarchy, State and Utopia*. New York: Basic Books.

O'Neill, O. (1993). 'Kantian Ethics', in P. Singer (ed.), *A Companion to Ethics*. Oxford: Blackwell, 175–85.

Parfit, D. (1984). *Reasons and Persons*. Oxford: Oxford University Press.

Parker, M. (2002). *Against Management*. Cambridge: Polity.

Patton, M.Q. (1990). *Qualitative Evaluation and Research Methods*. Nerbury Park: Sage.

Pettigrew, A. and McNulty, T. (1995). 'Power and Influence in and around the Boardroom', *Human Relations*, 48/8: 845–73.

Phillips, R. (2003). *Stakeholder Theory and Organizational Ethics*. San Fransisco: Berrett-Koehler.

Polt, R. (1999). *Heidegger: An Introduction*. London: Routledge.

Prasad, P. (1993). 'Symbolic Processes in the Implementation of Technological Change: A Symbolic Interactionist Study of Work Computerization', *Academy of Management Journal*, 36/6: 1400–29.

Price, T.L. (2003). 'The Ethics of Authentic Transformational Leadership', *The Leadership Quarterly*, 14: 67–81.

Pusey, M. (1987). *Jürgen Habermas*. London: Tavistock.

Pye, A. (2005). 'Leadership and Organizing: Sensemaking in Action', *Leadership*, 1/1: 31–49.

Rhodes, C. and Parker, M. (2008). 'Images of Organizing in Popular Culture', *Organization*, 15/5: 627–37.

Rosen, A.D. (1996). *Kant's Theory of Justice*. New York: Cornell University Press.

Rosener, J.B. (1990). 'Ways Women Lead', *Harvard Business Review*, November–December: 119–25.

Rost, J.C. (1991). *Leadership for the Twenty-First Century*. New York: Praeger.

Ruschman, N.L. (2002). 'Servant Leadership and the Best Companies to Work For in America', in L.C. Spears and M. Lawrence (eds.), *Focus on Leadership: Servant Leadership for the 21st Century*. New York: Wiley, 123–40.

Sarkasian, S.C. (1981). 'A Personal Perspective', in R.S. Ruch and L.J. Korb (eds.), *Military Leadership*. Beverly Hills: Sage, 243–7.

Sartre, J-P. (1965 [1944]). *The Philosophy of Jean Paul Sartre*, R.D. Cumming (ed.). New York: Random House.

—— (1973 [1946]). *Existentialism and Humanism*, P. Mairet (transl.). London: Methuen.

—— (2003 [1943]). *Being and Nothingness*, H.E. Barnes (transl.). Oxford: Routledge.

Selznick, P. (1957). *Leadership in Administration*. New York: Harper Row.

Showkeir, J.D. (2002). 'The Business Case for Servant Leadership', in L.C. Spears and M. Lawrence (eds.), *Focus on Leadership: Servant Leadership for the 21st Century*. New York: Wiley, 153–66.

Skinner, E.W. (1969). 'Relationships Between Leadership Behaviour Patterns and Organizational Situational Variables', *Personal Psychology*, 22: 489–94.

Smircich, L. and Morgan, G. (1982). 'Leadership: The Management of Meaning', *Journal of Applied Behavioural Science*, 18/3: 265–79.

Smith, A. (1998 [1776]). *Wealth of Nations*, K. Sutherland (ed.). Oxford: Oxford University Press.

Solomon, R.C. (1993). *Ethics and Excellence: Cooperation and Integrity in Business*. Oxford: Oxford University Press.

Spears, L.C. (2002). 'Tracing the Past, Present and Future of Servant Leadership', in L.C. Spears and M. Lawrence (eds.), *Focus on Leadership: Servant Leadership for the 21st Century*. New York: Wiley, 1–16.

—— and Lawrence, M. (eds.) (2002). *Focus on Leadership: Servant Leadership for the 21st Century*. New York: Wiley.

Spence, L. (2000). 'What Ethics in the Employment Interview', in D. Winstanley and J. Woodall (eds.), *Ethical Issues in Contemporary Human Resource Management*. Basingstoke: Palgrave MacMillan, 43–58.

Stanworth, C. (2000). 'Flexible Working Patterns', in D. Winstanley and J. Woodall (eds.), *Ethical Issues in Contemporary Human Resource Management*. Basingstoke: Palgrave MacMillan, 137–55.

Sternberg, E. (1999). *The Stakeholder Concept: A Mistaken Doctrine*. Leeds: Leeds University Centre for Business and Professional Ethics.

—— (2000). *Just Business: Business Ethics in Action* (2nd edition). Oxford: Oxford University Press.

Stiglitz, J. (2001). *Globalisation and its Discontents*. London: Penguin.

Stoney, C. and Winstanley, D. (2001). 'Stakeholding: Confusion or Utopia? Mapping the Conceptual Terrain', *Journal of Management Studies*, 38/5: 603–26.

Strauss, A. and Corbin, J. (1990). *Basics of Qualitative Research: Grounded Theory Procedures and Techniques*. Newbury Park: Sage.

Taylor, C. (1991). *The Ethics of Authenticity*. Cambridge: Harvard University Press.

Taylor, F.W. (1997 [1912]). 'Scientific Management', in D. Pugh (ed.), *Organization Theory*. London: Penguin, 275–95.

Toulmin, S. (1990). *Cosmopolis*. Chicago: University of Chicago Press.

Turner, A. (2002). *Just Capital: The Liberal Economy*. London: Macmillan Pan.

Vidal, J. (2010). 'Nigeria's Agony Dwarfs the Gulf Oil Spill. All We Do is Ignore It', *Observer*, 30 May: 20–1.

Walzer, M. (1995). 'The Concept of Civil Society', in M. Walzer (ed.), *Toward a Global Civil Society*. Providence: Berghahn, 7–27.

Watson, T.J. (2001). 'Beyond Managism: Negotiated Narratives and Critical Management Education in Practice', *British Journal of Management*, 12: 385–96.

—— (2002). *Organising and Managing Work*. Harlow: Prentice-Hall.

Weber, M. (1947 [1924]). *The Theory of Social and Economic Organization*, A.M. Henderson and T. Parsons (transl. and ed.). New York: Free Press.

—— (1968 [1911–1920]). *Economy and Society*, Vols. 1, 2 and 3, G. Roth and C. Wittich (eds.). Berkeley: University of California Press.

Western, S. (2008). *Leadership: A Critical Text*. London: Sage.

Willmott, H. (1998). 'Towards a New Ethics? The Contributions of Poststructuralism and Posthumanism', in M. Parker (ed.), *Ethics and Organizations*. London: Sage, 76–121.

Winstanley, D. (2000). 'Conditions of Worth and the Performance Management Paradox', in D. Winstanley and J. Woodall (eds.), *Ethical Issues in Contemporary Human Resource Management*. Basingstoke: Palgrave MacMillan, 189–207.

Wolin, S.S. (1996). 'Fugitive Democracy', in S. Benhabib (ed.), *Democracy and Difference: Contesting the Boundaries of the Political*. Princeton: Princeton University Press, 31–45.

Woods, P.A. (2004). 'Democratic Leadership: Drawing Distinctions with Distributed Leadership', *International Journal of Leadership in Education*, 7/1: 3–26.

——, Bennett, N., Harvey, J.A., and Wise, C. (2004). 'Variabilities and Dualities in Distributed Leadership: Findings from a Systematic Literature Review', *Educational Management Administration and Leadership*, 32/4: 439–57.

Young, I.M. (1996). 'Communication and the Other: Beyond Deliberative Democracy', in S. Benhabib (ed.), *Democracy and Difference: Contesting the Boundaries of the Political*. New Jersey: Princeton University Press, 120–35.

Zaleznik, A. (1977). 'Managers and Leaders: Are They Different?', *Harvard Business Review*, May–June: 126–35.

Index